ETHNOLOGY OF INDIA

ETHNOLOGY OF INDIA.

BY

R. G. LATHAM, M. A., M. D., F. R. S.

GYAN

Published by

Gyan Publishing House
5, Ansari Road
Daryaganj, New Delhi-110002
Phone: 011-47034999, 9811692060
E-mail: books@gyanbooks.com

Distribution Network
gyanbooks.com
India, USA, Canada, UK, Australia, France

ISBN: 978-81-212-8314-4 (PB)
First Published, 1859

2nd Impression 2023

Printed at: Gyan Press, Delhi.

ETHNOLOGY OF INDIA
Author: R. G. LATHAM

ETHNOLOGY OF INDIA.

BY

R. G. LATHAM, M.A., M.D., F.R.S.,

LATE FELLOW OF KING'S COLLEGE, CAMBRIDGE, ETC.

LONDON:

JOHN VAN VOORST, PATERNOSTER ROW.

MDCCCLIX.

PREFACE.

THE following pages form an extract from a larger work, one in which a full and systematic description of the several varieties of mankind is attempted. That such an extract should be made,—in other words, that a particular portion of the work should be thus separated from the rest, and that that portion should be the notice of India and the districts of the Indian frontier, are circumstances of which the explanation lies in the special importance of the subject; a subject which, interesting as it is in a scientific view, is, at the present moment, one of vast practical magnitude. It commands much of our attention as Englishmen. It ought, perhaps, to command more.

The present notice gives the ethnology of British India, and something more. That the acquisitions of the Company are by no means limited to Hindostan is well known. It is well known that Arakan, Pegu, and the Tenasserim provinces, on the East; that portions of Caubul, on the West; and that certain Himalayan districts in the North, are, at one and the same time, British in respect to their political relations, and other than Indian in their ethnology. For this reason the Indian frontier has been considered in conjunction with India. In the eyes of many too much space may have been devoted to it.

The populations akin to the Tibetans and Burmese come first. They agree, to a great extent, in both language and physical form. The general character of their civilization (when it exists) and of their barbarism (when they are barbarians) is the same. They lie to the north and north-east of India proper; in Ladak, Nepaul, Sikkim, and the parts to the East of the Bay of Bengal. Some are decidedly Tibetan or Burmese. Others, like the Nepaulese, are, in many important respects, Hindu; whilst a few, like the Bodo and Garo, have actually been treated as Indians.

On the west and north-west the frontier is Persian. In the way of politics it is important; inasmuch as it gives us the tribes which bound our acquisitions in both the Punjaub and Sind. In the way of ethnology it is more important still, since, according to all hypotheses, it was from the west and north that the pre-eminently Indian characteristics of India were introduced.

In the details of India proper, I have relied, in all cases, upon first-hand evidence. The great repertories have, of course, been those numerous periodicals of which the Asiatic Researches, the Transactions of the Asiatic Society of London, and the Transactions of the Asiatic Society of Bengal are the chief representatives. Numerous reports, especially those of the Bombay Government, have also been investigated. When the authorities are of this kind, it is no easy matter, in all cases, to give the particular observer upon whose account you rely. For the most part, however, the authors of the chief monographs are named.

CONTENTS.

PART I.

PART II.

CHAPTER I.

CHAPTER II.

CHAPTER III.

CHAPTER IV.

CHAPTER V.

CHAPTER VI.

CHAPTER VII.

CHAPTER VIII.

CHAPTER IX.

CHAPTER XXI

CHAPTER XXII.

CHAPTER XXIII.

CHAPTER XXIV.

TIBETANS AND ALLIED FAMILIES

OF

INDIA.

CHAPTER I.

Ladak.—Kunawer.—Kumaon.—Doms.—Rawat.—Nepaul Bhot.

LADAK, like Bultistan, belongs to Gulab Singh, with the exception of two districts—Spiti and Lahúl, which constitute a part of British India. Spiti is wholly, Lahúl but partially, Bhot. It is Bhot along the banks of the Chandra, and Bhot along those of the Bhaga; but below the junction, and along the Chandra-Bhaga, or the result of the two combined streams, it is Hindu.

In Spiti the population is scantily spread along the banks of the river so called. In 316 houses, distributed in sixty villages, we find

Adult males	392
Boys under 12	191
Adult females	593
Girls under 12	238
Priests	193
	1607

Their chief enemy is the small-pox; weakness of the eyes being common — goitre rare. The men marry between twenty and twenty-one, the women from fifteen to twenty. Polyandry prevails; and, side by side with it, polygamy A man in good circumstances may have

B

two or three wives; but, then, the priest has none. Of food they have but little variety, being without poultry, without vegetables.

The whole area of Ladak is as follows:—

UNDER GULAB SINGH.

Districts.	Sq. Miles.	Mean Heights.
Nubra	9216	12,763
Ladak	3960	11,500
Zanskar	3080	13,154
Rukshu	5580	15,634
Purik, Suru, Dras	4200	11,196

BRITISH.

Districts.	Sq. Miles.	Mean Heights.
Spiti	2312	12,986
Lahúl	1872	11,063

Hungrung.—I know of no true ethnological difference between the Bhot of Hungrung and those of Ladak and Tibet. The district, however, belongs to the Rajah of Bisahur. The villages lie at different levels; ranging from 9,500 to 12,000 feet, the alluvia being numerous, and the climate, considering the altitude, favourable to cultivation.

On the very crest of the Hungrung pass, at a height of 14,800 feet, the dama grows in patches; the dama being the Tibetan name for the Caragana versicolor, a small shrub, that thrives at elevations where no other tree is to be found. This makes it valuable for fuel; the scarcest of the Bhot necessaries. The barleys are of two kinds, the common, and the Hordeum Ægiceros. Both are cultivated; and that after the ordinary Bhot fashion; *i. e.* by means of irrigation. On the lower levels are grown wheat, buckwheat, millet, a kind of rape, and apricots. On the higher, there are no fruit trees at all.

It is at Nako, in Hungrung, that Dr. Thompson finds occasion to remark upon the gradual character of the transition from India to Tibet, both morally and physically. It is by gradual transitions that Brahminism passes into Buddhism. It is by gradual transitions that the Hindu physiognomy becomes Bhot. The "gradual transition, in descending the Sutlej, from Hinduism to Buddhism is very remarkable, and not less so because it is accompanied by an equally gradual change in the physical aspect of the inhabitants; the Hindus of the Lower Sutlej appearing to pass by insensible gradations as we advance from village to village, till at last we arrive at a pure Tartar population. The people of Upper Piti have quite the Tartar physiognomy, the small stature and stout build of the inhabitants of Ladak, to whom they closely approximate in dress."

Kunawer.—In Lower Kunawer the language is Hindu rather than Bhot; in Upper Kunawer it is Bhot rather than Hindu. Nor is this all. There are dialects and sub-dialects. The Milchan is the language of Lower Kunawer; Milchan being the Rampúr term for the language in general. In Súngnúm the forms are truly provincial, and, as the word Theburskud, or Tibberskud is used as a name for all deviations from the ordinary speech, the Súngnúm dialect has been given as Theburskud. The Lubrung (or Kanam) and the Lidung (or Lippa) forms are varieties of the Milchan. The Súmchú is, perhaps, a fresh dialect.

English.	Milchan.	Theburskud.	Súmchú.
Man	mi	mi	mé
Women	chismi	eshrí	esplung
Head	bul	pisha	pisha
Tongue	le	le	le
Eye	mík	mé	mí
Ear	kanung	rupung	repung
Foot	bung	bunk	bunkun
Sun	yúnc	né	nímok
Moon	gulsung	gulsung	gulsung

English.	Milchan.	Theburskud.	Súmchú.
Star	skara	karma	karma
One	ít	té	ít
Two	nísh	níshí	nísh
Three	súm	súm	hûm
Four	pu	pí	pu
Five	gna	gnai	gna
Ten	saí	chúí	sa

The differences here are slight. The infinitives, however, have peculiar endings:—

Milchan	. . . . lonhmih'	or	lonhmig
Lippa	. . . . lodenh'	or	lodent
Kanam	. . . . logma		
Sángnúm	. . . . lopang		
Súmchú (?)	. . . lomma	or	loma.

Neither the Bhot nor the Hindu populations of Kunawer are truly pure. On the contrary, there are Bhot characters amongst the Hindus, Hindu characters amongst the Bhot. Buddhism, indeed, decreases in the central districts, and disappears in the southern. It is not, however, replaced by any pure form of Brahminism. Local gods and irregular priests appear here. Every hill has its deota or genius. Polyandry is general. To one family one wife; the elder brother being the more special husband. Minute and trenchant divisions of caste are wanting. There is, however, an approach to it. The Chumangs are regarded as outcasts, and no true Kanet * will eat with them, intermarry with them, or allow them to cross their threshold. Their skins are dark, and some are said to be woolly-haired. The same is said concerning the Rawi and Dom of Kumaon. They are not found in the Bhot districts. The people of the lower hills call them Koli; those of Rampúr, Chumars. Chumang is what they call themselves. They till the soil and weave.

* Population of *Kun*-awer, where a dialect called *Kan*-am is spoken.

Polyandry is one of their habits, as well as one of their superiors'. They are liable to be pressed as porters.

So are the Domang, whose name is, word for word, that of the Dom of Kumaon.

So is the class of carpenters.

Hence, even in Kunawer, with its Buddhist frontier and its Bhot characters, there are no less than three castes; each of which keeps its members to itself in the way of intermarriage. A Dom will not intermarry with a Chumang.

Gurwhal and Kumaon.—The productive and habitable portion of the Bhot area in Kumaon and Gurwhal is confined to the passes and their neighbourhood, all the rest being either snow or rock. Their minimum height is about 6000 feet. The paths to them coincide with the head-waters of the following rivers.

The Mana Pass is on the		Saraswati	Feeders of the Ganges.
The Nítí Pass	„	Duli	
The Juwâr Pass	„	Gaûri	Feeders of the Sarda or Gogra.
The Darma Pass	„	Dhouli	
The Byanse Pass	„	Kali	

The evidence to the gradual extension of the zone of snow is strong. The passmen state that ridges, which, within the memory of man, were covered with forests, are now covered with snow; that pastures to which their fathers drove their flocks in summer are now non-existent; that avalanches from the higher regions are, on melting, found to contain trees in their centre. With such a neighbourhood it is easy to imagine that the passes themselves are of no ordinary difficulty. The watercourses that run up to them require bridges; the roads by the side of them require continual repairs. The snow blocks them up; masses of rock obstruct them; beasts of burden are often unable to proceed alone, and must be raised or lowered by means of slings passed round their bodies. The Niti pass is the best, the Juwár the worst. Respecting the latter the story runs thus—that when a Bhot army, under Raja Bag Bahader Khan, invaded Kumaon, the commander inspected the making of the road himself, and paid a rupee for every cupful of earth. This is not given as a fact. It is given as a measure of the belief of the natives in the engineering difficulties that presented themselves during its construction. The number of well-built stone houses (for well-built houses of stone are required to stand their ground) in the Bhot districts is as follows:—

	Villages.	Houses.
In Mana	3	125
In Nítí	10	219
In Juwár	13	455
In Darma	24	342
In Byanse	9	184
	59	1326

A portion of the population consists of slaves, who, with their families, live under the same roof with their masters. They help in the cultivation of the soil; for here, as elsewhere, the Bhot is an agriculturist. Marse a species of amaranth, wheat, two kinds of barley, two kinds of buckwheat, are the chief products; to which add, as cultivated vegetables, turnips and leeks, and as wild ones, garlic, celery, rhubarb, a kind of frankincense. Few or no fruits receive any culture. The walnuts and hazel-nuts are small, the apricots and peaches ill-flavoured. Gooseberries, currants, strawberries, and pears, grow wild. The domestic animals are those of Ladak and Tibet.

In the Mana, Nítí, Juwár, and Byanse passes the population is generally believed to have emigrated from Tibet within the historical period, inasmuch as many of the chief families trace their family to some Tibetan locality.

They encroached upon an earlier body of Hindus, and drove them downwards. With the inhabitants of the Darma pass the case is different. They are considered to be descendants of a body of Mongols left in Kumaon by Timúr. If so, the difference of origin is considerable; if so, the occupants of the Darma pass are no true Bhots, but Mongols, who have learned the Bhot language. They differ from the rest in dress (especially that of the females) and in certain customs. All the passmen burn their dead; but the Darma make a general ceremony of the cremation and reserve it for the month Kartik. Those who die at any other time of the year are interred, but only for a time. When the month Kartik approaches they are taken out of the ground, and transferred to the funeral pile. But what if a Darma die away from his native village? In such a case his relations take a clue of worsted and draw it from the dead body to the house of the deceased, keeping it unbroken if they can. The object of this is to enable the spirit to join those of its ancestors.

The details, then, of the Bhot area in Kumaon require further investigation. Again,—in the districts of Dewara and Bágeswar vestiges of some population other than Hindu, and, perhaps, other than Bhot, are to be found. They consist, chiefly, of tombs constructed of large flat tiles, different in their external character from those of the other inhabitants, who call them the Mogul sepulchres.

At the same time the people repel the doctrine that makes them Mongol; the term Mogul being too closely associated with the Mahometan religion. Of their language we have no specimens. In their creed there are probably peculiarities; at any rate the practice of divination is spoken of as if it were more Darma than aught else. The omens are taken from the warm and reeking livers of sheep, sacrificed for the purpose, whenever an undertaking of importance is in hand.

Another distinction—the Mána, Níti, and Juwár Bhots pretend to consider the men of Darma as their inferiors;—but, as they have the same low opinion of those of Byanse, this either proves too little or too much. Are the Byanse Mongol also? The fact of their being classed with the Darma in the matter of caste is not their only Darma characteristic. The women of the two passes dress alike. A piece of cloth, folded round the body, descends from the waist to the ankles, like a petticoat, being fastened round the waist with a girdle. Above this is a shift without sleeves, reaching to the knee. Over the head is a hood, with a tail behind, which reaches nearly to the heels. The ornaments are remarkable for their mass; the pewter ear-rings being compared to large house-keys.

Again,—whilst the Mána, Níti, and Juwár Bhots abstain from beef of all kinds, the Darma and Byanse indulge in the flesh of the yak, and would not abstain from that of the common cow if the law permitted them to eat it. But there is, in the province, a general prohibition against the slaughter of this holy animal.

The difference of rank, along with the other details akin to it, is worth our notice, if it be only for its suggesting the probability of the Darma and Byanse populations being other than Bhot. But there is another reason for giving prominence to it. The feeling of caste is, by no means, Buddhist; and Bhots as Buddhists ought to have nothing whatever to do with it. They have it nevertheless. This is because their creed is no longer pure; but Buddhist *plus* certain Brahminic influences. The Hindu doctrines on one side contend with the Tibetan on the other; and the contest has not been wholly unfavourable to them. A Bhot, in want of a priest, will accept the services of either a Brahmin or a Lama. The Juwár Bhots go further in the direction of Hinduism. They affect many of the Hindu prejudices in regard to food. They occasionally practise Suttí. The use of the Hindu language is most widely diffused amongst them. Their trade is the most considerable.

Trade is important to the whole Bhot population of the passes; but it is most considerable within the Juwár country. A periodical fair for Tibetan goods takes place every September, at Gartokh, the residence of the Lahsa viceroy. The Bhots of Hindostan are freer to visit this fair than the Hindus; and the Juwars freer than the other Bhots of Hindostan.

The Bhots of the passes are subjects of the East India Company; without being, wholly and absolutely, disconnected from Tibet. Many of their suits are decided in Tibetan courts; and if a Bhot commit a crime on Tibetan soil, he is judged as a Tibetan. He seems to be responsible for the peaceable condition of the passes to the Chinese Government as well as to the Company's.

It is just through the Bhot of Kumaon that British India comes in contact with China; the passes in question being the roads from that portion of Hindostan which abuts upon the Chinese empire to the Tibetan province called Nari or Gnari. Westward of these passes lies Ladak, wherein the British provinces of Lahúl and Spiti are separated from the Chinese frontier by the Sikh possessions, whilst eastward are the independent rajahships of Nepaul and Sikkim. Beyond these, the northern frontier of Bengal touches the southern frontier of Bútan; but Bútan, though a Chinese dependency, is a dependency of a much looser kind than Tibet Proper.

For this reason I shall enlarge upon the government of the important province of Gnari—the province of China which the Bhot of Kumaon, about the five passes of Nítí, Mána, Juwár, Byanse, and Darma separate from British Hindostan. What is the machinery by which the Chinese keeps up its exclusiveness in these parts, an exclusiveness to which, as is reasonably believed, the Tibetans themselves are no parties ?

The general government of the province is entrusted to the two Garphan; one of which is called the Urgú Ma, the other the Urgú Ya. They are Tibetans; and natives of Lahsa. They hold their office for three years, and are, then, replaced. They reside at Gartokh.

Under the Garphan or governors of the province are the district officers; also two in number; and named Deb and Vazir. Like the Garphan, the Deb holds his office for the limited period of three years; the Vazir *quamdiu bene se gesserit*. They are Tibetans.

The troops seem to be either Turk or Mongol; or, perhaps, Mantshu. This is an inference from the notion which the Bhots entertain concerning their habits of eating. They are believed to feed upon horseflesh; which no Tibetan and no Chinese would do. The force consists of about 200 men. All beyond is native. Each town and village has its number of militiamen, who may be called out whenever their services are required. A horse post keeps up a rapid communication between Gartokh and Lhasa. The stages are from 15 to 20 miles apart, and four horses, with their riders, are kept at each.

As each district has its Deb and Vazir, and each Deb and each Vazir has his residence, there are so many little capitals. Four of these are named as follows:—(1) Chaprang, (2) Dapa, (3) Kiunlang, (4) Taklakol; with these, four out of the five passes coincide; each having its special and peculiar market to which it is limited. Thus:—

Mana is free of the market at				Chaprang.
Nití	„	„	„	Dapa.
Dharma	„	„	„	Kumlang.
Byanse	„	„	„	Taklakot.

The Juwári can trade with any and all of these.

The Rawat.—What are the Ráwat? The Ráwat, or Raji, are certain occupants of the forest districts of Kumaon. They pertinaciously adhere to certain customs other than Hindu; though the exact details as to what these are and what they are not are unknown. They are reduced to (say) twenty or thirty families—so, at least, runs the statement in Mr. Traill's report. They represent themselves as the descendants of one of the ancient princes of Kumaon who fled to the jungle when his country was invaded; and, on the strength of this royal pedigree, they refuse the ordinary salutation to all men alike, high or low. Whatever be your rank a Ráwat will show you no respect. Their language, by its "total dissimilitude" from the Hindu of the Kumaon, marks them out as a different race. What is this language? We have no specimens of it. What is it likely to be? It is likely to belong to the same class with the Bhot dialects, without being actually Bhot in the limited sense of the word. Against its being this is the probable antiquity of the Ráwat population. It is considered to represent the aborigines of the district. If so, it must differ from the Bhot, as well as resemble it.

The Doms.—What are the Doms? The lowest class of the Kumaon population are thus called. Many of them have dark, and almost black, complexions, with crisp curly hair. They are supposed to be the descendants of the aborigines. That these may be represented by the Ráwat has just been stated. It has also been stated that the Ráwat may belong to the same class with the Bhot. Hence, the Dom and Ráwat may be in the same category.

The Bhot of Nepaul and Sikkim.—These fall into two divisions, the civilized and the rude. Indentations of the proper Bhot area may easily occur, along the whole of the frontier. In this case the population will be neither more nor less than the Bhot population of Lahúl, Kunawer, and the Kumaon passes. But there may also be the analogues of the Ráwats.

A Serpa vocabulary of Mr. Hodgson's represents one, at least, of the Bhot populations of Nepaul. It is all but actual Tibetan.

English.	Serpa.	Tibetan.
Man	mi	mi
Head	go	go
Hair	ta	ta
Eye	mik	mik
Ear	amchuk	amcho
Tooth	so	so
Blood	thak	thak
Bone	ruba	ruko
Hand	lango	lango
Foot	kango	kango
Sky	nam	nam
Sun	nimo	nimo
Moon	oula	dawa
Star	karma	karma
Water	chhű	chhű
Stone	doh	do
Tree	dongo	shindong.

Far more interesting are three rude tribes named *Chepang*, *Haiyu* and *Kasanda;* of which, as far as there are degrees in rudeness, the Kusunda are the rudest. I give the only account of them in Mr. Hodgson's words:—

"Amid the dense forests of the central region of Népál, to the westward of the great valley, dwell, in scanty numbers and nearly in a state of nature, two broken tribes having no apparent affinity with the civilized races of that country, and seeming like the fragments of an earlier population.

"They toil not, neither do they spin; they pay no taxes, acknowledge no allegiance, but living entirely upon wild fruits and the produce of the chase, are wont to say that the Rajah is Lord of the cultivated country as they are of the unredeemed waste. They have bows and arrows, of which the iron arrow-heads are procured from their neighbours, but almost no other implement of civilization, and it is in the very skilful snaring of the beasts of the field and the fowls of the air that all their little intelligence is manifested.

"Boughs torn from trees and laid dexterously together constitute their only houses, the sites of which they are perpetually shifting according to the exigencies or fancies of the hour. In short, they are altogether as near to what is usually called the state of nature as anything in human shape can well be, especially the Kusundas, for the Chépángs are a few degrees above their confrères, and are beginning to hold some slight intercourse with civilized beings and to adopt the most simple of their arts and habits. It is due, however, to these rude foresters to say that, though they stand wholly aloof from society, they are not actively offensive against it, and that neither the Government nor individuals tax them with any aggressions against the wealth they despise or the comforts and conveniences they have no conception of the value of.

"They are, in fact, not noxious but helpless, not vicious but aimless, both morally and intellectually, so that no one could without distress behold their careless unconscious inaptitude."

He continues—

"During a long residence in Népâl, I never could gain the least access to the Kusundas, though aided by all the authority of the Durbar: but, so aided, I once in the course of an ostensible shooting excursion persuaded some Chépángs to let me see and converse with them for three or four days through the medium of some Gúrúngs of their acquaintance. On that occasion I obtained the accompanying ample specimen of their language; and, whilst they were doling forth the words to my interpreters I was enabled to study and to sketch the characteristic traits of their forms and faces. Compared with the mountaineers among whom they are found the Chépángs are a slight but not actually-deformed race, though their large bellies and thin legs indicate strongly the precarious amount and innutritious quality of their food. In height they are scarcely below the standard of the tribes around them—who, however, are notoriously short of stature—but in colour they are very decidedly darker or of a nigrescent brown. They have elongated (fore and aft) heads, protuberant large mouths, low narrow foreheads, large cheekbones, flat faces, and small eyes. But the protuberance of the mouth does not amount to prognathous deformity, nor has the small suspicious eye much, if anything, of the Mongolian obliqueness of direction or set in the head. Having frequently questioned the Durbar whilst resident at Káthmándú as to the relations and origin of the Chépángs and Kusundas, I was invariably answered that no one could give the least account of them, but that they were generally supposed to be autochthones, or primitive inhabitants of the country. For a long time such also was my own opinion, based chiefly upon their physical characteristics as above noted and upon the absence of all traceable lingual or other affinity with the tribes around them. So that I took them to be fragments of an original hill population prior to the present Tibetan inhabitants of these mountains; and to be of Tamulian extraction, from their great resemblance of form and colour to the Aborigines of the plains, particularly the Kóls. It did not for several years occur to me to look for lingual affinities beyond the proximate tribes, nor was I, save by dint of observation, made fully aware that the Mongolian type of mankind belongs not only to the races of known northern pedigree, such as the mass of the sub-Himálayan population, but equally so to all the Aborigines of the plains, at least to all those of Central India. Having of late, however, become domiciled much to the eastward of Káthmándú, and having had more leisure for systematic and extended researches, those attributes of the general subject which had previously perplexed me were no longer hindrances to me in the investigation of any particular race or people. I now saw in the Mongolian features of the Chépángs a mark equally reconcilable with Tamulian *or* Tibetan affinities; in their dark colour and slender frame, characteristics at first sight indeed rather Tamulian than Tibetan, but such as might, even in a Tibetan race, be accounted for by the extreme privations to which the Chépángs had for ages been subject; and in their physical attributes taken altogether I perceived that I had to deal with a test of affinity too nice and dubious to afford a solution of the question of origin. I therefore turned to the other or lingual test; and, pursuing this branch of the inquiry, I found that with the southern Aborigines there was not a vestige of connection, whilst, to my surprise I confess, I discovered in the lusty Lhópás of Bhútán the unquestionable origin and stock of the far removed, and physically very differently characterized Chépángs!"

That their language is akin to the Lhopa is clear from the specimen; clearer from the table which Mr. Hodgson has given of the affinities. Whether they are more especially Lhopa than Tibetan is doubtful. I give the table as it is given by its author:—

English.	Chepang.	Lhopa.	Tibetan.
Sun	nyam	nyim	nyimá
Sky	nam	nam	namkháh
Mountain	rías	rong	rí
Star	kar	kam	karma
Free	sing-tak	shing	jon-shing
Salt	chhé	chhá	tsá
Road	liam	lam	lam
House	kyim	khim	khyim
Fire	mí	mí	mé
Arrow	láh	dáh	dáh
Dog	kúī	khi	khyi
Buffalo	mísha	méshi	mahi
Fish	gná	gná	nyá
Hog	piak	phag	phag
Horn	róng	róng	rá
Two	nhí-zho	nyi	nyis
Three	súm-zho	súm	súm
Give	búī	bin	búh
Take	lí	ling	lan

Are the Chepang, Haiyu, and Kusunda remnants of the earlier occupants of the soil? or are they wanderers from Tibet degenerated? I only submit that they are in the same category with Ráwat, so that what the Chepang are, that are the Ráwat also.

CHAPTER II.

The Nepaul Tribes.—The Sunwar.—The Magar.—Gurung.—Jareya.—Newar.—Murmi.—Kirata or Kichak.—Limbu.—Lepcha.—The Denwar, Durré, and Bramho.

The Sunwar.—Of these I only know that they lie in the north-west, and at a high level, conterminous (I believe) with the true Bhot. Then come

The Magar.—It is the *lower* levels, chiefly on the *east* of the Kali, which are occupied by the Magar. They are the occupants of the lower levels; a point worth notice, because when we approach the mountain-tops the population changes. The forces which have changed the character of the indigenæ of western Nepaul, Gurwhal, and Kumaon are in continuance, directing themselves eastwards. Hence, the Magar may, at some future time, be what their neighbours to the west are at present, thoroughly Indianized. Their present condition is, more or less, transitional. Their physical conformation is their own, being that of the Bhot in general. At the same time there has been much intermarriage, and amongst the Hindus we may find the flat faces of the aborigines; amongst the aborigines the oval outlines and prominent, regular, or delicate features of their conquerors.

The language of the Magar is their own; essentially what is called monosyllabic; essentially in the same great class with the Tibetan, Chinese, Burmese, and Siamese. If it were not so they would scarcely find their place in this part of the work. There are elements, however, here which betoken transition, inasmuch as numerous words of Hindu origin have become incorporate. Besides this, many Hindus speak the Magar; whilst many Magar have either unlearnt their own tongue or use the Hindu in preference. This is more especially the case with the soldiers, many of whom are separated for long periods of time from their fellow countrymen at home, doing service in garrisons in other parts of the kingdom.

Upon the whole, the approximation to the Hindu type has been sufficient to lead more than one author to designate the Magar as Kshatrias—Hindu Khsatrias, neither more nor less. They are not this. On the contrary, they are members of the same great group with the Bhot, &c.

The Magar alphabet is of Indian origin; indeed, this may be said of the alphabets of all the languages now coming under notice in general. In one or two cases we may hear of a native alphabet. If such exist it will still be of Indian origin, having been introduced earlier, having been adapted differently, having been modified by the course of time. A truly native alphabet is to be found neither at the foot of the Himalayas nor at their sides, nor yet at their tops, nor yet anywhere round about them. There has been (in the very decided opinion, at least, of the present writer) but one native alphabet in the world.

But the real hybridity appears in the religion. Without being scrupulous in other meats the Magar abstains from beef. Utterly unscrupulous in the way of drinks, he indulges freely in the use of fermented liquors, and makes anything in the way of a feast or festival an occasion and excuse for intoxication. His excess in this matter is notable.

Then he has his own priesthood, or, at any rate, an Indian priesthood, with a Magar nomenclature. His

Brahmins are all Achars. In the pagan times a priest was called a Dami; Dami being the name for a priest in more than one of the tribes akin to the Magar at the present moment. We shall meet with the word when we get to the Bodo and Dhimal. Have we not, indeed, met with it already? There is a change in form and a change in sense—both being slight—but, surely, the Dami of the Magar is, word for word, the Jam and Tham of the Bulti populations, and of others far away from Bultistan.

Imperfect as is our information for the early history and social constitution of the Magar, we know that a trace of a tribual division (why not say an actual division into tribes?) is to be found. There are twelve thums. All individuals belonging to the same thum are supposed to be descended from the same male ancestor; descent from the same great mother being by no means necessary. So husband and wife must belong to different thums. Within one and the same there is no marriage. Do you wish for a wife? If so, look to the thum of your neighbour; at any rate, look beyond your own. This is the first time I have found occasion to mention this practice. It will not be the last; on the contrary, the principle it suggests is so common as to be almost universal. We shall find it in Australia; we shall find it in North and South America; we shall find it in Africa; we shall find it in Europe; we shall suspect and infer it in many places where the actual evidence of its existence is incomplete.

(2.) *The Gurung.*—The tribes that lie equally westward with the Magar, but differ from them in occupying a higher place on the mountain sides, are those of the Gurung. These are decidedly and eminently pastoral; the breeders of sheep. They use, too, the sheep as a beast of burden, and lay upon its patient back such light loads as their chapmanship requires them to move about with. The higher the level of his occupancy the more the Gurung is said to thrive. The heat of the plains is better borne by the Magar.

Their language is their own; different from that of the Hindus; different from that of the Magar; not very well known even to professed philologues; but known from a sufficiency of samples to enable us to place—or rather to isolate—it. It is the medium by which the Gurung priests propagate a Buddhist creed; for the Hindu religion, though not unknown to some of the Gurung, has yet to make its way to any notable extent. That it will encroach on the earlier creed is likely. On the other hand, it is not certain that even Buddhism has wholly replaced the original Paganism. A tribe, or collection of tribes, called Bhujal Gharti, is accused of numerous impurities in the way of food; for they eat anything except, perhaps, milk. At any rate they eat beef. When the details of the Bhujal superstitions are known they will probably turn out to be those of the Bodo and Dhimal; neither Buddhist nor Brahminic, but yet tinctured with an early Brahminism, which, in its present state, is either a rudiment of something that has to be developed, or a fragment of something that has fallen into decay. Like the Magar the Gurung fall into tribes; some of which are the Nisi, the Ghali, and the Thagsi; the Thagsi being the occupants of the highest altitudes, and constituting the truly Alpine division of the family.

(3.) *The Jareyas.*—Of the Jareyas I can give but an indifferent account. They lie to the south of the Gurung, with whom they are intermixed, and with whom they intermarry. Hamilton says that they have a peculiar dialect; but of this he gives no specimen. Mr. Hodgson denies the existence of a Jareya form of speech altogether. They are eminently Hindu both in creed and manners, notwithstanding which they may easily be as separate from both Gurung and the Magar, as those two families form one another. But they may also be either Gurung, or Magar, or Newar.

(4.) *The Newar.*—For now comes the notice of a new section thus named. The main portion of the central valley of Nepaul Proper was originally Newar, and Newar it is now, save and except the Hindu populations of the conquest. Favoured in respect to both soil and climate, at a lower level than the sheep-feeding Gurung, the Newar occupy a strong clay soil, fitted for brick-making, tile-making, and tilth. And this determines their industry and their architecture. The Newar are agriculturists and masons. No better cultivation, no better domestic architecture, is to be found than that of the Newar. The houses, as a general rule, are well-built and three stories high. They form large villages or small towns. The morals their occupants exhibit in the way of the sexes is by no means exemplary; indeed, the freedom (to use no stronger term) of the women is notorious.

Of their primitive Paganism no traces have been noticed. Perhaps they have no definite and tangible existence. Analogues to the Bujal Gharti amongst the Gurung there are none; so, at least, runs the evidence as it stands. On the other hand, there is no small portion of Hinduism engrafted upon the original Buddhism. There is also a great deal of true, or slightly-modified, Brahminism. Still it is Brahminism with a difference. A Newar priest is not a Hindu Brahmin, but a native Achar. Then there is the class of surgeons and physicians called Jausi. These are the sons of Brahmin fathers and Newar mothers.

A little before the Ghurkha conquest Hinduism took root in the Newar country, when some influential proselytes to the worship of Siva were made. These have developed themselves and their successors into a definite division of the population. Nowhere, however, is there absolute purity. Like the Magar the Newar eat beef; like the Magar the Newar drink alcoholic liquors. We have seen that, like the Magar, they have a priesthood, Brahminic in many respects, but not Brahminic in name and origin. A worshipper of Siva will both kill and eat his beef; one of Buddha will eat but not kill it. They burn their dead.

On the 11th of August a curious operation is effected in the matter of frogs. The Newar farmer on that day goes forth into the field, takes with him some mashed rice, looks out to find the frogs, and gives them the rice to eat.

English.	Sunwar.	Magar.	Gurung.	Newar.
Man	muru	bharmi	mhi	mijang
Head	piya	mitalu	kra	chhong
Hair	chang	chham	moi	song
Hand	table	hutpiak	lapta	palaha
Foot	kweli	mihil	bhale	pali
Eye	michi	mik	mi	mikha
Ear	nopha	nakyeh	nabe	nhaipong
Bone	nishe	miryaros	nugri	kwe
Blood	usi	hyu	koh	hi
Tooth	kryu	siak	sak	wa
Day	nathi	namsin	dini	nhi
Sun	na	namkhan	dhini	suja
Star	soru	bhuga	pira	nagu
Fire	mi	mhe	mi	mi
Water	pankhu	di	kyn	lau
Tree	rawa	sing	sindu	sinia
Stone	phunglu	thung	yuma	lohong
One	ka	kat	kri	chhi
Two	nishi	nis	ni	ni
Three	sang	song	song	son
Four	le	buli	pli	pi

English.	Suuwar.	Magar.	Gurung.	Newar.
Five	gno	banga	gna	gna
Six	ruk	—	tu	khu
Seven	chani	—	nis	nhe
Eight	yoh	—	pre	chya
Nine	guh	—	kuh	gunh
Ten	sashi	—	chuk	sanho

(5.) *The Murmi.* (6.) *The Kirata* or *Kichak.* The Sikkim frontier is now near, so that the remaining populations, in all probability, belong to the two kingdoms. Of the four that stand over for notice, the first two are the Murmi and the Kirata.

Of the former I only know that they are Buddhists, with a less amount of Hinduism amongst them than any of the aforesaid.

Of the Kirata, or Kichak, half may be Buddhist, half Brahminic. Brahminic, however, as that half is, it either eats beef or unwillingly abstains from it.

(7.) *The Limbu.*—The Limbu are called Chung by the Lepcha.

The Limbu intermarry with the Kirata, and are somewhat less Buddhist, and somewhat more Brahminic than their situation leads us to expect. It has been the policy of the Nepaul rulers to conciliate them.

The few known notices concerning the Limbu make them hardy and hardworking. They cultivate grain, feed cows, pigs, and poultry. Their huts are neat and well made; the walls being of split bamboo, the roofs of the leaves of the wild ginger and cardamon. They are guyed down to the ground by long rattans, to steady them against the winds—violent, frequent, unexpected.

A glimpse at the nature of a Limbu festival is got from Captain Sherwill's narrative. All the men, women, and children, amounting to about twenty, were drunk. And they were hospitable. The best of what they had was laid out before his party of sixteen—*chee* (the *chong* of Bútan) to drink, fowls and rice as food; and not only fowls and rice but milk, against which so many of the populations akin to the Limbu have a prejudice. At the house of the principal man of the neighbourhood some thirty men and women were sitting on the ground, drinking hot chee. Some beat drums. In the middle a young girl, highly excited, in a fantastic dress fringed with the teeth of beasts, the beaks and spurs of birds, the claws of bears, and cocks' tail feathers, was dancing. Her action was slow and monotonous at first, then livelier and more rapid, then most lively and most rapid, then hurried and irregular, then frenzied and uncontrollable. The noise, too, increased; the humming or singing became a shout; the drums beat louder and more discordantly. There was a fire in the middle of the circle; the poor girl dashed into it, and with her naked feet sent the burning ashes over the floor. Then a propensity to mischief set in. She would pull down the frames upon which the domestic utensils were hung; she would burn down the house. The next morning she was as quiet and demure as any decent little Limbu could be.

(8.) *The Lepcha.*—The Lepcha is hemmed in between the Newar and the other tribes of Nepaul, and the Lhopa of Bútan; the Lepcha area being barely sixty miles in breadth. Darjeling is the town wherein the Lepcha is most found; Sikkim the district which he more peculiarly calls his own. His decidedly Mongolian physiognomy has been admitted and insisted on by all who have noticed him—by Hodgson, Hooker, &c. The latter expressly states that of his Mongolian kindred he is more specially Tibetan than either Newar or Lhopa—"he differs from his Tibetan prototype, though not so decidedly as from the Nepalese and Bhotanese." The stature is short, varying from four feet eight inches (which is *very* short) to five feet; the face broad and flat, nose depressed, eye oblique, chin beardless, skin sallow or olive; the lip shows a little moustache. Broad-chested and strong-armed the Lepcha is still fine-boned; at least, his hands are small, and his wrists thin. In like manner the legs of the Lepchas are stout, the feet small. The expression of their features is more mild and frank than cunning and quarrelsome, and this seems to agree with their real character. The Ghorkas are brave and fierce, the Lhopa quarrelsome and cruel, but not brave; the Lepcha timid and peaceful; such, at least, is Hooker's statement. He adds, that in their dealing with each other they are an honest people.

The chief article in a Lepcha dress, scantier and cooler than the altitude of their occupancy would suggest, is a cotton cloak, which is loosely thrown round the body, so as to leave the arms free, striped with blue, and worked with white and red. In cold weather an upper garment, with loose sleeves, is added. The hat, when worn, which is only on occasions, is made of the leaves of one of the *Scitamineæ* spread out between two thin plates of bamboo, extravagantly broad, wide-brimmed, and with a hemi-spherical crown. This is when the weather is rainy. When dry it is changed for a conical one, ornamented with peacock's feathers, and flakes of talc. The umbrella is a hood rather than a true umbrella, reaching from the head to the thighs. A Lepcha in a shower is like a snail with its shell on.

The ornaments—amulets as well as ornaments—are chiefly of Tibetan make, some of great beauty, others of great value, having in them little idols, charms, copies of prayers, bones, hairs, and nail-parings of Lamas. The hair, an object of pride and care, in the dressing of which a female will assist a male, is collected into a large tail—simple or plaited, flat or round. The women wear two tails, and when in full dress are much less ungainly in their costume than the men. Besides the skirt and petticoat they wear a small sleeveless woollen cloak, covered with crosses, and fastened by a girdle of silver chains. A coronet of scarlet cloth adorns the head. The common dress (as with the Bodo) is of silk, coarse in kind, and spun by a worm peculiar to the country which feeds on the leaves of the castor-oil plant.

The Lepcha knife is long, heavy, and straight, serving for all purposes to which a knife can by any human ingenuity be applied; it is always worn, but rarely drawn in anger. They drink out of little cups turned in the knots of maple and other woods. A common one costs but 4*d.* or 6*d.*; but, besides these, there are several fancy articles (so to say) polished or mounted in silver. These are dearer. If made of a peculiar wood, paler than the common material, they are supposed to serve as antidotes, and of these the price is extravagant—say forty times as much as that of the common ones. Mr. Hooker gave a guinea for one hardly different from the ordinary kind in its outward appearance. The knots, from which they are shaped, are the modified roots of the oak, &c., as attacked by the balanophora, a parasite.

Their stimulus is the fermented juice of the Eleusine Coracana (Murwa grain). It is acidulous, refreshing, slightly intoxicating, and not unlike hock or sauterne in its flavour; is not common, above 6000 feet elevation; is presented in a joint of a bamboo, and sucked through a hollow reed. Word for word it is Murmi *chee*, the Bútani *chong*.

The only musical instrument, described as Lepcha, is a kind of flute, made of the cane of the bamboo, with four or six holes burnt in it considerably below the mouth-piece. The tone is low and sweet, and its sound monotonous, but not unpleasant, like that of the Æolian harp. The Lepcha songs are monotonous also.

Marriages are contracted in nonage, and even in childhood. Brides are purchased either by money or service. The violation of the marriage tie is sharply punished. The children of mixed marriages belong to the country of the father.

Though the Lepcha is no Buddhist, the Buddhist religion has considerably modified some of his customs and ceremonies. The priests, for instance, called Bijua, profess mendicancy, like the begging friars of Tibet; carry the Mani or prayer-machine, and wear Buddhist rosaries and amulets. The natives, who treat them with no little respect, liberally answer to their applications for charity, and so freely admit their sanctity, that a little energy in the business of conversion would, doubtless, be followed by a large amount of Lepcha proselytism. As it is, however, the original creed is but little interfered with. In this the priest is the medicine-man, the exorcist, and the director of feasts, ceremonies, and sacrifices. These are to the evil rather than the good spirits. "Why should we sacrifice to *them?* They do us no harm. The evil spirits, who dwell in every rock, grove, and mountain, are constantly at mischief, and to them we must pray, for it is they who hurt us."

Omens are sought for in the entrails of fowls, and superstitions of all kinds are rife and common. A list of Lepcha charms is long and heterogeneous. The dog-tooth of a leopard, the dog-tooth of the barking deer, an ornamented brass bead, a piece of ginger, a clove of garlic, the hard seeds of some tree—all these at once strung on a thread did Major Sherwill see on the neck of a Lepcha child.

A list of Lepcha vegetables is peculiar. Mountain spinach, fern tops, fungi, are what a Lepcha will contrive to exist on amongst the hills ; but he adds to his mess of spinach a sauce of stinging-nettles, crushed, but raw.

The Lepchas are one of the many rude tribes who are skilful in kindling a light by means of two pieces of wood. One lies horizontally, and has a hole in it ; another is worked vertically, and is sharpened to a point. Both are prepared beforehand, highly-dried, and smoked. The point of the vertical, is fixed in the hole of the horizontal, piece, and rapidly revolved ; the friction at the points of contact soon produces fire. This is just how it is done amongst the Dyaks of Borneo, also amongst some of the American tribes. It is effective. When "lucifers, matches, flint-and-steel, and several other modes of procuring fire were utterly unavailing in these damp mountains, the Lepchas were never at a loss." They rubbed the sticks and got a light. After about a minute's working the wood catches fire. It is the wood of a particular tree, and resembles willow. Two men do the revolutionary part of the operation. One begins at the top of the upright stick. As his hand gradually slides downwards another succeeds. So that before the light is kindled four hands are in action.

The Lepchas believe that dysentery is infectious, and, accordingly, take certain sanitary precautions to prevent its spread. It was at Hee when Major Sherwill was on his survey. The people begged him not to go there, refusing to follow him if he did. Ere long he came upon two upright posts, one on each side of the path. They were connected at top by a horizontal pole—

gallows-fashion. From this pole hung two bundles of sticks, near them two cudgels; a few feet further stood two more posts, but without any pole or bar to join. The meaning whereof is this. Any one coming from the side of the two unconnected posts may pass on; any one coming from the side of the two connected ones must not pass on. If he do he will be beaten by the cudgels, and fined thirty rupees; thirty being the number of the sticks in the two bundles—fifteen in each.

The chief Lepcha diseases are small-pox (the most dreaded of all), goitre, remittent fevers, and rheumatism.

The dead are burnt or buried, sometimes burnt first and buried afterwards.

English.	Murmi.	Kiranti.	Limbu.	Lepcha.
Man	mi	mana	yapme	maro
—	—	—	yembocha	tagri
Head	thobo	tang	thagek	athiak
Hair	kra	moa	thagi	achom
Hand	ya	chukuphema	huktaphe	kaliok
Foot	bale	ukhuro	laugdapphe	dianghok
Eye	mi	mak	mik	amik
Ear	nape	naba	nekho	anyor
Bone	nakhu	saiba	sayet	arhet
Blood	ka	hau	makhi	vi
Tooth	swa	kang	hebo	apho
Day	dini	len	lendik	sakne
Sun	dini	nam	nam	sakhak
Moon	ladima	lava	lavo	dau
Star	karchin	sangyen	kesva	sahor
Fire	me	mi	me	mi
Water	kwi	chawa	chua	ong
Tree	dhong	sangtang	sing	kung
Stone	yumba	lungta	lung	long
One	grik	ektai	thit	kat
Two	gni	hasat	nyetsh	nyet
Three	som	sumya	syumsh	sam
Four	bli	laya	lish	phali
Fire	gna	gnaya	gnash	phagnon
Six	dhu	tukya	tuksh	tarok
Seren	nis	bhagya	nuksh	kakyok

English.	Murmi.	Kiranti.	Limbu.	Lepcha.
Eight	pre	reya	yetsh	kaken
Nine	kuh	phangya	phangsh	kakyot
Ten	chiwai	kip	thibong	kati

Three other populations seem to belong to the same group with the Ráwat, Kúsúnda, Haiyu, and Chepang. They occupy the districts where the soil is moist, the air hot, the effluvia miasmatic. They are named, but not described in full, by Mr. Hodgson as Durre, Denwar, and Bramho. Word for word, I believe these names to be Tharu, Dunghur, and (possibly) Rawi. No specimen of their language is published. It may be akin to the Chepang; it may be more akin to the Dhimal and Bodo of the next chapter.

CHAPTER III.

The Kocch.—Dhimal and Bodo.—Western Bodo of Sikkim and the Bútan frontier.—Eastern Bodo, or Borro, of Asam and Cachar.—The Garo.—The Kasia.—The Mikir.

The Kocch (*Koktsh, Koksh,* or *Kúksh*).—The Kocch are the Kavach of the Yogini Tantra, where they are noticed as Mlekhs, or barbarians; as, without doubt, they *then* were, one and all. They are not all barbarians now; but, on the contrary, fall into three divisions; two of which are sufficiently modified to disguise their real affinities. Two are disguised after the manner of the modified Magars and Newars; or rather they are in the condition of the Jareyas where the concealment of the original character is greater. What this arises from we can anticipate; though not altogether. Brahminism has something to do with it. Has Buddhism also? No. We are anticipating too much here. We are no longer in Tibet and Nepaul, but in India, where Buddhism is said to be banished. It is not, then, a case of Brahminism and Buddhism, but one of Mahometanism, and Brahminism. When the Mahometan power was established in Bengal the kingdom of the Kocch bounded it on the north, extending from 88 to 93° E. L., and from 26 to 27° N. L. It may have touched the south-eastern extremity of Nepaul. At any rate it lay along the southern frontier of Sikkim, and Bútan, extending itself into Asam, with Kocch Bahar for its metropolis. Such a kingdom as this was powerful; and, although the Hindu and Mahometans called it the Kingdom of Kavach, or Kocch, its ethnological constituents were heterogeneous. In fact, they consisted of all the tribes under notice; one being as much Kocch as the other, the name being, when first given, general, though now exceedingly limited. At present a Kocch is one thing, a Dhimal another, a Bodo another. Some centuries ago they were all Kocch. Suppose the sub-alpine regions of Lombardy and Piedmont to have been called Barbary, by the Romans, without distinction of the tribes which composed their population. Suppose this population to have been heterogeneous. Suppose some portion of one division of it to have become Romanized; and, so changed, to have abandoned the name of Barbari; the remainder retaining it. The name would, in all probability, be anything but a complimentary one. Meanwhile, the kingdom breaks up, and the other divisions are no longer blended with the general mass of Barbars, but known in details; or, supposing them to be taken *en masse*, the name by which they are known to the Romans is changed. What could now befall the primitive Barbari, *i. e.* those who were not Romanized? They would be the only section of the population that retained the original name, which would now have become special and particular—general and collective though it had been originally. They might or might not be proud of it. They might be proud of it if left alone; yet easily made to abandon it by being acted upon from without. Its discreditable nature might be enlarged on: and, in the course of time, its application might become equivocal. *Mutatis mutandis*, this seems to have been the case with the word under notice. The Bodo of the immediate neighbourhood call the population we are considering Kocch. The more distant Bodo of Asam call them Hásá. The Dhimal call them Kamul (? Dhimal). But what do they call themselves? The Mahometan and Hindu members of the class have, as aforesaid, abandoned the name. But the unconverted portion; what of it? They called themselves Koocch when "not perplexed with Brahminical devices;" by which I understand that, when they are persuaded that the same is a badge of rudeness, they are easily put out of love with it.

The unconverted Kocch, the only ones at present under consideration, live in the woods, and cultivate the soil with the hoe. They move from spot to spot as the soil gets exhausted. They are well fed and fairly clothed; of average strength and vigour. They abstain from beef; but respect and admire the Garo who do not, and *because* they do not; for they hold that the less a tribe is restricted the more exalted it is. They eat no tame animal without sacrificing some part of it to the gods, two of whom are Pushi and his wife Jago. They sacrifice, too, to the sun, moon, and stars, to the deities of the rivers, hills and woods, to their deceased parents. The chief feast is at the harvest. The end, too, of the rainy season is a time for solemn sacrifices. The sacrificant priest is called a Deoshi. He is chosen by his employer, marries, and works like the rest, and has no hereditary authority. Of the victims, the blood goes to the deities, the flesh to their worshippers. The dead are kept two days, during which time the family mourn, the friends feast. They are then burnt, by a river's side, where the mourners bathe and have done with their mourning. There is also a sacrifice of pigs. Whoever marries out of his tribe incurs a fine, and whoever incurs a fine without paying it must become a bondsman until his wife can redeem him. And here we come in contact with a strange piece of social economy. The property of the husband is made over to the wife; when she dies it goes to her daughters, and when he marries he lives with his wife's mother. Marriages are arranged in the nonage of the parties concerned;

though not without consulting the inclination of the contemplated bride. Ante-nuptial frailties are overlooked, and a girl can always marry her lover. After marriage however, the morality becomes strict, and polygamy or polyandria, concubinage and adultery, are punished with fines. The general character of the social organization of the Pani Kocch is patriarchal. The elder of the settlement decides between contesting parties.

The northern parts of Rungpúr, Púrnea, Dinajpúr, and Mymansing, are the chief Kocch localities.

At the risk of being accused of improperly rationalizing on historical statements I cannot forbear taking an exception to the account of the Kocch kingdom during the days of its supremacy, as given in Buchanan, and endorsed by Hodgson. It is to the effect that its founder's name was Hájo, that he lived more than three hundred years ago, at the end of the fifteenth, or the beginning of the sixteenth, century, that he had no son, that his daughter was his heiress, that he gave her to a Bodo chief in marriage, that he thus founded the kingdom, and successfully defended it against its three most formidable enemies, the Sauman, the Plov, and the Javan. In all this there is nothing intrinsically improbable, and if it were not for two out of the five names in the narrative no objection would arise. But Hájo is a suspicious denomination. It has all the appearance of being such a word as Romulus in the history of Rome and Hellen in that of the Hellenes. We shall see the name Hojai as that of a population before we get three degrees eastward, if we have not seen it already in the word Hásá. I suggest, then, that Hájo is a fabulous individual, no real founder of the Kocch or any empire; but an eponymus hero. Then comes Javan. In the ordinary translation of ordinary statements it is rendered Greek, being neither more nor less than Ion and Javan. Here, however, it is said to mean Mahometan; Saumar meaning the Ahoms of Upper Asam, and Plava the men of Bútan; Phih or Pruh being the name by which the Lepchas designate the Bútani.

The Dhimál.—The Dhimál live to the north and east of the Kocch, between the open plains and the higher levels of the mountains (both of which they avoid); also between the rivers Konki and Dhorla, touching the Bodo districts as well as the Kocch; indeed, the Bodo and Dhimál are intermixed, though each population occupies separate villages.

Neither do the two divisions intermarry. Of these the Dhimál is the smaller, amounting to no more than some 15,000 souls, a number that decreases rather than increases. It was the opinion of Mr. Hodgson, founded upon four months' intercourse with the Dhimál as well as the Bodo, that their traditions were nothing worth; that their area, however, had once heen larger than it is he inferred from the fact of there being a tract in North Bengal still called Dhimáli, lying considerably beyond the present limits of the reduced and receding Dhimáls. Again, although no chief of the Dhimál tribes now exists, a migration from Kamba to the Tengwa, and from the Tengwa to the Konki, in order to escape the oppressions of the Ghurkas of Nepaul, a migration from west to east, is still within the memory of man, having happened no more than sixty years ago.

I am probably wrong in departing from the plan so well illustrated by Mr. Hodgson in his valuable monograph on these tribes, wherein, on the strength of the little difference between them, and the great extent to which an account of the one serves as an account of the other, the two divisions of the Bodo and Dhimál are treated together, the *minutiæ* in which they differ being pointed out as they arise. Nevertheless, as it is my wish to give special details rather than to advance generalities, I adhere to the distinctions with which I have begun, and continue the notice of Dhimál as one separate from that of the Bodo, though not wholly, as will be seen in the sequel. Whatever may be their similarity in other respects—

1. The languages of the two populations are different.

2. The Pantheon of the two populations is different. This, however, is a difference of less importance than it appears to be at first sight, inasmuch as the chief objects of reverence with both the Bodo and the Dhimál are the rivers of their respective districts, which are sometimes invoked under the name of the deity that is supposed to preside over them, sometimes by the simple geographical designation. Thus, as examples of the former, we have the names Timai, Lakhim, and Chima, denoting the Teeshta, the Mahamada, and Kosi Rivers respectively, Timai, Lakhim, Chima, being three sisters. On the other hand, however, the names of the Konki, Mechi, Soran, Boas, and Dubelly Rivers are simply Kankai, Menchi, Sonusi, Bonasi, and Dhulpi. Some of these are of the masculine, others of the feminine gender; *i. e.* some are gods, others goddesses.

3. The details of the marriage ceremony are different. The Dhimál priest propitiates Dáta and Bidáta by invocations and offerings of betel-leaf and red-lead—Dáta and Bidáta being the deities who preside over wedlock. This is a cheaper operation with the Bodo than with the Dhimál; for with the Dhimál the marriage feast may be prolonged to the third day, and cost from thirty to forty rupees; whereas the Bodo ceremony may be gone through for four or six. When Dáta and Bidáta have been invoked, the bride and groom are placed side by side, each with five

pauns, with which they feed each other; the parents of the groom then cover the couple with a sheet, when the priest completes the nuptials by sprinkling them with water.

4. If the Dhimál weddings are dearer than those of the Bodo, their funerals are cheaper, for the Bodo practise more formality. A Bodo, when the funeral feast is ready, repairs with his assembled mourners to the grave of the deceased, and, if he be the nearest of kin, takes a little food, and presents it to the departed one with these words:—" 'Take and eat: heretofore you have eaten and drunk with us; you can do so no more: you were one of us; you can be so no longer: we come no more to you; come you not to us.' After this each member of the meeting breaks and casts on the grave a bracelet of thread; proceeds to the river and bathes, and having thus lustrated himself, repairs to the banquet, and eats, drinks, and makes merry."

5. That the names of the Dhimál festivals should differ is nothing more than what we expect from the difference of language. There are differences, however, in their number and details as well—not very important, nor yet calling for description. Still they are differences.

Word for word, I believe Dhimál, Kamul, and Tamul to be the same.

The Bodo.—The Bodo area extends much further than the Dhimál, the Bodo population being by far the more important of the two. Its western branch belongs to Bahar and Bengal, to the Sikkim and Bútan frontiers; and it is described in the valuable and well-known monograph of Mr. Hodgson, along with the Kocch and Dhimál. The eastern branch occupies Asam and Cachar.

The western Bodo build their houses and lay out their little villages in the same manner as the Dhimál; and building houses, and clearing grounds, are matters in which the two populations intermix and help each other. The chief material with which they work are the jungle grass and the bamboo. From ten to forty of the huts thus rudely made form a village. If the family be large each house forms a court or enclosure. First, the main dwelling-house; secondly, a cattle-shed, stable, or fold opposite it. Then, if needed, there are two wings on each side so as to form a quadrangle. The roof projects. The body of the houses falls into two compartments, one to sleep, the other to cook in. A bedstead, a few stools, a few mats and shelves, constitute the furniture—all home-made, as is, also, the earthenware. For the metal pans there must be a little barter at Kocch markets. They are all of brass—none of copper, none of iron. Neither is there any manufacture or use of leather. Ropes of grass, and baskets of cane do instead. In the way of clothing, they use silk and cotton, (but no wool); which they spin, weave, and dye. Their sandals are of wood: their ornaments, few in number, like their pots and pans, are purchased. Rice, maize, millet, fresh-water fish, and a fair allowance of meat, constitute the chief Bodo aliment, and Jo their chief drink. This is made of rice or millet, the grain of which is boiled, and flavoured by the root of a plant called Agai-chito. It then stands, nearly in a dry state, to ferment for two days. Water is then added, and the whole, after three or four days, is fit for drinking. The plant is grown for the purpose. Hodgson compares the Jo of the Bodo with the Aji-mana of the Newari of Nepaul. I think he might have done more. He might have suggested that the name of the Newari beverage was the name of the Bodo plant (Aji-mana, Agai-chito). Beside their Jo, the Bodo use tobacco—both freely; but not hemp, nor yet opium.

The Bodo are tillers of the soil; but their agriculture is imperfect, and quasi-nomadic; since they are not fixed but erratic or migratory cultivators. They have no name for a village, no sheep, no oxen, no *fixed* property in the soil. Like the ancient Germans, *arva in annos mutant, et superest ager*. They clear a jungle, crop it as long as it will yield an average produce, and then remove themselves elsewhere.

The Bodo villages are small communities of from ten to forty huts. The head of these communities is called the Grá. It is the Grá who is responsible to the foreign government (British, Tibetan, or Nepaulese), for the order of the community, and for the payment of its tribute. In cases of perplexity the Grás of three or four neighbouring communities meet in deliberation. Offenders against the customs of the community may be admonished, fined, or excomunicated.

The Bodo religious ordinances are simple. The birth, the weaning, and the naming of children are all unattended with ceremonies requiring the presence of a priest. At funerals and marriages, however, the priest presides. This he does, not so much as a minister to the essential ceremony, as for the sake of the feast that accompanies it. No Bodo or Dhimál will touch flesh which has not been offered to the gods: and this offering a priest must make.

Marriage is a contract rather than a rite. Polygamy or concubinage is rare: the adoption of children common. All the sons inherit equally; daughters not at all. A Bodo can only marry to one of his own people. Divorce, though practicable and easy, is rare; the wife and daughter have their due influence. Children are named as soon as the mother comes abroad, which is generally four or five days after her confinement. The idea that the delivery involves a temporal impurity is recognized;

so that all births (and deaths also) necessitate a temporary segregation and certain purificatory forms.

A price—Jan—must be paid by the bridegroom elect for the intended bride. If the former have no means of discharging this sum, he must go to the house of his father-in-law elect, and there literally earn his wife by the sweat of his brow, and labour for a term of years.

When any person is afflicted by witchcraft "the elders assemble and summon three Ojhás or exorcists, with whose aid and that of a cane freely used, they endeavour to extort from the witch a confession of the fact and the motives. By dint of questioning and of beating, the witch is generally brought to confession, when he or she is asked to remove the spell, and to heal the sufferer; means of propitiating preternatural allies (if their agency be alleged) being at the same time tendered to the witch, who is, however, forthwith expelled the district, and put across the next river, with the concurrence of the local authorities."

"When sickness takes place, it is not the physician but the exorcist who is summoned to the sick man's aid. The exorcist is called, both by the Bodo and Dhimáls, Ojhá, and he operates as follows. Thirteen leaves, each with a few grains of rice upon it, are placed by the exorcist in a segment of a circle before him to represent the deities. The Ojhá, squatting on his hams before the leaves, causes a pendulum attached to his thumb by a string to vibrate before them, repeating invocations the while. The god who has possessed the sick man, is indicated by the exclusive vibration of the pendulum towards his representative leaf, which is then taken apart, and the god in question is asked, what sacrifice he requires? a buffalo, a hog, a fowl, or a duck to spare the sufferer. He answers (the Ojhá best knows how!) a *hog*; and it is forthwith vowed by the sick man and promised by the exorcist, but only paid when the former has recovered. On recovery the animal is sacrificed, and its blood offered to the offended deity. I witnessed the ceremony myself among the Dhimáls, on which occasion the thirteen deities invoked were Póchima or Waráng, Timai or Béráng, Lákhim, Konoksiri, Ménchi, Chímá, Danto, Chádúng, Aphói, Biphói, Andhéman (Aphún), Tátopátia (Báphún), and Shúti. A Bodo exorcist would proceed precisely in the same manner, the only difference in the ceremony being the invocation of the Bodo gods instead of the Dhimál ones."

The great Bodo festivals are four; the Shúrkar, held in December or January, when the cotton-crop is got in; the Wagaleno for February or March; the Phúlthépno for July or August, when the rice comes into ear; and the Aihúno in October, or bamboo festival.

The Wagaleno was witnessed by Dr. Campbell and Mr. Hodgson. A noise of voices by the wayside between Siligori and Pankhabari drew them from the direct road to the spot whence it came. This was the bed of the river, where they found thirteen Bodo men, in a circle, facing each other, and each carrying a long bamboo pole, with different articles of wearing apparel streaming forth as its ornaments and a yak's tail at the end. Of three men who stood within the circle, the first danced to the singing (for the thirteen around him were solemnly chanting a kind of chorus) and gesticulated. The second was a priest; the third a servitor or assistant. It was a priest, clothed in red cotton, who set the tune to the thirteen chanters. The servitor had a brush and a water-pot. More important, however, than either servitor or priest was another actor, the seer, prophet, or inspired one. He it was who, full of the God, answered such questions as were put to him about the prospects of the coming seasons. He was Déódá, or Possessed. "When we first discerned him, he was sitting on the ground panting, and rolling his eyes so significantly that I at once conjectured his function. Shortly afterwards, the rite still proceeding, the Déódá got up, entered the circle, and commenced dancing with the rest, but more wildly. He held a short staff in his hand, with which, from time to time, he struck the bedizened poles, one by one; lowering it as he struck. The chief dancer, with the odd-shaped instrument, waxed more and more vehement in his dance; the inspired grew more and more maniacal; the music more and more rapid; the incantation more and more solemn and earnest; till at last, amid a general lowering of the heads of the decked bamboo poles, so that they met and formed a canopy over him, the Déódá went off in an unaffected fit, and the ceremony closed without any revelation—a circumstance which must be ascribed to the presence of the sceptical strangers."

The Aihúno is a domestic ceremony. The "friends and family being assembled, including as many persons as the master of the house can afford to feast, the Déóshi or priest enters the enclosure or yard of the house, in the centre of which is invariably planted a Sij or Euphorbia, as the representative of Báthó who is the family as well as national god of the Bodo. The Báthó, thus represented, the Déóshi offers prayers, and sacrifices a cock. He then proceeds into the house, adores Mainou, and sacrifices to her a hog. Next, the priest, the family, and all the friends proceed to some convenient and pleasant spot in the vicinity, previously selected, and at which a little temporary shed has been erected as an altar, and there, with due ceremonies, another hog is sacrificed to Agráng, a he-goat to Manásho and to Búli, and a fowl, duck, or pigeon (black, red, or white, according to the special and well-known taste of each god) to each of the remaining nine of the Noöni madai. The blood of the sacrifice belongs to the gods—the flesh to his worshippers, and these now hold a high feast, at which beer and tobacco are freely used to animate the joyous conclave, but not spirits, nor opium, nor hemp."

Mannou is the wife of Báthó, an eminently domestic goddess. She is found in every house, under the guise of a bamboo pole, about 3 feet high, with one end in the earth, and with a small earthenware cup of rice on the other. Such the symbol; which has its annual and its monthly offerings. The annual one has been described; the sacrifice being that of a hog. The monthly offerings are eggs, and they are made by the females.

The Borro of Cachar.—The Eastern Bodo (Borro), or Cachar, are divided into the Cachars of the hill-country and the Cachars of the plains; and these again are subdivided according to their difference of creed. A hill Cachar may be either a Hindu or a Pagan, though he is oftener the latter; and a Cachar of the lower levels may be the same, though he is generally, perhaps always, the former.

A Cachar of the plains is called a Hazai, Hojai, or Hajong, and this is what is meant by the Hojangs of Asam, and the parts about are spoken of. They are Hindu in creed, more or less Hindu in language and manners, Cachar in blood.

The Hojai have had rajahs of their own. Again, the title Burmon, or Brahmin, is applied as a mark of distinction to some of their nobler families, families which, notwithstanding their title, are a tribual aristocracy rather than an aristocracy of caste. Of this they have little; so little as to make them but loose and imperfect Hindus. They eat freely of both fowls and pigs. They sacrifice them to their deities. They indulge freely in fermented liquors; in short, they depart widely from what a Brahmin of Benares would consider orthodox. Their education is Hindu, their alphabet of Hindu origin. Those that read and write are prone to leave their ordinary agricultural industry and become collectors, policemen, and the like; showing no want of intelligence or activity in their new employments, but by no means showing the simplicity of character they maintained as cultivators of the rice and cotton of their fertile soil. In office they become adepts in chicanery, corruption, and oppression, imitating the worst practices of the Bengali.

The hill Cachar is more simple and unsophisticated, stouter, hardier, and more turbulent; more formidable, too, in the eyes of the neighbouring marauders of the Naga family. However little an Anjami Naga may hesitate to attack a Mikir village, he generally abstains from the occupancies of the hill Cachar.

Of the hill Cachars each head of a family lives in a separate house, of which from 20 to 100 go to constitute the village; the batchelors living in the *dekha chung*, or *warrior's house*. This is a large building in the centre of the village more like a club than an ordinary dwelling. The young men who have attained a certain age and have not chosen for themselves a wife, support it, and in it they live, their parents having eliminated them from the houses of their nativity. The Nagas have the same practice.

The great locality of the Borro of Asam is a frontier district, named Chatgari, between Desh, During, and the

Bútan hills, where their numbers may amount to 30,000, half the whole Borro population.

English.	Kocch.	Dhimál.	Bodo.
Man	beta-choá	waval	hiwa
——	———	diang	manshi
Head	mura	purung	khoro
Ear	kan	nhatong	khoma
Eye	chaku	mi	mogon
Blood	lohu	hiki	thoi
Bone	harwa	hara	begeng
Tooth	dant	sitong	hathai
Hand	hath	khur	akhai
Foot	bhori	khokoi	yapha
Sun	bela	bela	shan
Moon	chand	tali	nokhabir
Star	tara	phuro	hathotkhi
Fire	agni	men	wat
Water	jal	chi	doi
Stone	pathai	unthur	onthai
One	ek	elong	manche
Two	du	nhelong	manne
Three	tin	sumlang	mantham
Four	char	dealong	mambre
Five	panch	nalong	manba
Six	choe	tulong	mando
Seven	sat	nhilong	manchini
Eight	ath	yelong	———
Nine	noze	kuhalong	———
Ten	das	telong	———

The Garo.—The mountaineers of the Garo Hills, to the north-east of Bengal, have long commanded the attention of investigators, and a good account of them is to be found in the third volume of the Asiatic Researches, by Mr. Eliot. Their language, of which a specimen is there given, is left unplaced in the Asia Polyglotta of Klaproth. It is, however, a member of the class under notice, and was known to be so when the Bodo and Dhimál were considered Indian.

The Garo, like so many mountaineers, are hardy, stout, and surly-looking, with a flattened nose, blue or brown eyes, large mouth, thick lips, round face, and brown complexion. They have a prejudice against milk; but in the matter of other sorts of food are omnivorous. Their houses, called *chaungs,* are built on piles, from three to four feet from the ground, from ten to forty in breadth, and from thirty to one hundred and fifty in length. They drink, feast, and dance freely; and, in their matrimonial forms, much resemble the Bodo. The youngest daughter inherits. The widow marries the brother of the deceased; if he die, the next; if all, the father.

The dead are kept for four days; then burnt. Then the ashes are buried in a hole on the place where the fire was. A small thatched building is next raised over them, which is afterwards railed in. For a month, or more, a lamp is lit every night in this building. The clothes of the deceased hang on poles—one at each corner of the railing. When the pile is set fire to, there is great feasting and drunkenness.

The Garo are no Hindús. Neither are they unmodified Pagans. Mahadeva they invoke; perhaps worship. Nevertheless, their creed is mixed. They worship the sun and the moon, or rather the sun *or* the moon; since they ascertain which is to be invoked by taking a cup of water and some wheat. The priest then calls on the name of the sun, and drops corn into the water. If it sink, the sun is worshipped. If not, a similar experiment is tried with the name of the moon. Misfortunes are attributed to supernatural agency; and averted by sacrifice.

Sometimes they swear on a stone; sometimes they take a tiger's bone between their teeth and then tell their tale.

Among them "a madness exists, which they call transformation into a tiger, from the person who is afflicted with this malady walking about like that animal, shunning all society. It is said, that, on their being first seized with this complaint, they tear their hair and the rings from their ears, with such force as to break the lobe. It is supposed to be occasioned by a medicine applied to the forehead: but I endeavoured to procure some of the medicine thus used, without effect. I imagine it rather to be created by frequent intoxications, as the malady goes off in the course of a week or fortnight. During the time the person is in this state, it is with the utmost difficulty he is made to eat or drink. I questioned a man, who had thus been afflicted, as to the manner of his being seized, and he told me he only felt a giddiness without any pain, and that afterwards he did not know what happened to him."

In a paper by Captain C. S. Reynolds, we have the notice of a hitherto undescribed superstition; that of the *Korah.* A *Korah* is a dish of bell-metal, of uncertain manufacture. A small kind, called Deo Korah, is hung up as a household god and worshipped. Should the monthly sacrifice of a fowl be omitted, punishment is expected. If "a person perform his devotion to the spirit which inhabits the Korah with increasing fervour and devotion, he is generally rewarded by seeing the embossed figures gradually expand. The Garo believe that when the whole household is wrapped in sleep, the Deo Korahs make expeditions in search of food, and when they have satisfied their appetites return to their snug retreats unobserved."

The greater part of the Garo population is independent. A part, however, is British.

It is the northern members of the family that are in this predicament; their area being on the boundary of the Calúmalúpara pergunnah. This pergunnah is divided into shares of six and of ten annas; a fact which has engendered the names Cheanni (6 anna) and Dusanni (10 anna). There is Cheanni portion of Calúmalúpara, and there is Dusanni portion also; and it is the Calúmalúpara people who are either Dusanni or Cheanni. The terms, however, have been extended to the Garo, who lie along the frontier, those opposite the Cheanni parts being Cheanni; those opposite the Dusanni parts being Dusanni. Though "we have hitherto considered the Dusanni and Cheanni Garows as separate tribes, I believe that they are both of one Abengyas, and that this distinction is without a difference. They consider themselves one and the same people." Word for word, *abengyas* is, doubtless, the same as *buniah*, a term used by Eliot, and applied to the Garo chiefs. In the passage before us it seems to mean chieftaincy.

In 1822–23 the pergunnah of Calúmalúpara was sold to the Company, and the Garo mehauls seem to have gone along with it. These were troublesome possessions, for the Garo of Currybari were in actual revolt, and the whole occupancy had been a source of annoyance rather than gain.

Soon after its transfer the chiefs made their submission, and agreed to pay a revenue of 196 rupees *per annum;* the chiefs of each village paying it. In 1832, however, there were arrears, a demonstration against them, and a settlement which lasted till 1848; when another demonstration was necessary. A murder had been committed; and, as the murderer was not given up, Captain Reynolds, from whose narrative this notice is taken, made an inroad into their territory, burnt a village, and exacted promises of better behaviour for the future. He found the road barricaded in several places, and planted with panjis, or bamboo stakes, short, sharp, and dangerous. One end is set in the ground. The other wounds the feet of those who tread on it. So effective are they, that the troops, in one place, were an hour and a half getting over 200 yards of ground. They had to shave them off close to the soil before they could proceed. I draw attention to this, because, in another notice of the mode of warfare of the tribes of south-eastern Asia, these panjis will appear again. Several Malay tribes use them, and find them more formidable than either spear or sword. They are not above four inches long—little better than strong thorns. The whole weight, however, of the body, comes down on them, so that they penetrate to the bone—and this through the sole of a shoe or boot.

The expedition ended in the following agreement, signed by fifteen Locmas of village chiefs. It gives us a better insight into what the people are, and what the Company wishes them to be, than a longer notice.

"*Art. 1st.*—We agree to abstain from committing murder, either in our own clan or in any other, nor will we permit any amongst us to do so, or to commit any other heinous offences that we may be able to prevent.

"*Art. 2nd.*—It was our former custom to hang human skulls in our houses, we hereby agree to abstain therefrom for the future.

"*Art. 3rd.*—All disputes which may occur in our jurisdiction requiring investigation, we will endeavour to settle with the assistance of a punchyat of four or five of the most influential chiefs amongst us, and in presence of the disputing parties, and should we be unable to settle it ourselves, we will report the same to the Hunt Mohurir, with a view to its being settled by your lordship.

"*Art. 4th.*—When any officer or government servant may have occasion to travel through our country, we agree to clear the roads in our several jurisdictions, and to furnish him with coolies, and render him every assistance in our power.

"*Art.* 5*th.*—When any officer or his deputy may arrive at Bengal Katta and summon us to attend him, we will instantly do so, and if it is necessary for us to attend him at any other place, we agree to do so on his summons.

"*Art.* 6*th.*—We agree to prevent any independent Garros from entering the government territories through our jurisdictions with intent to murder or commit any other disturbances.

"*Art.* 7*th.*—When any officer or government servant arrives at our Doar, we agree, on being called on, to pay, without delay, the revenue due by us.

"*Art.* 8*th.*—The road which has been cleared from Bhayamara to Kuntanangiri, and Bengal Katta to Ripoogiri, we agree to keep clear every year throughout our respective jurisdictions from twenty-four to thirty feet wide."

The Dusanni Garo occupy twenty villages, the smallest consisting of a single house paying one rupee, and the largest of 100, paying 100. The whole number of houses is 306, each holding (say) ten persons. Hence, the total population of the Dusannis is 3060. In the Cheanni country the number of villages is twenty-five. In each district the names of them end in either *-giri* or *-parrah*, as Repúgiri, Rungtupara. This, however, is Indian, so that the British Garo, at least, have been Indianized in respect to their language, always assuming that the names in question are native, *i. e.* names given by the Garo themselves, and not names given by the Hindus of the frontier.

English.	Garo.	Borro.	Bodo.
Man	mande	manse	hiwa
Head	skho	khoro	khoro
Eye	mikran	nigan	mogon
Ear	nachil	khama	khoma

English.	Garo.	Borro.	Bodo.
Tooth	wagom	hathai	hathai
Blood	anchi	thoi	thoi
Bone	greng	begeng	begeng
Hand	jak	nakhai	akhai
Foot	jatheng	atheng	yapha
Sun	sal	san	shan
Star	jashki	hatolthi	hathotki
Fire	wal	wat	wat
Water	chi	doi	doi
Stone	rong	lanthai	onthai

Due east of the Garo country comes that of

The Kasia, which falls into petty rajahships, and, by so doing, exhibits a little more political organization than that of their western neighbours, where the constitution seems to be simply patriarchal. The difference between the Garo and Kasia tribes seems but slight. Both abstain from milk. Both chew pawn. A Kasia man expresses his contempt of a Bengali by saying that he "has white teeth."

In his accounts of rude tribes an ethnologist must take what he can get in the way of information without asking too minutely whether each particular fact tallies with the rest of his description. He is in the hands of his informants, and it rarely happens that they examine the phenomena which come under their notice from the same point of view. One describes the dress, another the customs, another the manners of a country, a fourth its religion. Others notice certain facts because they are common, others because they are rare. Two tribes may be so closely allied as to have, in all fundamental points, the same ethnological character. The details, with few exceptions, may be the same. Yet if the descriptions of them be imperfect (as most descriptions are and must be), it is possible that the similarity may be concealed. Let one writer note what the other omits, and this will be the case.

I have no doubt but that many isolated facts in the description of a Garo apply to a Kasia also, though in the notices of the Kasia they may be non-apparent, and *vice versâ*. I find, for instance, no notice of the Kasia believing in men becoming tigers; yet it is, probably, a Kasia superstition. The Kasia, on the other hand, have an especial fear of the snake. The Garo *may* have this also. No account, however, has been taken of it. From the Garo alone, or from the Kasia alone, we get but a slight notion of the mythology of the parts to which those families belong. Combine the two and our *data* increase. One account becomes the complement to the other. The fragmentary character of our material is at the bottom of this. If every section of every class had its full and complete description we might condense, generalize, connect; as it is we must take facts when we can get them, not caring overmuch whether they be isolated or systematically connected.

The construction of the Garo house is, at present, an isolated fact. When we get further southwards, and further eastwards, we shall find that the large house on a frame of piles is the ordinary structure.

The Garo panjis are in the same predicament. As has been stated, they will re-appear in Borneo.

Numerous rude nations catch fish by means of traps. I find, however, the Kasia fish-trap particularly noticed. Like the large houses, and the panji spikes, it will be noticed again, *i. e.* in Java, Borneo, and Sumatra.

Most of the tribes of the Bhot alliance are not only thirsty drinkers, but skilful distillers. No one, however, has told us this as a general fact; on the contrary, a certain number of observers have stated that such and such tribes practised such and such contrivances, and indulged in such and such potations.

So it is. There are some facts which we must note because they are peculiar, others because they are common. They may be trifling; still they should be noted. Of course when they appear and re-appear too frequently they may be pretermitted. Until, however, they have re-appeared once or twice they should be noted. Otherwise we may assume likenesses improperly.

The *living* bridges of the Kasia country may be commoner elsewhere than the existing descriptions make them. In the present state of our knowledge, however, they claim attention. On the bank of the river that runs between Ringhot and Cherra grows a large India-rubber tree. Whilst its fibres are young and pliable they are stretched across the stream, and fastened by their free ends on the soil at the other side. They take root, grow, and form a bridge of live wood. Sometimes two trees are planted on the two sides of the river opposite each other, in which case their fibres join in the middle. I subjoin Captain Yule's account. The tree throws out "a multitude of roots. Two or three of the long fibres, whilst still easily pliable, have been stretched across the stream, and their free ends fastened on the other bank. There they have stuck firmly into the earth, and now form a living bridge of great and yearly-increasing strength. Two great roots run directly one over the other, and the secondary shoots from the upper have been bound round and grown into the lower, so that the former affords at once a hand-rail and suspending chain, the latter a footway. Other roots have been laced and twisted into a sort of ladder as an ascent from the bank to the bridge. The greatest thickness of the upper root is a foot, from which it tapers to six or seven inches. The length of the bridge is about eighty feet, and its height about twenty above the water in the dry season.

"This bridge was constructed by the people of the village of Ringhot, and forms their communication with Cherra during the rains; the present generation say it was made by their grandfathers. This was the first and most remarkable bridge of the kind that I saw in the Kasia Hills, and I supposed it to be unique, perhaps half accidental. But I afterwards found it to be an instance of a regular practice, and saw such bridges in every stage, from that of two slender fibres hung across the stream, to such as I have described above, and there are not less than half a dozen within as many miles of Cherra. One I measured ninety feet in clear span. They were generally composed of the roots of two opposite trees (apparently planted for the purpose) bound together in the middle."

From living bridges to dead stone the transition is, perhaps, abrupt. The analogues, however, of the Cromlechs and Stonehenges, numerous in most countries, have been specially described in Kasia. Groups of erect oblong pillars, hewn or unhewn, are common; the number generally odd—from three to thirteen. The middle one is generally the highest, and is sometimes surmounted by a circular disk. A flat table stone near the village of Sailankot stood five feet above the ground, was two feet thick, and thirty-two by fifteen in circumference. Many of the villages take their name from these monuments. Mau means stone; and the villages Mau-smai, Mau-inlu, Mau-flong, and Mau-mlu, mean the Stone of the Oath, the Stone of Salt, the Grassy Stone, the Upturned Stone, &c. The upright stones are said to be cenotaphs, and if a Kasia be asked why his ancestors erected it, the answer will be that "he did it to preserve his name." Yet the name is rarely remembered. So much for the credit due to the traditions of rude nations. Others are believed to have been erected as memorials of a compact. "There was war between Cherra and Mausmai, and when they made peace and swore to it, they erected the stone as a witness." So said Umang, an intelligent native. Nevertheless, the stone may be older than the war, and the oath have been sworn on it because it was where it was, not because it was erected for the occasion. The name, however, favours Umang's view. Then there is the Mau-mlu, or the Salt Stone. To eat salt from the point of a sword is said to be a Kasia mode of oath-taking.

The names of persons are short, as Tess, Bepp, Mang, Sor, Mir, Bi; and fathers are sometimes addressed by a title taken from their children. "How is it with Pabobon, the father of Bobon? How is it with Pahaimon, the father of Haimon?" Not that the link between fathers and sons is of the strongest. On the contrary, when a child has grown up he leaves his father, and all but treats him as a stranger. The details of this account want criticism. The son of the sister inherits. The male child of a Raja may be a labourer, whilst his cousin may succeed to a large property once his (*i.e.* the labourer's) father's. As a rule, the matrimonial relations are lax. In other matters the habits of the people are such as encourage the missionary. The heads of a large village near Cherra invited one (Mr. Jones) to settle amongst them, offering, if he would do so, to build a house for him. This was in 1842.

The children spin peg-tops. In how many more countries do they do the same? No man knows. How to observe has yet to be applied to children's games. There is ethnology, however, in all things—even in peg-tops.

One of their ordeals is that of water. The man who can hold his head under water longest, wins.

They draw omens from broken eggs, noting the way in which they break.

The moon, once a month, falls in love with his wife's mother: she, to repel his addresses, throws ashes in his face. In days of old the stars were so many individuals, who climbed to the top of a tree. Others from below cut this tree. The company in its upper branches are the stars. The group of the Pleiads is called the Hen-man (man and chickens).

Every fourth day is a market-day in each village; the great and little markets being held alternately. The space between two of these is the Kasia week.

A Kasia before drinking a glass of brandy dipped his finger four times in the glass, first filliping a drop of the spirit over each shoulder, then dropping one along each side. "Why do you do this?" "For the name of the God." The name, however, of the deity is not given. It seems that Nat worship is the culture of the Kasia.

A superstition in respect to snakes has been alluded to. It is this. If a snake dwell in your house you may sell and consume what you like and your store will not diminish.

Kano Likai, or Lika's Leap, is a waterfall near Cherra. "Once on a time, a man of foreign race came to the hills, married a woman named Likai, and settled with his wife in a village north of Maumlu. They had two children, a boy and a girl. One day the woman betook herself to the forest as usual to cut firewood, and in her absence the father killed his two little children, and cooked them; on his wife's return, he invited her to feast on what he had prepared, and she did so; he then disclosed what she had eaten. Then said Likai, 'It is no longer good to remain in this world,' and, hurrying to the adjoining precipice, leapt over."

Another legend, concerning the wife of Ula. "Ula was a great warrior at the court of the Raja of Linkardyem, and the Raja married his sister.

"Now in those days there were but twelve households in Cherra, and the Raja of Linkardyem, making war on the Raja of Cherra, drove him with his people to the woods, where they ate leather, and the rind of certain fruits. But the Raja of Linkardyem was a savage, and abused his wife, the sister of the brave Ula. For he placed her on a frame of bamboos, and lighted a fire beneath; and so, being roasted, she died. So Ula was wroth, and he went to the Raja of Cherra, and said, 'Make me a great man and I will avenge thee on thine enemy.' So he of Cherra agreed; and Ula, having cut off the head of the Raja of Linkardyem, brought it to him of Cherra, and so became first counsellor of the Raja.

"One day, as Ula was going forth on his avocations, with others of the village, he said to his wife, 'Clothe thyself with my arms and garments.' Meantime the new Raja of Linkardyem came against Cherra with a mighty host of four thousand men. Now the village of Cherra was well girt with palisades and ditches, and the wife of Ula went forth to the barriers in her husband's arms and clothing, and the other women, doing likewise, went with her; and when the army of Linkardyem beheld the arms and the shield, they shouted in terror, 'Ula! Ula!' and turned their backs in flight, for great was their fear of Ula; and the wives of Cherra and the men who remained, went forth with the wife of Ula, and chased the Linkardyemians, and smote them sorely. From these twelve households come the twelve tribes which now exist in Cherra. My informant was of the house of Ula."

The Jaintia Tribes.—East of the Kasia range, lies that of the Jaintia Hills, the occupants of which may differ from the Kasia about as much as the Kasia differed from the Garo. Instead of being independent, these are under the Company. Instead of being nearly pagan, they are tinctured with Hinduism; the Saiva form of worship being partially and recently introduced.

Of the tribes *in situ*, or in their actual Jaintia occupancies amongst the hills, I have seen no full account. There is a population in Cachar and Asam which is considered to represent them. Whether it do so or not is another question. This is that of—

The Mikir.—In Cachar, and in the Asam district of Nowgong, the Mikir, whose name is, I believe, word for word, that of the Mekhs, occupy a considerable area; the lowest computation of their numbers amounts to 26,000. They cultivate rice and cotton, changing their localities every four or five years. *Arva in annos*, &c. We have seen this already. *Arva in annos*, &c. We may quote the sentence *ad libitum* in the notices of these parts.

The Mikir are, in the matter of name, Mekhs, Mlecchas or impure infidels; the word being of Hindu origin. So, at least, it seems; although I am not able to affirm that they call themselves differently. And they are what their designation is supposed to suggest, either unbelievers or imperfect converts. The latter are forbidden to drink spirits, but allowed to chew opium; and in this they indulge.

They hold, too, as many of their original superstitions as are compatible with the profession of Brahminism—and these are numerous. This is the story of the Converted and Unconverted Kocch over again. Like the Bodo, the Unconverted Mikir delight in festivals, and in the drunkenness which attends them. Like the Bodo, they have no prejudices in the way of eating. The cow is rarely killed; but this is because it is inconvenient rather than because there is any prejudice against beef. Pork is eaten freely. The sacrifices of fowls are common. These they offer to the sun, the moon, and the invisible deities attached to trees and rocks remarkable for either size or shape.

There are the Mikir of the plains, and the Mikir of the hills; the Cachar distribution over again. The Mikir of the plains belong to Nowgong in Asam rather than to Northern Cachar; the Mikir of the hills belong to Northern Cachar rather than Asam. The evidence of their connection with the Jaintia tribes is partly inference, partly what is called tradition. It is capable of improvement.

Stewart writes that they were *originally* settled in or near their present districts; that they lived under chiefs of their own; that the Cachar Rajas oppressed them; that they fled to the Jaintia Hills; that they were oppressed there; and that they returned. He merely, however, says that this is tradition. I take exception to it. The descent from the Jaintia Hills is, probably, true. The previous occupancy of Cachar is doubtful. The single movement is historical. There is no evidence of the double ones. On the contrary, the statement that in settling in Cachar they were only retaking their own, is one likely to develope itself from a *minimum* amount of fact.

Robinson says that they have a tradition that their ancestors came from the Jaintia Hills, and he adds that they have a few Jaintia words in their vocabularies. But he superadds that he has not compared the two forms of speech.

Again—the Mikir physiognomy is Kasia. So is the Mikir dress, which consists of two pieces of striped cotton cloth made bag fashion and with holes for the head and arms.

If the Jaintia tribes be Kasia, these affinities may be real. But what are the Jaintia tribes? I wait for a full account of them. Meanwhile, I remark that whatever they may be, and whatever may be the relation between them and the Mikir, the latter have decided Naga affinities in the way of language. It is probable that in these parts the transition from the Garo to the Naga may be found. It is possible, too, that the Mikir may always have been where they are; that they may know as a matter of fact that they resemble the Jaintia tribes in language and customs, and that they may explain this likeness by the assumption of a descent. Extremes meet. Learned ethnologists theorize thus, and savages do the same; one consciously, the other unconsciously.

The Mikir of North Cachar are the mildest and least courageous of the numerous populations of that district. The Kutcha and Angami Nagas of their neighbourhood, attack the hill Mikir with impunity, burn their villages, enslave their women and children. And the Mikir resist slowly and inefficiently; the story running that, long ago they attempted to throw off the dominion of the Rajah of Asam, failed, and were disarmed; that habitual cowardice arose out of the disuse of their weapons; that it has become hereditary, and has been transmitted to the present generation. The present Mikir carry the dhao; carry the spear—but they do not use them for actual warfare.

Their arts are the arts of peace. They are manageable, industrious, regular. They keep clear of the courts of law, grow rice and cotton, sell them to the Kasia, and pay their taxes regularly. When not at work in the fields they fell timber, make canoes, float them down to Lower Asam, and realize profits on their labour, and humble enterprize. The ground that they work is forest-land rather than jungle, and (as such) requires more clearing. They are obliged to work harder than their neighbours, and have established a more industrial character accordingly.

They build their houses on platforms. One of them may contain as many as forty individuals; men, women, and children, members of the same family, or of different ones, as the case may be. Of these large houses, jointly occupied, we have seen something, and shall see more.

English.	Kasia.	Mikir.	Naga.
Man	uman	arleng	minyan
——	——	penso	——
Woman	ka kantei	arloso	dehiek
Head	kakli	iphu	kho
Eye	ka kamat	mek	mit
Ear	ka skor	ino	na
Nose	ka kamut	inokan	kho
Mouth	ka shintur	ingho	tun
Tooth	ka baniat	isso	pa
Tongue	——	ade	——
Hand	ka thallid	ripa	thali
Foot	ka kajat	kengpak	da
Sun	ka sngi	arni	san
Moon	ubanai	cheklo	da
Star	uklur	*cheklo longsho	merik
Fire	kading	me	van
Water	kaum	lang	jo
Stone	man	arlong	long
Wood	kading	theng	pan

* Little moons.

CHAPTER IV.

The Hill-tribes of Asam.—Northern Boundary.—Aka, Dofla, Abor, and Miri Tribes.—The Bor Abor.—Eastern extremity and South-eastern margin.—The Mishmi.—The Muttuk, Singpho, and Jili.

THE main part of the valley of Asam is either Indian or Indianized. Not so the hills round it.

The mountain-range that forms the northern boundary is a continuation of the hills of Bútan, the occupancy of the tribes whose languages are represented by the Tak and Changlo vocabularies.

The details of the Bútan frontier are but imperfectly known; since the populations are rude, inaccessible, and independent. We know, however, that the four following belong to the same class; at any rate their languages are closely allied.

The Aka.—On the western extremity of the northern range lie the Aka tribes, of which, though there is a sample of the language, there is no good description. I can only say that they are succeeded by

The Dofla.—No less than 180 petty chiefs are said to hold authority in the numerous Dofla villages of the Char Dwar.

Char Dwar means the Four Marches; the Char Dwar being but one of the Dofla areas.

The Dofla are succeeded by—

The Abor.—The hills on the right bank of the Dihong belong to the Pasial and Mayong, those of the left to the Padú, Sibú, Nibú, and Goliwar, Abor; tribes which were visited in 1825 by Major Bedford, whose notice of them finds place in Major Wilcox's report upon Asam.

In the matter of food they were well-nigh omnivorous; but expressed a horror for those who eat beef. Whether or no they drank milk is not stated. The generality of the mountain tribes of the Himalaya eschew it. Each warrior had a bow and quiver; some of the arrows being poisoned. Their dress was from the bark of the Uddal tree. It was tied round the loins and hung down behind in loose strips. It served for a rug to sit down on by day, and for a pillow to sleep on at night. Some wore basket caps; some caps made of cane and skin; some caps made like helmets, and ornamented with stained hair. Every man had something woollen in his possession; sometimes a waistcoat, sometimes a blanket; sometimes coloured, sometimes figured. When first visited they were in the habit of making periodical descents from their highlands and taking tribute, or levying black mail, from the villagers of the level country. They also took slaves; for amongst the Abors of Pasial many Asamese captives were found. This has now been put a stop to.

The buffalo is the animal they most especially hunt. They wound him with a poisoned arrow, and follow his tract, until they find him either dead or dying. The favourite ornament for their caps is the beak of one of the toucans, or horn-bills, the Buceros (? Nepalensis). With this at the front, and a red chowry behind, the appearance of their head-gear is imposing.

If the derivation of the word *Abor* be accurate, the term *Bor Abor* is something like a contradiction. *Bor* means *tribute;* whilst *a* (like the Greek *α*) = *not.* Hence, *Abor* = *free from tribute.* It is no native word at all; but one used to the Asamese; consequently, it can be applied to more populations than one. They may, for instance, be Bor Naga who pay tribute, and Abor Naga who do not; the latter being called simply Nagas. But what if one tribe more pre-eminently independent than the rest get called Abor, κατ' ἐξοχὴν? Such a thing may easily be. And what if a portion of it lose its independence, as it may easily do? In such a case it becomes Bor Abor, or the Tributary Independent, and we get an oxymoron.

This really happens. The population which the Asamese call Abor call themselves Padam, of which they are two divisions, the Bor and the Abor, the payers of no tribute, and the payers of tribute.

This really happens if the current explanation of the words Abor and Bor be accurate. But I take exception to it. The Bor Abors are the stronger, the more distant, the more independent population. Besides which, there is a branch of the Khamti called the Bor Khamti. Does Bor mean great? I have seen a statement to this effect; indeed, it appears in the very paper wherein we find the other etymology. It should be remembered, however, that it may do this and not mean much in the way of superiority of magnitude. Magna Græcia was not so large as ordinary Greece. Can it mean the mother country? In some cases it seems to do so. What it means in the case of the Bor Abor and the Bor Khamti remains to be decided.

A Padam village on the river Shiku consisted of 100 houses, with granaries at a distance (for security against fire), and a morang in the centre. The morang is a large building for the reception of strangers, for the transaction of public business, and for the residence of the unmarried men, who live in it as in a common club or boarding-house. At the dawn of day the boys go round like watchmen, bawl out the time, and tell the half-awakened sleepers that it is time for them to be at work.

In their politics there is unlimited freedom, both of

voting and of speaking. The people pass the resolutions, each individual having a vote. And this they cherish carefully, jealously; their constitution being essentially democratic. Age and oratory have some weight. Upon the whole, however, the legislation lies with the masses, small though they be.

Their creed is simple. They sacrifice to certain deities of the woods and hills. The conical mountain, Regam, is the abode of an ill-natured, not to say malignant demon, who would cause the death of any one who should pry into the secrets of his dwelling, which is at the very top of the peak.

The Miri.—The Miri are in closer relation to the Asam government than the Abor, for it is against the Abor that the Asam government protects them. The bow and arrow—the arrow poisoned—are the chief Miri weapons. Their occupancy is on the eastern frontier of the Abor area.

English.	Doďa.	Abor.	Miri.
Man	bangni	amie	ami
Hair	dùmùk	dumid	dumid
Head	dompo	dumpong	tupko
Ear	niorung	narung	ierung
Eye	nyuk	aming	amida
Blood	ui	yi	yie
Bone	solo	along	along
Foot	laga	ale	leppa
Hand	lak	elag	elag
Sun	dani	arung	dainya
Moon	polo	polo	polo
Star	takar	tekar	takar
Fire	ami	emme	umma
Water	esi	asi	achye
One	aken	ako	ako
Two	ani	ani	aniko
Three	aam	angom	aumko
Four	apli	api	apiko
Five	ango	pilango	angoko
Six	akple	akye	akengko
Seven	kanag	konange	kinitko
Eight	plagnag	pini	piniko
Nine	kayo	kinide	konangk
Ten	rang	iinge	uyingko

The Bor Abor.—The Bor Abor, probably, belong to the same division of the same class as the Abor. The evidence, however, of their speaking the same language is incomplete. They lie to the back of the Abor, on the higher hills, and in a more inaccessible country. They are rude, independent, powerful, and but little known.

As we approach the head of the valley, and prepare for urning round towards its south-eastern margin, we come to the country of

The Mishmi.—The Mishmi frontier touches that of the Padam, or Abor, being on the drainage of the Dihong and Dibong. The details of the area beyond it are unknown. Its villages are small. Jillee and Anundea contain from thirty to forty families, Mabúm ten, Alonga twenty, Chunda twelve; making, in all, eighty.

The Mishmi, differing from the Padam in language, and in the shrine at which they worship, acknowledge them as relations, and are acknowledged by them; a common origin being claimed by the two populations. They also eat together. On the other hand, they quarrel and fight, and when the Mishmi of the above-named villages were visited by Captain Wilcox, they were at variance with the Padam of the Dihong and certain members of their own stock as well. They were variously dressed. None, however, were observed to wear anything woollen. Some wore rings beneath the knee, some caps of cane. Their ears were pierced, and their ear-rings various; now of metal, now of wood. Their arrows were poisoned so effectively that they were said to kill elephants. The wounded part was cut out; the rest eaten.

They described the tribes with which they were at war, but which were as Mishmi as themselves, unfavourably. Those of Bubhajia were accused of cannibalism.

The hut of the chief of the Thethong Mishmi was

strangely and filthily ornamented. Long poles of bamboo were hung with the blackened, smoke-dried skulls of all the animals with which the owner had ever feasted his friends and retainers. The smokiness of the huts has told upon the physiognomy of the Mishmi. They habitually contract their eyebrows. What is the mortality of the children? In Iceland, and the island of St. Kilda, where the reek is as impure as it is profuse, the deaths of infants from *trismus neonatorum* are inordinately numerous.

Some of the tribes turn up the hair and tie it in a knot, whilst others are closely cropped. The lower classes dress scantily; the chiefs well; in Chinese and Tibetan cloths, and with Chinese and Tibetan ornaments. The cross-bow is a common weapon.

Polygamy is common; the limit to the number of wives being the means of the husband. For each wife so many heads of cattle. Ghalim, one of the more powerful chiefs, had ten or twelve in his house, and a large remainder in separate establishments, or quartered amongst their relations. The women mix with the men, and join them in every labour but that of the chase.

For even ten wives a man must have a large house. Ghalim's was about one hundred and thirty feet long, and eleven wide. It was raised on posts. He was proud of the skulls that adorned it. It showed the number of cattle he had killed in the exercise of a noble hospitality. When he dies they will all be cleared away, and buried near the burial-place of the chief himself. And then his son will take his pride and pleasure in filling the house afresh. A chief who was either shabby or ostentatious retained the skulls of his father's time, and bragged of them as his own. He was voted an impostor accordingly.

The calf of the leg of the daughter of the Gam of Dilling measured more round than both Captain Wilcox's put together. What was the size of the captain's? Was the enlargement natural? In more than one savage country artificial means of thickening the legs are resorted to. Men should remember this, and make inquiries accordingly, when the legs of young ladies are twice as thick as their own.

When trouble comes upon a Mishmi he sacrifices fowls or pigs to the rural deities, and places the branch of a tree over his door to inform strangers that his house is under a temporary ban, and that it must not be entered.

The Mishmi are traders. Every man amongst them will either buy or sell. They are also blacksmiths, and forge their own spear-heads, though they buy them as well. They are skilful, too, in making suspension bridges.

The Taying and Mijhu of the following table are Mishmi tribes; the Miri being Abors, Dofla, or Aka, rather than Mishmi.

English.	Taying.	Mijhu.	Miri.
Man	nme	ktchong	ami
Head	mkau	kau	tupko
Eye	mollom	mik	amida
Ear	nkruna	ing	ierung
Blood	rhwei	vi	yie
Bone	lubunglubra	zak	along
Hand	ptoya	yop	elag
Foot	mgrung	mpla	leppa
Sun	ring-nging	lemik	dainya
Moon	hho	lai	polo
Fire	naming	mai	umma
Water	machi	ti	achyc
One	eking	kmo	ako
Two	kaying	kaning	aniko
Three	kachong	kacham	aumko
Four	kaprei	kambum	apiko
Five	mangu	kalei	angoko
Six	tharo	katham	akengko
Seven	.uwe	nun	kinitko
Eight	elyeni	ngun	piniko
Nine	konyong	nyet	kouangk
Ten	halong	kyep	uyingko

The Singpho, &c.—The group that now comes under notice seems to fall into three (or more) divisions; (1) the Muttuk, (2) the Singpho Proper, (3) the Jili. There may be others. These, however, are all we know; and these we know imperfectly. Error, therefore, in the classification is excusable.

Up to the very bank of the river, on its southern rather than its northern side, and at no great distance from its entrance into the valley from the north-east, lies the country of—

(1.) *The Muttuk.*—Muttuk, Moran, and Moameria, or Mowameria, are all names of the same population, the subjects of the Barsenaputi, a vassal of the Raja of Asam.

The Muttuk are Hindu in creed, worshippers of Vishnu, but worshippers of a very equivocal orthodoxy.

I have no vocabulary of their language *eo nomine.* The statements, however, concerning it are these—that though spoken by a small population, and in districts not more than a day's journey apart, it falls into no less than seven dialects, sufficiently unlike each other to be understood with difficulty. That of the Khaphok tribe is just intelligible to a Singpho. In Khanung there is still a resemblance to the Singpho; but no mutual intelligibility. The Khalang and the Nogmún forms of speech are, again, like the

(2.) *The Singpho Proper.*—The Singpho Proper are a powerful intrusive population, of the physical appearance of the populations with which they come in contact, partly in Asam, partly in Manipur, partly in the unexplored tracts to the east. Their religion is Buddhism, tinctured with Paganism, or Paganism modified by Buddhism. They live in separate villages under chiefs, captains, or elders called Gams.

CHAPTER V.

The Hill Tribes of Asam.—The Nagas.

THE valley of Asam is Indian, or Indianized. Not so the hills around it.

On the eastern frontier of the Mikir and Cachar comes a population rude and pagan; or, if not wholly pagan, with a *minimum* amount of Buddhism or Brahminism. The numerous tribes which compose it are on the boundary of the British dominions—some of them within it. Expeditions have been made by British officers against them. Like all pagans, however, they are fitter objects for the missionary than the soldier; and missionaries are finding their way to them. The fullest notice of their dialects is to be found in the American Oriental Society (vol. ii.), where specimens of no less than ten of their dialects are to be found. They fall into four groups.

(1.)

English.	Namsang, &c.	Joboka, &c.
Man	minyan	mi
Woman	dehick	tunaunu
Head	kho	khangra
Hair	kacho	kho
Eye	mit	mik
Ear	na	na
Tooth	pa	va
Hand	dak	chak
Foot	da	tsha
Sky	rangtung	rangphum
Sun	san	ranghan
Moon	da	letlu
Star	merik	letsi
Fire	van	van
Water	jo	ti

English.	Namsang, &c.	Joboka, &c.
Stone	long	long
One	vanthe	tuta
Two	vanyi	anyi
Three	vanram	azam
Four	beli	ali
Five	banga	aga
Six	irok	azok
Seven	ingit	annat
Eight	isat	achat
Nine	ikhu	aku
Ten	ichi	ban

(2.)

English.	Mulung, &c.	Tablung, &c.
One	eha	eha
Two	ih	ih
Three	lem	lem
Four	peli	peli
Five	nga	nga
Six	vok	vok
Seven	niath	neth
Eight	thuth	thuth
Nine	ther	thu
Ten	pan	pan

(3.)

English.	Tengsa, &c.	Khari.
One	khatu	akhet
Two	annat	anne
Three	asam	asam
Four	phale	phali
Five	phungu	phanga
Six	thelok	tarok
Seven	thanyet	tani
Eight	thesep	sachet
Nine	thaku	taken
Ten	thelu	tarah

(4.)

English.	Angami.	Mozome Angami.
One	po	po
Two	kena	kane
Three	she	sus
Four	da	deh
Five	pengu	pangu
Six	soru	soru
Seven	thena	thene
Eight	thetha	thetha
Nine	theku	thaku
Ten	kerr	kurr

The Naga houses differ from the Mikir; so does the Naga dress—or rather un-dress. From this they are supposed to have taken their name, which is anything but native. Indeed, it is not likely to be so. Few tribes so rude as these mountaineers have any general or collective name at all amongst themselves. Amongst themselves everything is particular or specific. Each tribe has its name, but the whole stock none. It is the neighbours who know them in their collective capacity. Now, in the languages of the plains, *nunga* equals *naked.* I do not, however, find that the Nagas are actually this: they have some clothing, though not much. It is, moreover, home-made; manufactured by the Naga women, dyed by them.

The name Naga, as we may easily believe, is, in general, foreign to the Nagas. There is one tribe, however, in North Cachar that so denominates itself. The Aroong Nagas call themselves what the neighbours call them.

In one respect they differ from the Mikir, Kukis and Cachar, with whom (in some portions of their area at least) they come in contact; and that notably. All the above-named tribes, though not migratory, are easily moved to a change of residence. They crop the ground around their settlements, and when it is exhausted go elsewhere. The Nagas crop the ground also, and exhaust it; but when, having done this, they find it necessary to make a fresh choice of ground, they go to a distance, cultivate their allotments, and never mind the trouble and labour of bringing the produce home. This is the sacrifice they make for the love of their old localities. The field is changed; the house remains where it was. Of Naga houses, some twenty, thirty, or one hundred constitute a village, the situation of which is generally on the tops of the hills. Can this extraordinary affection for particular spots be accounted for in an otherwise not over-active community? I think the suggestion of Stewart is correct—viz. that the habit of burying the dead near the houses promotes it. The Nagas inter their deceased relations at the very threshold of their homes, rolling a stone over the grave to mark the spot. The village streets are full of these rude memorials, some falling into neglect, but others fenced-in and ornamented with flowers.

When no blood has to be avenged the Naga is simple, social, and peaceful. His government is so pre-eminently patriarchal as to be no government at all. A quarrel, however, between two villages, or even between two families of the same village, leads to miserable results—blood for blood, treacherous surprises, cruel punishments.

The first deity of the Naga Pantheon is Semeo, the god of riches.

The next (perhaps) is the god of the harvest, or Kuchimpai.

The chief malignant deity is Rupiaba, a Cyclops, not only with one eye, but with that in the middle of his forehead, even as the eye of Polyphemus. But—

Inter cæcos regnat luscus. His assistant Kangniba, bad-tempered and malicious, is blind altogether. He must, however, be propitiated. And this can be done cheaply. A fowl is the sacrifice; but the sickliest and smallest of the roost will do. He can only feel what room it takes. So the crafty Nagas put the little bird in a big basket, and so deceive Kangniba the sightless.

The custom of the Genna is this. When certain occasions call for the preliminary rite, the whole village is closed. Work is suspended. The fires are put out. Eating and drinking, however, are believed to go on with more than usual vigour. A buffalo, or some animal, is sacrificed. When a fresh piece of jungle is cleared the ceremony of the Genna precedes; and the fire used for the purpose is made by rubbing two pieces of wood together. The ordinary light of a household hearth would be improper.

English.	Cachar.	Kuki.	Angami.	Mikir.
Man	subung	mi	ma	arleng
Woman	masainjoo	wamei	thennma	arloso
Head	khoro	loo	uchu	iphu
Eye	ma	met	umhi	mek
Ear	kumao	bill	uneu	ino
Nose	gung	na	unheu	inokan
Mouth	khu	kum	ume	ingho
Tooth	hatai	ha	uhu	isso
Hand	yao	khutpang	ubiju	ripa
Foot	yapha	kengpang	uphi-ju	kengpak
Sky	nakhasu	vanpi	keruke	shineng
Day	saing	ni	ja	arni
Sun	saing	ni	naki	arni
Moon	daing	lha	thirr	cheklo
Star	hatri	ashi	themu	cheklo longsho
Fire	wai	mei	mi	me
Water	di	tui	zu	lang
Stone	lonthai	shong	keche	arlong
Wood	bon	thing	si	theng
One	masi	khut	po	hisi
Two	maguni	ni	kana	hini
Three	magtham	thum	se	kithom
Four	mabri	le	da	phili
Five	mabonga	nga	pengu	phanga
Six	mado	gup	shuru	therok
Seven	masni	suggi	thena	theroksi
Eight	majai	get	thata	nerkep
Nine	masku	ko	theku	sirkep
Ten	maji	som	kerr	kep

CHAPTER VI.

The Burmese Group.—The Khumia and Kuki of Sylhet, Tipperah, and Chittagong.—The Old and New Kuki of Cachar.—The Mugs of Arakan.—Tribes of the Koladyn River.—Mhru, Kami, and Kumi.—Sak.—Shendu, or Heuma.—The Khen of the Yoma Range.—The Karien.

THE Naga dialects lead so decidedly to those of Munipúr, and the northern portions of the area now coming under notice, that the present chapter is, in many respects, their proper place. It was chiefly for the sake of the reader that they were separated. It was convenient to carry him round the great Asam valley as continuously as possible.

We have seen how it is bounded on the south. First come the Garo, then the Kasia, then the Jaintia Hills; then the occupancies of the Nagas in North Cachar, and Nowgong; then those of the Singpho, which take us up to the great bend of the Brahmaputra. Now all the native populations of all these localities, so far as they have already been enumerated, are, more or less, akin to the populations of the Burmese Empire; the Naga being somewhat less so than the rest.

South of the Nagas lies Munipúr and its dependencies; leading to Ava.

South of the Jaintia, Kasia, and Garo ranges lie the districts of Tipperah, Sylhet, and Chittagong, leading to Aracan.

In all these the population is equally Burmese. But it is not equally unmixed. The nearer we are to Hindostan, the greater the amount of foreign influences; the greater, too, the amount of Hindu blood. Sylhet, Tipperah, and Chittagong are like Asam—Indian, or Indianized.

Khumia and Kuki.—Khum means village; Khumia, a villager. The Khumia occupy the skirts, the Kuki the tops, of the hills. Except so far as the difference of level may develop differences in their mode of life, a Kuki is a Khumia, a Khumia a Kuki.

The Kuki, however, are, as may be expected, the ruder, and more truly pagan tribe; the creed being, nevertheless, tinctured with Indian elements. They "have an idea of "a future state, where they are rewarded or punished, ac-"cording to their merits in this world. They conceive "that nothing is more pleasing to the Deity, or more "certainly ensures future happiness, than destroying a "number of their enemies. The Supreme Being they "conceive to be omnipotent, and the Creator of the "World, and all that it contains. The term in their "language for the Supreme Being is Khogein Pootteeang. "They also worship an inferior deity under the name of "Sheem Sauk, to whom they address their prayers, as a "mediator with the Supreme Being, and as more imme-"diately interesting himself with the concerns of indi-"viduals. To the Supreme Being they offer, in sacrifice, "a gyal as being their most valued animal; while to "Sheem Sauk they sacrifice a goat only. In every "parah they have a rudely-formed figure of wood, of the "human shape, representing Sheem Sauk; it is generally "placed under a tree, and to it they offer up their prayers "before they set out on any excursion or enterprize, as "the Deity that controls and directs their actions and "destiny. Whenever, therefore, they return successful, "whether from the chase, or the attack of an enemy, they "religiously place before Sheem Sauk all the heads of the "slain, or of their game killed, as expressive of their de-

" votion, and to record their exploits. Each warrior has " his own particular pile of heads; and according to the " number it consists of, his character as a hunter and " warrior is established in the tribe. These piles are " sacred; and no man dares attempt to filch away his " neighbour's fame by stealing from them to add to his " own. They likewise worship the moon, as conceiving " it to influence their fortunes in some degree. And in " every house there is a particular post, consecrated to the " Deity, before which they always place a certain portion " of whatever food they are about to eat. In the month " of January they have a solemn sacrifice and festival in " honour of the Deity; when the inhabitants of several " neighbouring parahs (if on friendly terms) often unite, " and kill gyals, and all kinds of animals, on which they " feast; and dance, and drink together for several days. " They have no professed ministers of religion, but each " adores the Deity in such manner as he thinks proper. " They have no emblem, as of Sheem Sauk, to represent " the Supreme Being." (*Account of the Kookies, or Lunctas, by J. Macrae, Esq. Asiatic Res.*, vol. vii. 1801, p. 195.)

Such is the belief of the Kuki of Sylhet, Tipperah, and Chittagong, of whom the Kuki of Cachar are an offset.

The Kuki, who about sixty years ago came from the jungles of Tipperah to settle in Cachar, were, at first, in the same category with the Nagas, *i. e.* naked. In the course of time they ceased to deserve the name. They not only wear clothes now, but are skilful in the cultivation and weaving of cotton. They are well clothed and well fed; on a level with the Angami Nagas for physical strength, as also with the Kasia—these being the ablest-bodied of the frontagers of Asam.

In Cachar they are called the Old Kuki. They fall

into three divisions—the Rhângkûl, the Khelma, and the Betch, the first being the largest. The whole, however, are under 4000.

The Old Kuki of Cachar have a New Kuki to match. Both came from the south—both from the ruder parts of Tipperah and Chittagong. They came, however, as the name implies, at different times, and, as their language suggests, from different districts. The New Kuki form of speech is not always intelligible to an Old Kuki. Mr. Stewart saw one of the Khelma tribe as much puzzled with what a New Kuki was saying to him as he would have been with a perfect stranger. On the other hand, the Manipur dialects and the New Kuki are mutually intelligible. I do not think that the vocabularies verify this doctrine; either in the way of likeness or of difference. It may, nevertheless, be accurate.

It was the Lushai (Looshais) who caused the flight of the New Kuki into Cachar; the Lushai who inhabited the same parts only further to the south, the Lushai who spoke (and speak) a Kuki dialect, the Lushai against whom we had to protect the fugitives. In 1848-49 four Kuki tribes—the Thadon, the Shingshon, the Chúngsen, and the Lumgúm—driven from their native districts, poured themselves into Cachar, and were pursued by the Lushai. Three hundred men of the Sylhet Light Infantry Battalion, under Colonel Lister, were not long in coercing them. They drove them beyond the frontier, and returned to settle and protect the Kuki.

Some had settled themselves. Some, however, hung on the skirts of the Lushai, and only waited for the opportunity of being revenged on them. To prevent the chronic state of warfare that would have originated from this, Colonel Lister enlisted them as soldiers, officered by their own clansmen, but trained and disciplined according to English tactics. The measure succeeded. The Kuki soldiers are found to constitute excellent posts on the frontiers of both the Lushai and the Angami countries.

Of the fugitives some fixed themselves in Manipur, some in South Kachar, some in North.

The Lushai I hold the same population, as that which in the paper of Macrae's, just quoted, is called Luncta; a population scarcely differing from the ordinary Kuki, or rather, a population of ordinary Kuki, under another name.

The best observer of the New Kukis credits them with clearer and more definite notions in the way of religion than any of the tribes of their neighbourhood. This is, perhaps, the actual fact. It may, however, be otherwise. The Kuki creed may simply be the one best known. It recognizes one deity, more important than the rest, whose name is Puthen. His passions are human; though, on the whole, he is benevolent, and is interested in the welfare and virtue of the Kuki family; perhaps in that of the world at large. He visits sin with sickness in this world; punishes it in a world beyond the grave. He is sometimes invoked in order that he may abate his own anger; sometimes that he may intercede with other deities. Sometimes animals are sacrificed to him.

The family of Puthen is large; though it is not certain that every one charged upon it is a true member. Ghumoishe, for instance, is doubtful. He is the deity who exercises the worst influence on mankind. He does a great deal of mischief, and delights in doing it; for his disposition is naturally malevolent. If he show himself to a Kuki, death ensues. If he inflict disease, the symptoms are of the worst sort. What, however, is his relation to Puthen? Some say that he is his illegitimate son. Some deny the paternity altogether.

Ghumoishe has a wife—and a very bad one too—whose name is Khuchom, and whose special delight is to inflict colic and pains in the stomach. It is no good praying to either of them. You may avert their wrath by sacrifices, but you will never get any positive services. You may obtain, too, the intercession of Puthen; but direct prayer in reliance of any amiability on the part of either Ghumoishe or Kuchom is useless. Hila, the daughter, is the Goddess of Poisons, or, at least, of indigestion. She can make viands otherwise edible poisonous, disturbing healthy stomachs by means of wholesome food. To keep her from mischief you must apply to Puthen.

Thus far Puthen may or may not be the father of a family; Ghumoishe's best claim being but a bastard one. With Nongjai and Thila the case is different. The former is the wife, the latter the son. Thila, without being absolutely malignant or diabolical, is harsh, ill-conditioned, and vindictive. His anger, however, can be averted by prayers and sacrifices; either at first-hand (in which case they are made direct to him) or mediately, through the intercession of Puthen or Nongjai.

If Thila has *his* faults, his wife has *hers*. Ghumnu is her name; a name which, even when you pray to Thila, it is not well to omit. She is pre-eminently sensitive on this point. When you pray to her husband, pray to her also. If you don't you may take a headache, a toothache, or some similar ailment.

Khomungnu is the household, Thingbulgna the forest, god. Then there are the gods with the compound names; names wherein Puthen simply means deity. Such are Tui Puthen the Water God, Thi Puthen the Iron God.

From the Pantheon to its priests is but a short step. The Thempu are initiated priests, skilful (in the case of god-sent diseases) to divine the offended deity, to point out the propitiations he expects, to conduct the propitiatory ceremonies. In a large Pantheon, whereof more than one member is mischievous, the office of a Thempu is a medical necessity. As often as disease occurs, his services are wanted. Necessary, however, as they are, they are not always to be obtained. The Thempu are not a caste. Novices from the people at large who choose to undergo the initiatory ordeal, may become Thempu. But so formidable is the initiation that few covet the honour. Indeed, so great is the fear—physical or superstitious—of its pains or dangers, that, in order to prevent the order from dying out, the rajahs have, on occasions, been obliged to coerce their unwilling subjects into the privilege of holding communion with the deities. The details of the initiation are unknown. One, however, of its formulas is a prayer of indemnity on the part of the neophyte. Should anything go wrong during the ceremony, let the punishment fall on his head—not on the heads of his teachers. Another known fact is the use of a mysterious language, unintelligible to the people at large. Judging from what we know elsewhere, it is, probably, a mixture of slang and archaism.

The details of the initiation are unknown. Not so, however, the professional practice of the Thempu. When a villager feels ill, he gets the Thempu to feel his pulse, and ask him certain questions concerning the place and time of the first ailment, the nature of his recent occupations. On this he meditates. He then names the offended god, and enjoins the necessary propitiation. The sacrifice may be a fowl; in which case the remedy is cheap. Or it may be a pig, a dog, or a goat; in which case there is an entertainment as well as an oblation. Or it may be a cow, or methin; in which case there is an expensive feast, and the remedy is as bad as the disease.

The Kuki country lies to the south of the Garo, Kasia, and Mikir areas or the hill-ranges of Garo, Jaintia, and Cachar, in Sylhet, Tipperah, and Chittagong.

Manipur lies to the south of the Naga districts, eastward of the Kuki area, and on the drainage of the Irawadi.

Of the frontier between the southern members of the group represented by the Nagas and the northern tribes of Manipur, I can give no account. It seems, however, that over and above the civilized and Buddhist occupants of the capital and the parts around, the phenomena which we have seen in the Naga districts repeat themselves. From the southern slope of the Patkoe range the feeders of the western branch of the Irawadi cut channels and fertilize valleys; the occupancies of rude tribes, whose dialects differ notably from each other. Eleven of these are known, through vocabularies; the percentage of proper Manipur words in each being as follows:—

In the	Songpú	21
,,	Kapwi	41
,,	Koreng	18
,,	Maram	25
,,	Champhung	28
,,	Luhuppa	31
,,	North Tankhul	28
,,	Middle ,,	35
,,	South ,,	33
,,	Khoibu	40
,,	Maring	50

When we have said this, we have said nearly all we can say. The three Tankhul forms of speech are said to be all but mutually unintelligible. The Kapwi is a very small tribe. The Champhung consists of but thirty or forty families. The resemblance between the words Songpú and Singpho should be noticed. So should the re-appearance of the root *mr* in Maram and Maring. It has already appeared as Miri, and will do so again as Mru and Mrung. Luhuppa is very like Lhopa and (?) Lepcha. At any rate the terminations *-pa, -po, -pu,* are old acquaintances. Then there are the names for Manipur, some of which appear in the maps as Moitay and Kathi, or Kassay; which is Kasia.

East of Chittagong lies the Jo country; the language of which is neither more nor less than a rude dialect of the ordinary Burmese; the population being Burmese also.

The same is the case with the Mugs; Mug being the name by which the native population of the towns and villages of Arakan is designated. The Mugs amount to about six-tenths of the whole population; one-tenth being Burmese, and the remainder Hindu. The only town of importance is the capital. Some of the Mug villages lie but just above the level of the sea; others are on the sides, others on the tops, of hills. The early history of Arakan, so far as it may be dignified by that name, makes it an independent state, sometimes with Chittagong and Tipperah in subjection to it, sometimes with Chittagong and Tipperah separate.

The island of Ramri, Cheduba and Sandoway are parts of Arakan; Mug in languages, British in politics.

In the hill-country the type is changed, and instead of the comparatively-civilized Mug we get tribes like the Kuki and Naga. The best known of these are—

The Tribes of the Koladyn River.—The tribes of the Koladyn River form a convenient if not a strictly-natural group. The Koladyn being the chief river of Arakan, and Arakan being a British possession, the opportunities for collecting information have been favourable; nor have they been neglected. Of the names of tribes, and of specimens of tribes, we have no want; rather an *embarras de richesse.* There Buddhism, as a general rule, is partial and imperfect; partial as being found in some tribes only, imperfect as being strongly tinctured with the original Paganism when it is found. And of unmodified Paganism there is, probably, not a little. The forms of speech fall into strongly-marked dialects; in some, into separate languages; by which I mean that, in some cases, they may be mutually unintelligible. The government seems to be patriarchal during a time of peace, ducal during a time of war; ducal meaning that a tribe, or a confederacy of tribes, may find themselves, for the time, under the command of some general chief. That such occasions are by no means unfrequent, we infer from the history of certain sections of the population rather than from any direct account of their wars. The story of almost every tribe is the same. It came upon its present locality a few generations back, having originally dwelt elsewhere; somewhere northwards, somewhere to the south, somewhere to the east. It dispossessed certain earlier occupants. But these earlier occupants may, in their turn, be found in fragments, consisting of a single village, or of a few families. The form that the history (if so it may be called) of these marchings and countermarchings, of these fusions and amalgamations, of these encroachments and displacements assumes, is deserving of notice. Ask a Khyen how he came to be where he is, and he will answer that his ancestors came there as soldiers and invaders in some Burmese army long ago, that they remained on the spot, settled, propagated their kind, and left issue. Is this true? No. Is it a tradition? No. What is it? It is an inference. It is the narrator's mode of accounting for a phenomenon which he knows as a fact, but has not ethnology enough to explain. It is his mode of accounting for the likeness in language between himself and more powerful neighbours. Lest any one should condemn this as so much rationalism out of place, I will add that it is not in one place, nor in two, but in many that these accounts are to be found. We shall find them amongst the Shans, *mutatis mutandis*. Now there cannot well have been a succession of armies with a succession of stragglers who became colonists. More than this, the story is sometimes absurd. In one case it runs that the part which was left behind consisted of lazy or tired men who fell asleep, and stayed where they were, whilst the others kept awake and left them behind. Child's play this. Child's play, but still dignified by the name of tradition. Traditions do not grow on every tree. The Mring state that their ancestors were brought as captives from the Tipperah hills. This is more probable, since removals of this kind are commoner than armies leaving stragglers. At the same time it is not safe, even here, to believe more than this, viz. that the tribes who tell the story believe that they have congeners in the quarters where they lay its venue; their belief being *primâ facie* evidence of the fact.

Does any one believe this, viz. that one of the forms of tribute to one of the conquerors of one of the branches of the Khyens was the payment of a certain number of beautiful women? To avoid this the beautiful women tattooed themselves, so as to become ugly. This is why they are tattooed at the present time. So runs the tale. In reality, they are tattooed because they are savages. The narrative about the conqueror is their way of explaining it. Should you doubt this, turn to Mr. Turner's account of Tibet, where the same story repeats itself, *mutatis mutandis*. The women of a certain town were too handsome to be looked at with impunity; for, as their virtue was proportionately easy, the morals of the people suffered. So a sort of sumptuary law against an excess of good looks was enacted; from the date of which to the present time the women, whenever they go abroad, smear their faces with a dingy dirty-coloured oil and varnish, and succeed in concealing such natural charms as they might otherwise exhibit.

There is another class of inferences; for which, however, learned men in Calcutta and London are chiefly answerable. Some of the tribes are darker-skinned than others. The inference is that they have Indian blood in their veins. They may have this. The fact, however, should rest upon its proper evidence. I venture to guess that, in most cases where this darkness of complexion occurs, the soil will have more to do with it than any intercourse with the Hindus. There will be least of it on the hill-tops, less on the hill-sides, most of it in the swampy bottoms and hot jungles. At the same time, *some* Indian influences are actually at work.

The tribe which, most probably, is in the closest geographical contact with the Kuki of Chittagong is the

Mrú, or *Túng Mrú*.—The name is native. It is also Rukheng. It means in Rukheng, or the language of Arakan, over and above the particular tribes under notice, all the hill-men of the surrounding district; this being the high country between Arakan and Chittagong. That the Mrú are the same as the Mrúng, who deduce their origin from Tipperah, I have no doubt; though I doubt the origin. They were all parts of one and the same division. At the present moment, the Mrú are in low condition; fallen from their ancient high estate. For at one time, a Mrú chief was chosen king of Arakan; and when the Rukheng conqueror invaded the country, the country was Mrú. However, at present, the Mrú are despised. Their number in Arakan amounts to about 2800. Their present occupancy is somewhat west of their older one. This was on the Upper Koladyn; whence they were expelled by—

The Kami, or *Kumi*.—The Kámi or Kumi are themselves suffering from encroachments; gradually being driven westwards and southwards. They state that they once dwelt on the hills now held by the Khyens. What this means, however, is uncertain. The Khyens of a forthcoming section lie south of the Koladyn on the Yuma mountains. If these, then, were the men who displaced the Kami and Kumi, the Kami and the Kumi, when they moved upon the Mrú, moved northwards. But this need not have been the case. Khyen is a name given to more populations than one; and the very Mrú of the last noticed are sometimes called Khyen. If so, it may have been from one part of the Mrú country that the Kami and Kumi moved against another part. I do not give this as history; scarcely as speculation. I only give it as a sample of the complications of the subject.

Word for word, I consider the Kami and Kumi to be neither more nor less than the name of the Khumia of Chittagong. I also think that Mrú is Miri.

The Kami (Kumi) of British Arakan amount to 4129 souls.

The Sak, or *Thak*.—The Sak, or Thak, are a small tribe on the river Nauf.

English.	Mrú.	Kúmi.	Kami.	Sak.
Head	lú	a-lú	a-lú	a-khú
Hair	s'hám	s'hám	a-s'hám	kú-mí
Eye	min	me	a-mí	a-mí
Ear	pa-rám	ka-no	a-ga-ná	a-ka-ná
Tooth	yun	he	a-fhá	a-*tha*-wá
Mouth	naur	li-boung	a-má-ká	áng-sí
Hand	rút	ka	akú	ta-kú
Foot	khouk	khou	a-kho	a-tar
Skin	pí	pé	a-phú	mi-lak
Blood	wi	a-thí	a-thí	thé
Bone	a-hot	a-hú	a-hú	a-mrá
One	loung	há	ha	sú-war
Two	pré	nhú	ní	nein
Three	shún	túm	ka-tún	thin
Four	ta-lí	pa-lú	ma-lí	prí
Five	ta-ngá	pán	páng-ngá	ngá
Six	ta-rú	ta-rú	ta-ú	khyouk
Seven	ra-nhit	sa-rú	sa-ri	tha-ni
Eight	rí-yát	ta-yá	ka-yá	a-tseit
Nine	ta-kú	ta-kau	ta-ko	ta-fu
Ten	há	hau	ha-suh	si-su
Sun	ta-nin	ka-ni	ka-ní	sa-mi
Moon	pú-lá	hlo	lá	*that*-ta
Star	ki-rek	ka-si	a-shi	*tha*-geing-*thi*
Fire	má-i	mhá-i	má-i	há-in
Water	tú-í	tú-í	tú-í	mi (?)
Bird	ta wá	ta-wú	ka-vá	wa-si
Fish	dám	ngho	moí	pan-na
Snake	ta-ro-a	pú-wi	ma-khu-í	ka-pú
Stone	ta-whá	lún-s'houng	ka-lún	ta-lon
Tree	tsing-dúng	din-koung	a-kún	púng-páng
Mountain	shung	mo-i	ta-kun	ta-ko
River	an	ka-wú	ka-vá	pi-si
Village	kwá	a-váng	váng	thing
House	kín	úm	in	kyín
Egg	diú	díu	du	wa-tí
Horn	anáng	ta-ki	at-ta-ki	a-rúng
Man	mrú	ku-mi	ka-mí	lú

The Heuma, or Shendu.—In 21° 15′ N. L. the Meeyk-young falls into the Koladyn from the east. It, of course, arises on some higher level, and this higher level is the watershed between it and the drainage of the Manipur rivers; the Manipur rivers being on the system of the Irawadi. And this watershed is the range of the Yeomatoung hills, the occupancy of a population with a like name; the occupancy of the Shendu, or, as they call themselves, Heuma. The hill-ranges themselves are low at first, but they soon arise mass upon mass, and tier upon tier, with jungle along their skirts, and deep, narrow water-courses down their sides.

What we know of the Heuma is from Captain Tickell, whose informant was one of their Aben, or chiefs, named Lebbey. Lebbey's village was on the Khoon (Khyen?) frontier. Its name was Búkí, and it consisted of 350 houses. Further to the north-east lay the following villages.

	Houses.
2. Thubban	400
3. Lalyang	100
4. Tumbú	100
5. Rúngfe	50
6. Yanglyng	250
7. Húthe	240

The numbers, here, are inordinately and improbably, high. I give them, however, as they stand.

In shooting elephants the Heuma use the trap-bow, or rather a pair of them, so set that a line pulls both triggers and shoots the huge animal on each side. The use of the musket is superseding that of the ruder and more native arms.

Men may marry two sisters at once, but not more; may not marry their stepmothers. This the Khumia *may* do. All property goes to the eldest son; provided he be unmarried. Should he have settled himself in life the property is divided amongst his brothers. Daughters get nothing: widows as little. They bury their dead.

They regard the sun and moon as deities, and sacrifice pigs and cattle to them at the beginning of the rainy season.

THE KHYEN.—Khyen is a general name for several of the rude tribes of Ava, some of which are independent, some subject to the Burmese, some within the dominions of the East India Company.

The Khyen, at present under notice, occupy the same range as the mountaineers already described. They lie, however, further to the south; the exact details of their area and frontier being uncertain. They say that their ancestors were at one time the occupants of the fertile plains of Ava, and the rich alluvia of Pegu. But strangers came down upon them, and drove them both northwards and eastwards. At first they kept up the appearance of friendship, but afterwards threw off the mask of dependance, and comported themselves as the lords of the soil. It was "contrary," said they, "to the dictates of nature for two kings to reign, or for two populations to live together." So they deposed the Khyen king, and banished the most powerful chiefs. These, along with others, fled to the hill-country, and, for a while, kept up a semblance of a sovereignty and a royal family. But the members of it died out, and now they have no one but their little village chiefs, captains, patriarchs, elders, or whatever they may be called.

In their religious matters their liberty and equality is somewhat less than in their secular. The Passin is the head of the Khyen Church. He resides on a mountain by the side of a river, and by his descendants in the male and female line the office of prophet, soothsayer, or priest, is continued. Passins officiate at weddings and funerals; expound doubtful points of law and custom; are the conservators of the traditions; are the exorcists in cases of sickness.

One of the objects of the simple worship of the Khyens is a thick bushy tree, bearing a small berry called subri, and under its branches they assemble at certain seasons, with all the members of their family, and with their cattle, feasting and making sacrifices of pigs and fowls; just the animals that so many other rude tribes are in the habit of offering.

Another object is the thunderbolt, or what passes for such. When a storm occurs they watch the lightning, see what it strikes, and if it strike a tree or building, or can be seen to touch the ground, wait anxiously for the weather to become calm, and then dig for the thunderbolt. They are unfortunate if something in the shape of a stone is not found, and when found supposed to have fallen with the lightning from heaven. It is thus invested with supernatural powers—has a hog and a bullock sacrificed to it—is delivered to the Passin, and kept as a talisman.

The souls of those who have acted well are transferred, after death, to the bodies of oxen or pigs; so that the Khyen creed admits of a rude kind of metempsychosis. Yet they kill their cattle without compunction, but not without the leave of the Passin.

When any one dies a feast is held over his remains. If they be those of a poor man they are buried in the immediate neighbourhood. The burial-places of the wealthy, however, are the two holy mountains of Keyúngnatin, or Yehantoung, to one of which they are conveyed, even when the death takes place at a distance. From the summit of Yehantoung "the whole world can be seen." Near the tombs there constructed a hut is erected, in which a certain number of people are left for the purpose of defending it against malignant spirits. Over the remains a rude carving converts a log into a likeness of the deceased.

Marriages are just so far religious ceremonies that the Passin is consulted about them. The contracting parties ask his sanction. When given, the bridegroom sends presents to the parents of the bride. A feast follows.

But the bride may prove unfaithful; if so, the adulterer is fined, and the wife is restored to former favour, her reputation being as good as before.

With unmarried women the custom is different. Simple discovery is fined. The birth of a child creates a claim on the part of the female. The offender must either marry her or pay the fine over again, and take the child—the fine being a bullock. The damsel starts *de novo* as a damsel.

Unless she be the daughter of a chief, when the fine is tripled, other things being as before; but three bullocks instead of one being the mulct.

Cousins marry, but not brothers and sisters. Intercourse, however, between even these is possible and contemplated. The fine for it is a bullock to the father.

A divorce costs a bullock.

A murder costs ninety rupees; the valuation being got at by the following process. The murderer is seized by the village chief, who requires of him either three of his friends to be given up to the family of the sufferer, or thirty rupees a man for each. But he may escape. If so, he must be given up, or war ensues unless he be given up. Given up, he is committed to slavery; bloodshed for offences being forbidden.

Ordinary theft is not much punished. The stealing, however, of corn is a felony. The culprit must either become a slave, or pay thirty rupees, *i. e.* the third of the price of a murder.

We know beforehand what the medical practice is. The thunderstone in the hands of the Passin will cure everything.

Are the Khyen hospitable? We are inclined to say yes; because hospitality is the virtue of rude tribes. We answer, however, *à priori*. So few strangers traverse their land that a precedent in the way of the reception of one is unknown. Those, however, from whom our authority (Mr. Trant) got his information, said that if a foreigner fell in with one of their nation "he would not be ill-treated; but that they did not remember such a visit having taken place."

Cotton grows in the Khyen country, and of cotton the Khyens spin enough to dress with and export. Black seems their favourite colour, or no colour. A black cloth, striped with red and white, is thrown across their shoulders. A black cloth goes round their loins. A black jacket is used occasionally. The women wear a black petticoat reaching the knees. Are they handsome? More so than they make themselves; for a story runs in the Khyen country that when it was overrun and conquered, the marauders, who drove the aborigines to the mountains, imposed upon them a tribute, in default of which they seized the most beautiful of their women, and laid them out before their king, who chose the flower of them for his harem. To save the race from extermination the men persuaded the maids to disfigure themselves. So they cheerfully complied, and tattooed their faces.

More important, more widely spread, and, to a certain extent, better known than the Khyen, but, like them, a wild, and (generally speaking) an independent race, are—

The Karen.—The ordinary way of speaking of the

Karen is to call them a population of remarkable geographical extent, both vertically (or from north to south) and horizontally (or from east to west). In fact they are said not only to be found within the British, Burmese, Siamese, and Chinese frontiers, but to extend from 28° to 10° N. L., if not further. Then there are the Karens of the *eastern* part of Siam, separated from those of the Burmese, or western, frontier by the Valley of the Menam, and the great bulk of the native T'hay population. In Bowring's map this eastern branch occupies the parts about Korat, and the foot of the mountains that form the watershed of the Mekhong.

Now the evidence that these are true Karen is unsatisfactory. It consists of the name only. Different populations, however, may easily have borne it, especially as it is not native. Nevertheless, the fact may be what the term suggests, and true Karen may have an actual existence in Eastern Siam.

The evidence to the Karen of the north is better. Mr. Cross met with one from the Chinese province of Yunnan, from whom he obtained the following information. The Karen of the parts between the Burmese empire and China, although some of them lie within the Chinese province of Yunnan, are, upon the whole, independent, though not beyond the reach of attacks from the Burmese. They are agricultural, with a patriarchal constitution. They reckon themselves by families, not by cities or villages, nor yet by tribes. Each family occupies but one house, and this house may be large enough to contain three or four hundred individuals. Its floor is raised some six or seven feet above the ground, the material being bamboo, with mattings and a thatch of palm-leaf. Strong posts sunk firmly into the ground constitute its foundation and frame-work. A raised floor made of beams is attached to them, with a matting of split bamboo laid over them. The whole house—a court or covered village rather than a house—is divided into compartments, one for eating, one for sleeping, and so on, with a regular household discipline to match.

Some of the tribes are Buddhists; but the two described by Mr. Cross, which may fairly serve as a sample of the stock, are Pagan. They are the Sgau and the Pgho; the former being the more primitive. They are also smaller and lighter-coloured than the Pgho.

The term Karen is Burmese; the native name being *Pgha-Kenyau* = *man*.

Word for word, Karen is Khyen; and so it is often sounded in Burmese.

Their government is patriarchal; but, besides the elders, two classes of men exercise considerable influence, the *bukho* and the *wí*.

The *bukho* is, perhaps, a priest rather than a prophet, inasmuch as he rarely commits himself to the prediction of future events, but limits himself to the regulation of feasts, and the conduct of ceremonials. He is also the great authority for magical formulæ. He is also, more or less, a physician.

The *wí*, on the other hand, is a shaman, capable of foretelling events, recalling departed spirits, seeing embodied ghosts—only, however, when in a particular physical condition. Of course, this is one of excitement, into which the *wí* is capable, like the Sibyls and Pythonesses of classical antiquity, of working himself. He writhes his limbs, he twists his features, he foams at the mouth, he affects an epilepsy. When the fit, real or affected, is over, he delivers his prophecy. Many of these relate to the political condition of his countrymen, and (amongst the dependent Karens) predict a deliverance from the grinding tyranny of the Avans. Some of these either suit, or are fitted to, the political and missionary advent of the English and Americans. I give the following *wí* prophecies as I find them in Mr. Cross.

"If deliverance come by water, rejoice, for you will be able to take breath.

"When the Karens have cleared the horn-bill city happiness will arrive.

"When the Karens and white foreigners shall fight happiness will arrive.

"The white foreigners possess the word of God, and will one day restore it to the Karens who have lost it."

The local, personal, and individual *genii* of the Karens are called *kelah.* Every object has one. If the rice-crop look unpromising, the rice *kelah* is supposed to be away, and has to be called back. "O come, rice kelah, come. Come to the field. Come to the rice. With seed of each gender come. Come from the river Kho. Come from the river Kaw. Come from the place where they meet. Come from the West. Come from the East. From the crop of the bird, from the maw of the ape, from the throat of the elephant, come. Come from the sources of rivers and their mouths. Come from the country of the Shan and Burman. From the distant kingdoms come. From all granaries come. O rice kelah, come to the rice."

The human kelah may leave the body and wander about, in which case it has to be recalled. For this there are various formulæ, which it is the business of the wí to understand.

This is a sketch of the first series of ideas attached to the word kelah. There is a second. The kelah is supposed to possess seven existences, seven yet one. The first seeks to render the person to whom it is attached mad, the second produces reckless folly, the third shamelessness, the fourth anger, and so with the rest of our bad passions and infirmities. All kelahs of this kind are essentially bad.

The moral principle, however, is *thah*. It is thah, rather than kelah, through whom we sin or act rightly. The following distinction is from a native Karen, though not (I imagine) an untaught one. "When we sin, or commit any offence, it is the *thah*, soul, which sins; and again, when we perform any good action, it is the *thah*. Praiseworthiness, or blame-worthiness, is attributed to the *thah* alone. By some the *kelah* is represented as the inner man, and with others the inner man is the *thah*. When the eyes are shut and in sleep the reflective organs are awake and active. This is sometimes attributed to the *kelah*. Hence the *kelah* is the author of dreams."

Another deity, spirit, demon, or genius is named Tso. Tso resides in the upper part of the human head, and as long as he keeps his seat no kelah can do any mischief. But, in order for him to do so, the head must be attended to. Its owner must attire it handsomely. He must keep it, too, out of the reach of danger; away from roofs that may fall in, or from trees that may break down.

The Karen vampires, goblins, *ethoc genus omne*, are named *kephoo*, *theret* (*theret thekah*), *tahmus* (or *tahkas*), *plupho* and *sekhahs*.

The kephoo is more of a raw-head-and-bloody-bones than aught else. It is the stomach of a wizard which prowls about at night to devour the kelahs of men in the shape of a human head and entrails.

The therets, too, feed on kelahs; the therets being the souls of men untimely slain, and malefactors, not wicked enough for a place in the seat of punishment, nor yet good enough for the full fruition of the region of bliss. Hence they wander about on earth.

The tahmus and tahkas are the spirits of pre-eminently wicked men, tyrants and Burmese most especially. After leaving the body they invest themselves with the forms of the lower animals; sometimes with that of a gigantic human being.

The sekhah is the spirit of an infant, or of an old man in his second childhood. Or it may be that of one forsaken by his *tso*.

Plu-pho is the occupant of Plu, which is Hades. In Plu the dead alive renew their earthy occupations. To go to Plu is the normal state for the deceased. To become a kephoo, theret, tahmus, tahkas, or sekhah is irregular and exceptional. The king of Plu is named Cootay or Theedo. He "holds his dominion in the country of *Plu*. When he comes to call our *kelahs*, our bodies die, and we become the inhabitants of *Plu*, and enter the dominions of *Cootay*. When he has called men, and they are under his dominion, if they by their endeavours please him, or are good, they are in due time dismissed to the region above, or heaven. But, on the contrary, if they are wicked, such as strike their fathers and mothers, they are delivered into the hands of the king of hell, and punished by being cast into hell."

Hell is called Lerah. It has two divisions, the Lerah of the milder, and the Lerah of the severer inflictions.

The tah-*nahs* or *nahs* (word for word the *nat* of the Burmese, &c.) are invisible beings, capable of taking the forms of animals, and endowed with a theret's appetite for kelahs. Some are worse, and more malignant than the others. The king of the more fiend-like nats is Mukauli.

Then there are the deities of the elements and atmospheric phenomena, the kelipho who create the winds with their fans, the tah-yumu, who cause eclipses, the cuda and laŭpho presiding over seasons. The dry season and the wet season fight for victory, each in its turn winning or losing.

The mukhas are worshipped with offerings. Though they are more gracious than malevolent, it is as well to keep on terms with them. Besides this there is a natural feeling of affection and respect for them, since they are the parents and ancestors of the Karens who have ascended into the upper regions, where they live under a king, in towns and cities. They are the creators of the present generation. The work that the mukhas themselves do is good; that of their king bad. He is too busy to allow himself time; so that the individuals which he sends into the world are lame, or ill-formed. The mukhas that preside over marriage take care the blood of the two producing parties is properly commingled.

Phíbí Yau sits on some lonely stump and watches the livelong day over the ears of corn as they ripen. She fills the granary, and is one of the best loved and the most beneficent deities of the Karen Pantheon.

A mother behaved herself so cruelly towards her daughters that they died; whereupon the mother repented of her harshness, and betook herself to a wí. The wí called to him first the spirit of the younger daughter, and entreated it to prevail upon the elder one to return. So they returned. But the mother kept on with the cruel usage that had before killed them, and, when they had died, again called upon the wí. This second time the younger daughter alone could be prevailed on. Nevertheless, she is cruelly treated for the third time. After this she retires to the world of shades, never more to be tempted by either the invocations of a wí or the ephemeral contrition of a cruel mother.

In revivifying the dead the wí operates upon, and

through, the living; his first step being to catch the spirit of some person alive and to divert it to the dead one. The Karen thus robbed of his animating principle sickens and dies. But as he can be revived by a similar process inflicted upon some one else, his death is only temporary. Some one is killed off (ex-animated so to say) in order to restore him to life; and so they go on, ex-animating and re-animating, *ad infinitum.*

The wís are the chief poets of the Karens.

The Thoung-thú.—If the Thoung-thú, a population of the Karen frontier be not actually Karen, it is one which, in language, at least, is closely allied.

English.	Sgau.	Pgho.	Thoung-thoo.
Sun	mu	mü	mu
Moon	lá	lá	lu
Star	tshá'	shá'	hsa
Fire	mé'u	mé'	may
Water	thi	thi	htí
Bird	thó'	thó'	á-wa
Fish	nyá'	yá'	lita
Snake	gu	wgü	h'm
Stone	lu	lón	lung
Tree	thé'	thén	thing-mu
Mountain	ka-tsü	khó'-lon	koung
River	thi-kló'	thi-kló	nhrong
Village	tha-wo	ta-wün	dung
House	hi	yén	sam
Egg	di'	di'	de
Horn	ku-nu	nón-	nung
Man	pó-khwá	pshá'	lan
Head	khó'	khó'	katu
Hair	khó-thu	khó-thu	tu-lu
Eye	me	me	may
Ear	ná	na	nau
Tooth	me	thwa	ta-gna
Mouth	thá-khó	nó	proung
Hand	tshü	tshu'	su
Foot	kho	khán'	khan
Skin	phi	phi	phro

English.	Sgau.	Pgho.	Thoung-thoo.
Blood	thwi	tshü thwi	thway
Bone	ghi	ghwi	htsot
One	ta	ka du	ta
Two	khi	ni	ne
Three	thu	thün	thung
Four	lwi	li	leet
Five	ye	yei	ngat
Six	ghu	ghü	ther
Seven	nwi	nwi	nwot
Eight	ghó	ghó	that
Nine	khwi	khwi	koot
Ten	ta-tshi	ka-tshi	tah-si.

Such is the notice of those members of the Burmese family with which the ethnologist most especially concerns himself, such the rude tribes of the hill and forest, always more important than the comparatively civilized men of the town or city; because they more truly exhibit humanity in its older and more primitive forms.

Still, a short notice of the civilized Burmese (many of whom are British subjects) is requisite. That their alphabet, without being exactly that of either Southern India, or the neighbouring countries of Pegu, Siam, Laos, and Kambojia, belongs to the same class with all these, and is of Indian origin, is what we expect from the fact of the religion being Buddhist. The same applies to the language of their Scriptures. It is a learned tongue, the Pali; the same as that of Siam, Ceylon, and the Buddh countries in general. The native language, however, has its secular literature, lyrical, historical, and dramatic; no composition being of any high antiquity, and none of any notable merit. There are songs for lyrics; a mixture of pantomime and dialogue (more or less extempore) for a drama; a Buddhist chronology, and a short period of trustworthy narrative for a history. When does this begin? In the mind of the present writer very little earlier than the time of the first European visitors.

Then there are the laws; full of cruel and degrading punishments, even as the laws of Siam and China. And, then, there is the ceremonial—full of degrading obeisances and absurd circumlocutions. There is one set of words for equals, one for inferiors, one for superiors; even as there is in Siam, Java, and elsewhere. A difference between the language of politeness and rudeness exists everywhere. The phenomenon of a court dialect, as contrasted with the dialect of ordinary life, exhibits itself in the greatest prominence in the south-east of Asia.

The character of the Burmese drama, in respect to its decency or indecency, is a matter upon which there are two opinions. It has found defenders. The presumptions, however, are against its purity, the fact of a given writer having seen or heard nothing improper in a given number of performances being of no great weight against a single statement in evidence of indecorum.

The general character of the population has not been given in very favourable terms. Allowance, however, must be made for the class with which our embassies have come in contact. Residents of towns, and the official classes, are never safe representatives of a nation. The character of the rural population is probably that of the pagan tribes out of the like whereof they originated. Now these form a class that generally gets its due (and over-due) meed of praise. Where the mode of living is simple, there is no want of either courage or energy. Simplicity of living, however, is the exception rather than the rule with any one who can indulge in sensualities. The stimulants are those of the neighbouring populations, opium, bang, and the betel nut. The Burmese tattoo themselves, and they are, perhaps, (after certain Turks,) the most civilized men and women that do so.

It was in the middle of the last century that the Burmese power developed itself into that of a leading nation, and the hero of its development was the adventurer Alompra, the founder of the present dynasty. What Sivaji was to the Mahrattas, Alompra was to the Burmese. In the direction of Asam, in the direction of China, in the direction of Kambojia, Alompra conquered. This means that he annexed portions of territory from Munipúr on the north, and from Siam on the east. He also conquered Arakan and Pegu; since ceded, along with the Tenasserim districts, to Great Britain. The rule of the Burmese over the tributary populations is said to be hard and grinding.

A minute knowledge of the history of the countries of the Transgangetic Peninsula in general is necessary to enable us to fix, with any degree of accuracy, the relations of Ava to its neighbours as a military power. Its people seem to be warlike and brave, and to make good soldiers. Under Alompra the prestige was in their favour. Yet the very fact of Alompra being the conqueror he was, and the sudden development of the Burmese power, suggests the likelihood of the military history having once been different. And such was the case. The prominent place held by Ava, at the present moment, seems to have been held by no less than three other States in turn, Tipperah, Munipúr, and Pegu; all now on the low level of third or fourth-rate powers. The relative strengths, too, of Ava and Siam have been different; and Siam has at times been more superior than equal.

English.	Burmese.	Rukheng.	Khyen.
Man	lu	youkkya	padau
Women	mairima	mingma	notau
Head	k'haung	gaung	lu
Eye	myitsi	myitsi	myik
Mouth	n'hok	kandwen	kako
Sun	na	ni	k'hu-n'hi
Moon	la	la	klau

English.	Burmese.	Rukheng.	Khyen.
Star	ke'nekkat	kre	ashe
Sky	moh	kaungkan	ane
Fire	mih	mi	mia
Water	re	ri	tui
River	myit	mrik	lik
Sea	pengle	panle	panlai
Stone	kyauk	kyauk	long
Mountain	toung	toung	song
One	tit	taik	pa-hat
Two	n'hit	n'haik	pa-n'hi
Three	thon	thong	pa-thong
Four	le	le	l'hi
Five	nga	na	n'han
Six	k'hyauk	khrauk	s'houk
Seven	k'how-n'hit	k'hu-naik	shi
Eight	s'hit	s'hit	s'hat
Nine	ko	ko	ko
Ten	tase	tase	ho.

In Arakan, where the Indian elements are numerous, two forms of Bengali are spoken ; the one by the Hindus, the other by the Mahometans.

CHAPTER VII.

THE T'HAY; OR SIAMESE GROUP.

The Khamti.—On the extremity of Asam, and within Asam itself, lies a portion of the Khamti.

It is the Siamese stock to which the Khamti belong. The Siamese are Khamti, the Khamti Siamese. The Khamti and Siamese belong not only to the same stock, but, in speech at least, to the same division of it. Between the language as it prevails on the frontier of Asam, and the language as it is spoken at Bankok, the difference is simply that which exists between the English of Somersetshire and the English of Aberdeen. In Brown's tables ninety-eight per cent. of the words are identical. Such a fact as this is worthy of notice, because it exemplifies what may be called the *vertical* direction of a language, *i. e.* a direction from north to south as opposed to one from east to west. The Khamti creed and alphabet are Siamese; indeed, the whole population seems to be but a northern branch of a division of the T'hay group which has already been alluded to as—

The Shan.—I have little doubt but that Shan is a political, rather than an ethnological, term. It means a man of the T'hay stock who is a subject of, or tributary to, the Burmese empire. Cross the frontier, and get into the Siamese dominions, and the name no longer prevails. Yet the population is essentially the same. So are the political relations. As certain petty chiefs are to the central government at Ava, so are certain petty chiefs to that of the metropolis of Siam. The authorities, however, of Bankok do not call them Shan, but Laos. Laos states are Shan, and Shan states are Laos, *mutatis nominibus*. If Shan, they are Burmese; if Laos, Siamese; in each case they are T'hay.

The Shans fall into so many small States. What shall we call them? Kingdoms? Principalities? Rajahships? We cannot, perhaps, do better than take the local and national title of the chiefs, Tsawbwa, and talk of so many Tsawbwaships. The Shan Tsawbwaships are hereditary in certain families; but nothing more. The individual who takes one is appointed at Umerapura. It is only necessary that he belong to the right family.

The number of the Shan Tsawbwaships, according to Captain Yule, is twelve; of which seven are on the west, five on the east of the Salwen. The further they are from Burma Proper, the more uncertain is their allegiance. Neither is their frontage a matter of unimportance. China has influence on the Chinese side, as we expect; besides which three of them are dangerously near the independent Red Karen. The nearest of these is Mobyé; and the Red Karen have so encroached upon its area as to have left the unhappy Tsawbwa little more than his dilapidated capital; a capital, which, in '37, contained no more than fifty-six houses. He sent to Ava for assistance; but in vain. So now he pays tribute, or black mail to the Karen, barbarians and pagans as they are.

The next State of Mokmó does the same; at least to a great extent. The town of Mokmó contains about 350 houses.

Nyúng-yuwé, with a metropolis of about 150, and a population, in all, of about 1000 houses, has been more flourishing than it is now; the Karen having done the mischief.

Conterminous with Nyúng-yuwé is the district of

Myelat. It is under no Tsawbwa at all, but pays its revenue direct to the king.

Moné comes next. Of all the Shan states this is the most important. It is the one too, in which the Burmese influence is strongest; indeed, it is the seat of the Burmese presidency, and the occupancy of many Burmese families. It extends to both sides of the Salwen; and is the largest of all the Shan capitals, a town about 2000 feet above the level of the sea, with as many as 8000 souls.

Of Legya and T'heinné I only give the names, remarking that, for area, T'heinné is the largest of the Shan Tsawbwaships, although not the most populous.

Mormeit and Túng-bain are in the predicament of Myelat, *i. e.* they are districts without any recognized Tsawbwa.

Beyond the Salwen to the north is either a single State, or a confederacy of two—Kaingma-Maingmaing. It is but little known, and is believed to be in closer relations to China than Ava. The nature of this relation is made intelligible by the State of—

Maing-leng-gyé, which pays tribute annually to Ava, and triennially to China. It seems to be divided into petty chieftaincies, which practise private war against each other. The Lawa area lies in or on the frontier of Maing-leng-gyé.

Kiang-hung lies on both sides of the Mekhong, or Kambojia River. It sends tribute to Ava once in three years. In other respects it is Chinese; produces tea, is occasionally placed within the limits of the Chinese province of Yunnan in our maps; has the wild tribes of the Kakui on its frontier; and is divided into as many as twelve petty and subordinate Tsawbwaships, which quarrel amongst themselves, and practise private war as in Maing-leng-gyé.

With Kiang-tung and Kiang-khen the list of Shan states ends. It ends because we cross from Burma to Siam.

The Laos, &c.—On crossing the frontier we reach Zimmay, also spelt Chang Mai, and Xieng Mai. It is easily found, even in an indifferent map. It lies on the Menam between 19° and 22° N. L.; due north of Siam Proper, due west of the Burmese frontier.

A small territory, with a capital of about 12,000 inhabitants, is dependent upon Zimmay, and seems to have followed its fortunes. It is named Laphun. Another district, Lakhon, is (perhaps) in the same category.

The Siamese proper.—The Siamese proper are agricultural, more or less nautical, not a little commercial, somewhat industrial, though in all these matters inferior to the Chinese settlers. They are this to the extent that a despotic government, a monopolist tariff, and a Buddhist creed allow. They are moderately warlike; wars with the Burmese, wars with the Kambojians having occasionally exercised their skill and prowess—indeed, the Burmese invasions have ever been formidable. Among the best of their qualities is the affection of the parents for the children, and the children for their parents, amongst their worst deceit and servility. The generalities of travellers, however, are to be distrusted. We may, in most cases, form a better judgment *à priori*, and from the analogy of nations under similar conditions. Polygamy, monachism, despotism, an enervating climate, a seclusion from the western world —the fruits of these are the same all the world over. Learning, such as it is, is valued and diffused. Neither is there any natural deficiency of intellect. The harvest, however, corresponds to the seed. To the ordinary gratifications of the senses there are few checks; few checks, too, in the use and abuse of stimulants. Opium is used freely; more than it used to be, less than it is likely to be. It has greatly extended within the last thirty years. It is prohibited to the Siamese; but the Chinese indulge in it, and the great proportion they bear to the native population has already been stated. It is not probable that, under such circumstances, its use is limited. The Malay habit, however, of chewing the areca, betel-nut, is more particularly T'hay. The use of the bang and khashish is T'hay, or native also. So is that of tobacco; more so than that of snuff. Boys—children of five or six years old—learn to smoke. Of alcoholic drinks the consumption is comparatively inconsiderable.

Siam itself is, as may be expected, the chief seat of the T'hay stock; probably the area which contains the greatest number of T'hay individuals; at any rate that where the T'hay civilization is at its maximum. Whether the blood be the purest is another question. It is probable that this is far from being the case. If the dormant population be of northern origin there is every chance that the conquest of the country was made by a male rather than a mixed population. And even if it were not so, there is an enormous amount of Chinese elements superadded to the original basis. Pallegoix's calculations make the sum total of the population of Siam 6,000,000. Dr. Bowring puts it at something between 4,500,000 and 5,000,000. Pallegoix's elements are as follows:—

T'hay	1,900,000
Laos	100,000
Karen, Khongs	50,000
Mon	50,000
Kambojians	500,000
Chinese	1,500,000
Malays	1,000,000

English.	Khamti.	Laos.	Siamese.
Man	kun	khŏn	khŏn
Hair	phom	phom	phom
Head	ho	ho	hoa
Ear	pu	pu	pu
Eye	ta	ta	ta
Blood	lüt	leut	leut
Bone	nuk	duk	kaduk
Foot	tin	tin	tin
Hand	mü	mü	mü
Tooth	khui	khiau	khiau
Sun	wan	kangwan	tawan
Moon	lün	deun	tawan
Star	nau	lau	dau
Fire	fai	fai	fai
Water	nam	nam	nam
Stone	pin	pin	pin
Tree	tun	ton	ton
One	nüng	nüng	nüng
Two	song	song	song
Three	sam	sam	sam
Four	si	si	si
Five	ha	ha	ha
Six	hok	hok	hok
Seven	tset	tset	chet
Eight	pet	pet	pet
Nine	kau	kau	kau
Ten	sip	sip	sip.

Like the Burmese, the Siamese have encroached on their neighbours. There has been a T'hay conquest of Asam. Kambojia pays tribute to both Siam and Cochinchina. In the Malay Peninsula, Ligore, Kedah, Patani, Perak, Kalantan, and Tringanu are, more or less, directly or indirectly, under Siamese control.

CHAPTER VIII.

The Môn of Pegu.

THE head-waters of the Irawadi are Burmese. So is the middle course. But not the Delta.

The Delta of the Irawadi is Môn; Môn being the name of the native population of Pegu and the provinces of Martaban. In both these districts there is a Burmese population. In both, however, it has the appearance of being foreign to the soil. The aborigines call themselves Môn. Their neighbours call them Talieng. The Môn, or Talieng, is the vernacular language of Pegu.

It is quite unintelligible to a Burmese; quite unintelligible to a Siamese. The alphabet, also, in which it is written is slightly different; though equally of Indian origin. Like the T'hay and Burmese it is essentially the alphabet of the Pali form of speech. Like all alphabets of this kind it embodies a Buddhist literature; of which, however, but little is known.

In the 16th century the king of Pegu seems to have been a powerful monarch; inasmuch as the T'hay histories speak of a Pegu invasion of Siam, and a Pegu conquest. Whether, however, the leading men in this event were actual Môn is uncertain. A conquest from the kingdom of Pegu may have been effected by Burmese.

The Môn are now British; Moulmein or Amherst having been ceded to us at the close of the Burmese war of 1825, and the remainder in 1853. The condition of the inhabitants under their previous rulers is believed, on fair evidence, to have been that of a very oppressed and misgoverned population.

English.	Môn.	T'hay.	Burmese.
Man	bani	manut	lu
Head	kadap	hoa	k'haung
Eye	mot	paned	myitsi
Mouth	pan	pak	n'hok
Sun	man-tangwe	p'hraatid	na
Moon	man-katok	p'hraachan	la
Star	nong	dao	ke'nckkat
Sky	taka	fa	moh
Fire	kamet	fai	mih
Water	dat	nam	re
River	bukbi	menam	myit
Sea	tallc	tallc	pengle
Stone	kamok	hin	kyauk
Mountain	tu	fukao	taung
One	mue	nung	tit
Two	ba	song	n'hit
Three	pai	sam	tong
Four	pol	si	le
Five	pasun	ha	nga
Six	ka-rao	hok	k'hyauk
Seven	ka-bok	chet	k'hown'hit
Eight	ka-cham	pet	s'hit
Nine	ka-chit	kao	ko
Ten	chok	sib	tase.

Word for word, the Burmese name of the Môn, *Talieng*, is *Telinga*. That an important and influential settlement was made in Pegu by certain Hindus of the Telinga districts is highly probable. More than this, in the way of a *direct* affinity between the Môn and Indians, cannot safely be asserted. The nearest relation to the language of Pegu seems to be that of the Kho, or Kamer, of Kambojia.

PART II.

BILUCHES, AFGHANS, ETC. OF THE INDIAN FRONTIER.

CHAPTER I.

The Biluch Tribes.

The Biluch.—Biluchistan is the land of the Biluches, just as Afghanistan is that of the Afghans, and Hindostan that of the Hindus.

Some of the Biluches live in mud houses; others even invest themselves in forts; but the usual lodging is the tent, or gedaun as it is called. This is made, like that of the Afghans, of black felt or camlet, stretched over a frame of wicker-work made of the tamarisk. An assemblage of gedauns constitutes a tumun or village, the occupancy of a kheil, the same word we have so often met with in Afghanistan. So many kheils form a tribe. As the locality of a Biluch tumun may vary, the name of the kheil may vary also; the name itself being taken from the locality, from the head-man in it, or from some real or accredited quality of the members of which it consists. In Western Biluchistan we may find one half of the kheil in gedauns, the other in huts.

A nation that lives in tents must needs be pastoral, and it is well if it be not predatory also. No Biluch is free from the character of a robber; least of all the Biluch of the west. Mounted on camels, frugally furnished with dates, bread and cheese, and a little water in a leathern bag, the depredators ride on with as few stoppages as possible till they come within a few miles of the spot upon which the attack is determined. Here they rest their camels. At night they remount, accomplish the small remainder of their journey, and make their merciless attack. The spoil being attained, they prefer to return home by a fresh route; always returning expeditiously. There is no care for camel flesh, and journeys of from eighty to ninety miles are often made within the four-and-twenty hours. The number of beasts exceeds that of the men; one of whom may manage as many as ten or twelve—all laden with spoil, and in danger of either pursuit or attacks by the way. At first the lot of such slaves as may have been taken is pre-eminently miserable. They are blindfolded as soon as caught, and tied on the camel that conveys them to the country of their future masters. The women's heads and the men's beards are then shaved, and the hair extirpated with lime. This is to disgrace them in the eyes of their countrymen should they succeed in returning to them. However, when once made safe, they are treated kindly, and soon become reconciled to their lot, attached to their masters, and (it is the master that speaks) so unwilling to change their condition "that the severest punishment we can inflict upon them is to turn them about their business."

The representative of the Biluches, in the way of politics, is the Khan of Kelaut. The field in which they show with the greatest historical prominence is North-Western India, as will be seen when we treat of Sind. How far, however, either the annals of the

Khanat, or the records of the (so-called) Biluch conquests of Sind and the neighbouring countries, are Biluch in the strict ethnological sense of the word, will be considered when the Brahúi tribes come under notice.

At present it is enough to say that a man may be a Biluchistani, or native of Biluchistan, without being a true Biluch, just as a man may be a native of Great Britain without being of British (*i. e.* Welsh or Cornish) blood.

CHAPTER II.

The Afghans.—The Western Tribes.—The Durani.—The Ghilzyes.—The Eastern Afghans.

AFGHANISTAN is the country of the Afghans; whose language is the Pushtú or Pukhtu.

In India this last name takes the form Patan; and an Afghan of India is a Patan.

The Western Afghans.—The Durani.—The western Afghans are more of a pastoral people than the eastern; not that the former are all shepherds, nor yet that the latter are all agriculturists. Neither assertion would be accurate. Even with the western Afghans, it is only certain that the extent of land devoted to flocks and herds is greater than the extent under the plough or spade. That the number of shepherds is greater than that of the settled villagers and townsmen is by no means certain. Elphinstone considers that it is less. Many tracts are highly cultivated. The summer station is called the *Eilauk*, which is a Turk word. The winter station is called the *Kishlauk*, which is a Turk word also. The tent, however, is called by a native Afghan term, *Kizhdee*. It is of coarse camlet and black in colour, so that the Turks call it *Karaullee*, and the Persians *Siahtshaudur*, both of which words mean *black tent*. The less a tribe moves the better its tent. Some, indeed, have two sorts, one spacious and commodious for the chief residence, the other lighter and less bulky for the migrations.

There are nine Durani tribes—the Mauku, the Khougani, and seven others, the names whereof all end in *-zye*. This means the same as *Beni* in the Arabic and Hebrew genealogies, or *Mac* in the Scotch. Hence (*e. g.*), the Baurik-*zye* are the *Beni Baurik*, the *Mac Bauriks*, or the *Children of Baurik*, a mode of expressing relationship which by no means implies the personal existence of any real individual so-called. Some, perhaps all, of these nine tribes are divided into *kheils;* thus the Suddo-zye is a division of the Popul-zye. Amongst these *kheils*, one has, generally, a pre-eminence, and supplies the chief, or khan, of the higher denomination. The Suddo-zye is the *Khan-kheil* of the Popul-zye, so far as the subordination of the former to the latter is a reality. So great, however, are the privileges of the Suddo-zye that it may pass for a separate clan rather than a branch of any tribe.

Following, however the classification of Elphinstone, we find that the names for the nine Durani tribes are as follows:—Popul-zye, Allekko-zye, Baurik-zye, Atchik-zye, Noor-zye, Ali-zye, Iskhauk-zye, and the two others first named, Khougani and Mauku. Of these, the first is the largest, the two last the smallest. The influence of the Amír is more visible among the Duranis than amongst the other tribes, and the nearer a Durani district is to Candahar the greater it is. With the more distant tribes, that of the Sirdars exceeds that of the Central Government.

In person the Durani are stout and well made, with a considerable variety of feature. Some have round and plump faces; with others the countenance is strongly marked; with most the cheek-bones are prominent. The beard is an object of care. The young men clip it into shape. All, however, encourage its growth. Some of the shepherds let their hair grow loose and to its full length, so as to present a wild and shaggy aspect. It is more usual, however, to dress it with some care. A shaven stripe down the middle of the head is the common fashion. Long curls are occasional.

They rarely go out armed, except for long journeys, a matchlock being the ordinary weapon. And this prepares us for a comparative absence of inter-tribual feuds so common amongst the eastern Afghans. The influence of the female is considerable, and few restraints are put upon her freedom. When the family is by itself, the men and women eat together; but at parties they separate. In a caravan in which Mr. Foster travelled a lady Afghan took the absolute command. Men marry between eighteen and twenty, women between fourteen and sixteen. The Durani dance is called the Attun. It is danced, almost every evening, with songs and tales to accompany it. This is when the business of the day and universal amusement of the chase is over. It is also after the duties of religion have been performed. In these the Atchikzye tribe alone is negligent; all the other Duranis being religiously given—religiously given, but not intolerant. There is no encampment without a Mollah, and no member of it who omits his prayers. The creed is Sunnite. Few of the lower orders read. Of the higher, many are familiar with the compositions of the Persian poets.

The love of his country is one of the strong passions of the Durani Afghan, and holy amongst the holy places of his land is the Durani city of Candahar. It is in Candahar that the powerful men of the tribe are chiefly buried; and, even when they die at a distance from Afghanistan, their bodies are carried thither to be entombed. As a general rule, however, a Durani travels but little, and rarely as a merchant or adventurer.

Their character is drawn favourably both by Elphinstone and others, and, what is more, the evidence of the rest of the Afghans is cited in confirmation of their good qualities. The tribes that least like their rule speak of them with respect, and praise them as compared with any third ruler, actual or possible. It is a merit of the Durani in the eyes of the other Afghans that they have replaced and keep out the Ghilzyes; for the Ghilzye rule is generally deprecated, and the Ghilzye ascendancy dreaded. Even the Ghilzyes themselves admit the hospitality and bravery of the Duranis.

From this favourable character one tribe must be excepted—that of the Children of Atshik, or the Atchikzye, a tribe whose highest numbers are under 5000. They are pre-eminently pastoral, keeping their flocks in the valleys and heights of the Khojeh Amram and the high country of Toba, and their camels in the sandy plain of Shorabuk, where they are conterminal with the Baraitshes. They wear their beards unclipped, their clothes unchanged for years; are large, strong, quarrelsome men; inhospitable; without mosques or Mollahs, careless in the performance of their religious duties (but withal intolerant), and inveterate robbers. The Durani, unwillingly owning them as kinsmen, admit their courage, their fidelity, and their value as soldiers.

The Ghilzye is the second great name in Afghanistan. The number of its divisions is eight, the Ghilzye analogues of the Populzye, &c., being as follows:—

1st and 2nd—the clans of Hotuki and Tohki, from the first of which have sprung the kings, from the second Vizirs, of the Ghilzye dynasty.

3rd, 4th, 5th, 6th, 7th—the clans of Solimaun-kheil, Ali-kheil, Suhauk, Under, and Turruki.

8th—the Kharoti.

To these add the division of the Shirpau, no true kheil or clan, but an association formed out of the other eight.

Of these, the Solimaun-kheil is by far the most important, amounting to between 30,000 and 35,000 families. The following are its subdivisions:—

The Kyser-kheil and Summul-zye (or Ismael-zye) who live in a state of comparative independence, and with migratory habits, to the south and east of Ghuzni;

The Staunizyes, and the

Ahmed-zyes—the former agricultural, the latter pastoral.

The Ghilzyes of the Durani frontier resemble the Duranis, with whom they most especially come in contact. Thus—it is chiefly in their form of government that the Tohki and Hotuki are other than Durani. The Turruki recede still more from the Durani type, and the Unders more than the Turruki. The direction of the Ghilzye country is from north-east to south-west, the Kyser-kheil and Kharoti being the most eastern, and the Ahmedzye, the Suhauk, and the tribes about the city of Caubul, being the most northern. Ghuzni, too, is Ghilzye, lying between the occupancies of the Unders and the Alikheil.

I have remarked that the first distinction drawn between a Ghilzye and a Durani is a political one. The Governments of the two divisions differ. Among the Durani, though the power of the Amír and the authority of the Sirdars were, to a great extent, in the inverse ratio to each other, there was, still, a large amount of authority on both sides. The Ghilzyes are much more lightly ruled. Their constitution, however, is less democratic than that of Eastern Afghans, the chief of whom are

The Berdurani tribes.—The Berduranis are the Afghans

of the north-eastern parts of Afghanistan, occupying the lower course of the Caubul river, and the parts between the Indus, the Hindu Cush, and the Salt Range. The Ghilzyes bound them on the west. On the north they touch the populations akin to the Siaposh, on the east the Indians of Hindostan. As a general rule, the Indus is their boundary. Here and there, however, there is a Berdurani occupancy beyond it. Peshawur is the chief Berdurani town.

The tribes of the parts about Peshawur are the following five—the Children of Mahomed, the Children of David (Mahomed-zye and Dawúd-zye), the Momunds, the Guggiani, and the Khulíls. The Mahomed-zye and Guggiani, strictly obedient to the Amír and their own chief, occupy the parts about Hust-nugger, or the Eight Villages. The Momunds of the plain, or Lower Momunds, are also British subjects; in this differing from the Upper Momunds, who will be noticed in the sequel.

The Khuttuks (British subjects) lie to the south of the Caubul river, and to the west of the Indus; a portion of them having extended itself into Hindostan. They fall into two divisions. The further they lie south the greater their independence. The northern Khuttuks are fairer in complexion than the tribes of Peshawur, though more or less Indian in dress and habits. The southern Khuttuks occupy a more impracticable country, and are ruder.

The Bungúsh (British subjects) occupy the valley so-called.

The Khyberis are the tribes of the famous Khyber Pass. Word for word, I believe their name to be Kafir. I think that the name is well explained by supposing that, after the infidels of the parts around them had thrown off their infidelity, the men of the inaccessible ranges of the

Khyber mountain continued to retain theirs, just as, at the present moment, the Kafirs of Kafiristan do. There is another point connected with this name that deserves notice. A supposed connection between the Afghans and the Jews has commanded no little attention from more learned men than one. Now, one of the points that favour, or are supposed to favour the doctrine, is the similarity between the words Kyber and Heber (Hebrew). The Khyber division consists of three independent tribes—the Shainwairis of little, the Urukzyes of great, and the Afridis of very great, political importance.

The Urukzye are herdsmen and soldiers, soldiers and herdsmen—herdsmen who are, more or less, migratory in their habits. In the winter they live along the lower levels of the Kohaut and Tiri hills. In the summer they drive their flocks and herds to the mountain tops. Three of the divisions—(*a*) the Shíkhan, (*b*) the Mishtí, and (*c*) the Rabewkheil, occupy districts on the British boundary.

The most important, however, of our frontagers are the Afridis, who are wholly independent, fierce, factious, inaccessible, and strong—said (and, perhaps, with reason) to be faithless.

The Afridis are important from their numbers. They are also important from the passes of which they are the custodians. They cut in between the British districts of Peshawur and Kohat, so that the road between them runs through the Afridi country. It runs through two passes, the Kohat, and the Gulli or Jewaki. Each of these has been the subject of more than one quarrel between either the Afridis amongst themselves, the Afridis and some neighbouring tribe, or the Afridis and the British Government. The tribes thus mixed up with the politics of the frontier are (besides the Bungush, already mentioned, and the Jewaki, Bori, Bussikheil, and Bustikheil sections of the Afridi name), those of

The Sipah . .	500	fighting men.
— Buzotu . .	300	

Small as these tribes are, they are independent.

The Khyber pass itself, to the west of Peshawur, is about twenty-five miles long, rugged, narrow, tortuous, and often enclosed by precipitous and perpendicular walls of rock. Essentially predatory, the tribes on each side of it are largely paid for the permission to pass; largely, but not always sufficiently; a Khyberi escort being, by no means, sufficient to ensure a safe passage through the Khyberi country.

The Khyberis are lean, but muscular, dark-skinned, with prominent cheek-bones and high noses. This is also the Kurd physiognomy. In the valleys they have the terraced houses so common in Afghanistan; in the mountains, movable huts of mat. In some parts they are truly troglodyte; occupants of excavations in the rock. A dark turban, a dark blue tunic, and sandals of straw—this is the dress of a Khyberi, whose arms are a sword, a short spear, and a matchlock with a wooden fork to serve as a rest. Their habits make them excellent marksmen and good soldiers, so far as they can be relied upon for keeping their hands from plunder; for they love this better than fighting, and may fall upon the baggage of the army to which they belong, if they find it unguarded. This they did in the battle that lost Shah Shujah his crown.

The Children of Joseph—the Eusof-zye—are, perhaps, the most uncontrolled of all the Afghans. They are also amongst the most quarrelsome. Divided into numerous small communities, chiefly democratic, their form of government is eminently patriarchal. Contrasted with the feudalism of the Duranis, the Eusofzye system reminds us of the Lesgian and Mizhdzhedzhi communities of eastern Caucasus as opposed to the Circassian aristocracies of the west.

The Eusofzye division is numerous—numerous, but closely packed; for it is agricultural rather than pastoral, and it occupies warm and fruitful valleys rather than bleak and barren mountains. Its eastern limits touch the Indus, and, at one point, cross it; for the district of Drumtour on the eastern side of that river is Eusofzye, just as another district, lower down, is Khuttuk. The limits of the Eusofzyes touch the Indus on one side and the Punjkora on the other. On the south they extend to the Caubul. The northern part of the plain of Peshawur is Eusofzye. So is the valley of Bunír. So also those of Swaut, Punjkora, and Chumla. In all these the Eusofzyes have been encroachers, and in all of them the older population, although it has retired, is still represented. As a general rule, the higher the level of the valley the more aboriginal and the less Eusofzye its character. Let us remember this; also remembering that between the valleys there are hill-ranges as well as at the head of them. The plain belongs to the Afghan, the hill-range to the tribes he has dispossessed.

The whole number of Eusofzyes, including their serfs and dependants, may amount to 900,000, though Elphinstone is unwilling to carry it higher than 700,000. The fakirs form more than half. Some of these are of Afghan blood, who have been reduced to migrate from their own district and become serfs in the country in which they found refuge. Some are of Indian origin—Hindkis and Cashmirians. The majority, however, are the old occupants of the land—Deggauns and Swautis.

Many of the Eusofzyes have fair complexions, grey

eyes, and red beards. They are stout and brave; quarrelsome, as has been said; proud, as living as masters among slaves. Their morality is best in the high country; worst in the plains, where it is bad; very bad—where idleness induces vice, gambling, bang-eating, opium-eating, and worse. The influence, on the other hand, of the Mollahs is great—tyrannical. For an omission of the regular prayers, or neglect of the fasts, they either inflict bodily punishment, or disgrace the offender by public exposure on an ass. The intolerance is in proportion to their immorality.

When an Eusofzye becomes impoverished, the spirit of clanship steps in to save him from disgrace. A subscription is raised to set him up again. Sometimes (though this is discreditable) he goes the round of the villages, and, stopping outside each, waves his *loongee*. This ensures a contribution. Or he may go on a pilgrimage to Mecca, or he may seek his fortunes in India. And this is a common resource. Notwithstanding the love of their country so general to mountaineers, and which is not less strong, but rather stronger, in Afghanistan than elsewhere, the numbers of Patans (for so they are called in India) in Hindostan, sometimes mixed with the native Indians, sometimes collected together under their own chiefs, is very great. Of the Afghan settlements in India by far the most important is that of the Rohillas, a settlement which will require a separate notice.

Next to the Eusofzye come the Turkaun (or Turcolauni) and the Othmankail, the former in Bajour, the latter in the hills between Bajour and Swaut. The Bauz, or chief of the Turcolauni, has great power over his tribe. There are no fakirs in the Turcolauni country.

The Upper Momunds are connected with the Khyberis rather than the Momunds of the plain of Peshawur, or

Lower Momunds. They occupy the hill-range between the Punjkora and the Kuner rivers. The Currapa, between Peshawur and Jellalabad, is in the Upper Momund country. Mulliks have considerable power over their separate clans, but not so much as to dispense with references to the Jirgas. The Khan is only powerful through his influence with the Mulliks, except in the time of war. He has no revenue from his tribe at all. He has, however, a salary from the Amír, from whom he also holds lands. This is the price for the Currapa pass being kept passable, and for a contingent to the royal army. A single Momund, as an escort, ensures the safety of a traveller through the Momund country. Without one you are sure of being robbed. Two kheils of the Upper Momunds are nomad, and move in the spring with their camels and black tents to the head waters of the Helmund.

For the remaining tribes we have no longer any general name like Berdurani, Ghilzye, or Durani. We may, however, for the sake of convenience, designate the majority of them as the Afghans of the Punjab frontier; some of them being the Afghans of the Damaun—the Damaun meaning the eastern skirt of the Solimani range. Others are true mountaineers.

The Turis touch the Upper Bungush; the Jaujis the Turis; the frontier being a scene of inveterate hostility. The Turis are Shiah, rather than Sunnite Mahometans. Some of the Jaujis live in houses half sunk in the earth.

The Esaukheil occupy not only the banks of the Indus, but some of its islands; cultivators of wheat and occupants of villages, but still lawless robbers.

In the valley of Bunnú, which belongs to British India, the population is mixed in origin. It has a bad name. Before the conquest of the Sikh empire there was chronic warfare along the whole Bunnú frontier; for the warlike Viziris were continually making raids upon the valley. The effect of this was to coop-up the Bunnúches in small high-walled villages, and to limit their locomotion to the parts immediately under their shelter. It is evident that Mr. Temple, from whose report the newer notices of the frontier tribes is, for the most part, taken, lays great stress upon what he calls "the propensity inherent in the Bunnúches to surround themselves with walls," and the "morbid desire to wall themselves in" as physical influences. He says that, as a general rule, they have lived, from their childhood, "within four square walls twenty feet high;" and that many of them have never been more than a few miles from their native village. Hence, they stand in an unfavourable contrast to their neighbours. Hence, they are under-sized, and sallow-skinned. As is the body, so is the mind. Their moral qualities are of the worst. They are capable of reckless perjury, of deliberate assassination. It is admitted, however, that they are quiet, orderly, and regular in revenue matters. It is suggested, too, that some noble characters have arisen amongst them. Upon the whole, however, their name is a bad one. The first settlement of the affairs of the Bunnú valley was effected by Major Edwards; in whose Year on the Frontier of the Punjab the first full account of the Bunnú population is given.

Bunnú is British, Dour is independent; or rather the Amír of Caubul is free to take it to himself. It has not been treated as a portion of the Sikh empire. Its population, like that of Bunnú, is mixed.

The Viziri is one of the more important names of Afghanistan. The tribes it embraces (divisions and subdivisions) are numerous. The men who bear it are brave, active, warlike, and predatory. They are amongst the rudest of the Afghans. They have the credit, perhaps, of being ruder than they are. Their occupancy is in the mountains, to the back, and on each side, of Bunnú and Dour. They may muster, perhaps, 30,000 men. They quarrel, however, amongst themselves; so that the whole force of the name is scarcely destined to be ever enlisted in the same cause.

I have said that the Bunnú valley has been the scene of inroad after inroad. It has, for the most part, been the Viziris who were the aggressors. Indeed, some of them have effected permanent settlements in the valley, transforming themselves into agriculturists. These are British subjects. A few of their mountaineer brethren may admit the authority of the Amír of Caubul. The mass, however, is, both in practice and theory, thoroughly independent.

The chief division is into the Ahmedzyes, and the Othmanzyes. To the former belong

The Hatti . . . kheil		The Sirke . . . kheil
— Sudun ——		— Omerzye
— Mohmund ——		— Paenduh kheil
— Bezund ——		— Bodín . . . ——

To the latter

The Bukki	The Jani

The Nurmi.

Other divisions are, the Toroe, the Khojul, the Gunge, the Husein, the Taze, and (more important, from the circumstance of their having been mixed up with the quarrels of the frontier) the Muhsúd, and the Kabulkheil.

The Murwuts are, I believe, wholly British. They are

stout active men, of mixed habits (*i. e.* they are, more or less, agricultural as well as pastoral) who have been once more predatory than they are now.

The Damaun tribes are more or less migratory. Many, too, are more or less mercantile. This gives a greater mixture of manners than we find amongst the Berduranis. Their dress is more Indian than their look; for many of them are fair rather than dark.

Of the particular tribes each has something characteristic and differential.

The Gundehpoors are, perhaps, the rudest; the Bauburs the most civilized. They have among them not only merchants but capitalists; and properties as large as £30,000, an immense treasure for these parts, are perfectly safe. A portion of the Bauburs live in Sehra, beyond the Solimani range, contiguous to the Shirauni, whom they resemble.

The Damaun tribes put a control upon their natural lawlessness by the election of temporary and responsible magistrates, armed with power sufficient to keep the peace, but not sufficient to endanger the freedom of the tribe. They are selected from each kheil in such proportions as to make up the number of forty in all; whence they are called Chelwashtis, from the Pushtu word chelwasht = forty. Their head, or fore man, is styled the Amír of the Chelwashtis. The whole tribe bind themselves by oath, on his election, to support his authority; being at the same time fully prepared, both to watch its exercise, and to check its abuse. The Meankheil has four Amírs, and suffers from the division of power and responsibility accordingly. The Chelwashti system, though a characteristic of the Damaun tribes, is by no means either universal throughout the Damaun, or limited thereto. Of the Damaun tribes two dispense with it. Of the tribes other than Damaun two or more adopt it—the Shiraunis, and the Gilzyes of Kuttawauz. The Chelwashti system has been noticed as Tajik. It is also Nausser.

The Meankheil tribe is remarkable for being but incompletely Afghan, inasmuch as one out of the four parts of which it consists is Baktiari, the Baktiari being Persians.

The Storianis are so thoroughly a frontier tribe that part of their area has been conquered from the Biluches. This serves as their winter station, their summer one being in the high country belonging to the Mussakheil Caukers. A quarrel, however, with one of the tribes whose land lay between the two points made the migrations impracticable. So half the tribe sold its flocks and took to tillage at once; and the other half, with the exception of two clans, did the same soon afterwards. These two pastoral clans of the Storiani have Spusta, on the south-western skirts of the Tukt-i-Soliman, as their summer settlement.

The Sheraunis are the occupants of the Tukt-i-Soliman. They are pre-eminently agricultural, cultivating wheat, practising irrigation, keeping but few horses or camels and more oxen than sheep—hardy and frugal. They have bold features, grey eyes, and high cheek-bones. They never kill an ox; but, should one die, cut its throat with certain ceremonies prescribed by their religion, and eat it in defiance of their religion; for the Koran forbids the use of flesh of animals that die of disease as human food. They marry late; and the father gives his daughter a dowry instead of selling her (as is usually the custom) for a price. They have no serfs, no domestic servants. The few artificers and tradesmen of their country are Hindus or settlers from the Damaun. All the tribes that make their annual migrations through the Sherauni country have to fight their way: a traveller, however, with a native escort may pass through it in safety. The chief of the Sheraunis is called Nika or grandfather. He is elected as the head of the oldest Sherauni family, and is believed to be under the special guidance of Heaven. From every keeper of sheep he receives a lamb annually; from every keeper of oxen a calf; to omit the payment of which is to ensure some misfortune to the family of the defaulter. The Nika is the only true and legitimate judge. He hears the case, puts up a prayer to be enabled to decide justly, and is sure of his injunction being obeyed, for the fear of divine punishment is its sanction. The Chelwashti system is most in force in the parts distant from the Nika's residence; the two authorities being in the inverse ratio to each other. There is a Mullah in each village, who takes a tythe.

The Khan of Murhail is under the Nika of the Sheraunis, the Murhai country being Spusta. The tribe itself is pre-eminently pastoral, and resides in tents.

The tribes of Hurrepaul and Kuppeep are branches of the Sherauni.

Where the Sherauni portion of the Solimani range ends, the Zmurri portion begins. The Zmurris are said to rob less than the Sheraunis; but in other respects to resemble them. They are the most southern Afghans of the main ridge of the Solimani range.

CHAPTER III.

The Paropamisans of the Oxus.—Cohistanis.—Kafirs, &c.

I NOW come to a class for which I propose the name Paropamisan, its chief area being the parts between the southern slope of the Hindukush and either the main stream of the Indus itself or that of its feeder the Caubul river. To these drainages, however, it is by no means limited. Some of its members are on the water system of the Oxus, some on that of the Yarkend river, some (perhaps) on that of the Amur. They are all mountaineers, most of them being independent, and some being either actual Kafirs (*i. e.* infidels) or imperfect converts to Mahometanism. Our knowledge of them is eminently imperfect. For this reason it is far from unlikely that some of the populations now coming under notice may be more properly denominated Tajik.

The language, however, of a Paropamisan is Indian rather than Persian. The language of a Tajik is Persian rather than Indian. If so, the class under notice is transitional. This I believe it to be. I repeat, however, the statement, that it is one concerning which our details are of the scantiest.

The valuable, though fragmentary, journal* of Mr. Gardiner, gives us the following account of the superstitions of the Therba and Shuli tribes.

Time—February 24th, 1830.

* Journal of the Asiatic Society of Bengal, vol. xxii.

Place—E. or N.E. of Bamían, near a place called Dror, where the new and iutrusive population is that of the Kalzubi Turkoman, the aboriginal that of the Thur, or Thurba, and Shu, or Shuli, tribes.

A small pool at the bottom of a deep valley is the site of Moh's death. It is believed to be bottomless. The water is bitter and bituminous; bubbling up with sulphuretted hydrogen, and surrounded by incrustations of sulphur. Lambent flames are said to occasionally play over its surface. Near it is a dark cave, and in this cave are the remains of idols—more than one. The chief of these represent Moh and his wife, Mábún, deities whom even the Mahometans of the district reverence. No one enters the cave with his shoes on.

Two other caves are dedicated to Sheh, the destroyer, and Zhei, the God of Fire. At each new moon the Therba (who reckon by months rather than years) make a fire-offering to Zhei.

Two other caves are dedicated to Hersh and Maul.

Small beads of gold and stone, found in these parts by natives who dig for them, are called Solomon's grains.

Moh created the earth, and his wife Mábún created the wilderness. From them sprung the first giant race. They slept alternately for 999 moons, and reigned 450,000 moons. After this period, three sons rebelled, viz. Sheh, the life-destroyer, Zhei, the fire-god, and Maul, the earth-quaker; and by their combined efforts, Moh was buried beneath the mountains. Confusion lasted 5000 moons, after which the three victors retired each to his own region for 10,000 moons. Maul was lost in darkness of his own creating, Sheh fled with his family towards the sun, which so much enraged Zhei, that he caused fire to spread over the earth; this was quenched by the spirit of Mábún, but not till the whole giant race was destroyed, and the earth remained a desert for 3000 moons. Then Hersh and Lethram, originally slaves of Moh, and great magicians, emerged from the north, and settled in these mountains. By some Lethram is considered as the incarnate spirit of Mábún and the Queen to whom Hersh was vizier. Hersh had three sons,* Uz, Muz, and All. These he left in charge of all their families, while with a large army he travelled toward the sun in pursuit of Sheh, who was supposed to be still living. So the three sons of Hersh and their descendants reigned happily for 18,000 moons, till Khoor (Cyrus?) invaded and conquered the country, but after many years' struggle, they expelled the invader, and retained the name Khoorskush (Cyrus killed) now Khirghiz. The descendants of Hersh continued to reign for 10,000 moons more till Khoondroo (Alexander?) invaded the country, after which no separate legend of them seems to be recollected.

In the same district stands the fort of Khornúshí, to which you ascend by a series of steep steps on hands and feet. Then comes a narrow ledge of rock, from which a ladder of skin-ropes, or a basket and windlass, takes the explorer upwards. At the top, a basin of bubbling brilliant water, hot in the winter and cold during the summer, always full, and never overflowing, gives rise to the following legend—an echo of remarkable clearness adding to the mysterious character of the spot.

When Noah was at Mecca, Khor, the chief of the district, went to pay homage to him. Thereat Noah was well pleased, and promised to grant him any favour for which he should ask. So Khor asked for water. But the voice

* Whose names seem retained in the Uztagh, Muztagh, and Altai mountains.

in which he spoke was rough and loud, and his manner coarse. At this the patriarch was offended. So that instead of blessing the land of Khor he cursed it, and condemned it to become solid rock. Nevertheless, he kept his promise in the matter of the water, and sent his grandson Shur to carry it into effect. The grandson cried Nu Shu. Echo answered Nu Shu. The sound Nu Shu reached Mecca. And now Nu Shu is the sound which the water murmurs, and which echo still conveys to Mecca; the place retaining the name of the three parties concerned—Khor, the prince who spoke so rudely; Noah, the patriarch who disliked Khor's manners; and Shu, the grandson who did the work in opening the basin and calling out the words which echo delighted in repeating.

Wood's legend of the valley of Meshid is to the effect that, in former days, it was overrun with scorpions, and that to avoid them a certain king whose name was Soliman, whose throne was the Tukt-i-Soliman, lived on the top of a hill, but had his meals prepared in the valley. A line of men handed up his dishes. In one of them, a spider was concealed in a bunch of grapes, which stung and killed him. The valley, now containing scarcely 100 families, once held 100,000 workmen.

Gardiner gives the following account. Esh is a desert. Its localities suit these parts. Its chief city was depopulated by snakes, that took the colour of the rocks on which they were found—blue to blue, green to green. The pass at the end of the valley really abounds in serpents.

Again, the Koh Umber mountain, central to Taulikhaun, Kunduz, and Huzrut Imaum, was transported to its present site from Hindostan; as a proof of which all the herbs indigenous to India, are to be found on its sides.

Again, the undulating plain of Reikshan is associated by a Badakshi with all the misfortunes of its country. Khan Khoja, a Mahometan fugitive, at the head of 400,000 men, cursed it. It was to be three times depopulated. It has, already, twice been conquered by the Uzbeks.

In the same districts are legends to a great amount, which Wood, *pudicitiæ causâ*, withholds.

I read all this thus:—there was a barren tract with Hindu legends.

Again, putting together, as I best can, the details of Gardiner, so as to give a geographical result, I come to the conclusion, that the following are the western Paropamisans, *i. e.* the Paropamisans of the Oxus, occupants of the parts to the west of the Belut Tagh.

1.	Kafirs of Esh, calculated at	15,000
2.	——— Ushah	12,000

These are generally called Kafirs.

3.	Khâl (Kheil ?) Kru	12,000
4.	Gob or Gabr (Guebre ?)	12,000
5.	Ghar	12,000
6.	Lah or Lashi	12,000
7.	Udú	12,000
8.	Phaluth or Phah	12,000
9.	Shuli, or Shu	15,000
10.	Khuruk, or Kru	12,000
11.	Therba, or Thur	12,000

These are other than Mahometan, but, still, not called Kafirs.

12.	Bhur	25,000
13.	Mhar	40,000

These are Nimchi Mussulmen, half Mahometans, or Mahometans with a certain amount of heathenhood.

Moguls are met with in the northern portion of this area.

The tribes who own these superstitions are especially stated to be connected with each other. Their language is specially stated to differ from both the Persian and Arabic; whilst Sanskrit affinities are suggested. That it is other than either Turk or Mongol, is shown in the context. I have but little doubt as to the ethuological place of the men and women who speak it. Their geographical position is obscure. A few may belong to the north-western part of the Cohistan of Caubul. The mass, however, are on the western slope of the Belut Tagh, on the Kafir frontier of Buduskun, and on the drainage of the Oxus. The most northern tribes appear to be in contact with the Paropamisans of the Yarkend river, of whom more will be said hereafter.

I now turn to

The Cohistanis of Caubul, occupants, more or less partially, of the valleys of the Ghorebund, the Punjir, the Nijrow, the Tugow, the Alishang and Alighur, and the Lower Kuner.

The Pushai, or *Pushye,* is one of their dialects, but little different from

The Lughmani of the district called Lugman, and

The Deggauni.—The name Deggaun applies to the tribes of the lower Kuner. It applies to others as well. The Deggauns, however, in the limited meaning of the word, are the natives of the valley of the Kuner, in the parts about its confluence with the Caubul river.

English.	Lughman.	Pushai.	Kashkar.*
Man	adam	panjai	moashi
Woman	mashi	zaif	kumedi
Head	shir	sir	sur
Nose	matht	nast	naskar
Tongue	jub	jib	legin
Eye	aneh	anch	ghach (?)
Ear	kad	kad	kad
Hand	atth	ast	——
Tooth	dan	dan	dond
Foot	——	pae	pong
Sun	thur	——	——
Moon	mae	mae	——
Day	lae	dawas	chhoi
Night	vell	vyal	paniya
Fire	angar	angar	ingar
Water	warg	wark	ugh
Tree	kati	kadi	——
Stone	wad	wad	——
Fish	mach	macch	——
One	í	í	i
Two	do	do	ju
Three	te	te	trui
Four	char	char	chod
Five	panj	panj	punj
Six	khe	she	chui
Seven	that	sat	sut
Eight	akht	ash	ansh
Nine	no	no	nehan
Ten	de	de	jash.

The Punjkora and *Lundye Valleys.*—East of the Kuner lies the country of the Turcolaini, Othmankheil, and Eusofzye, Afghans. It lies, however, in the valleys rather than the hills; the valleys of the Punjkora and Lundye rivers. The skirts of mountains, and the mountains themselves, however, preserve the remains of an older class of occupants, Swautis of the valley of Swaut, &c., of which the details are obscure. The evidence that their affinities are with the tribes to the north is satisfactory.

* Spoken in Chitral, or upper part of the Kuner river.

I imagine that the following short vocabulary of the speech of the highlanders of Der best represents the Swauti language.

English.	Deer.	Tirhai.
Man	mish	——
Woman	is	——
Head	shish	——
Foot	khor	——
Eye	achhi	achha
Nose	nistur	nasth
Tongue	jib	zhibba
Tooth	dand	danda
Hand	thoho	hast
Lip	dudh	——
Ear	kan	kan
Day	dus	das
Water	wahe	wa
Milk	shid	dudh
One	yak	ik
Two	do	du
Three	shta	tra
Four	chor	tsor
Five	panch	pants
Six	sho	kao
Seven	shat	sat
Eight	pasht	akt
Nine	noh	nao
Ten	das	das.

The Puraunchehs are, by Elphinstone, who only knows them as a class of carriers, called Hindki. He adds, however, that Baber gave them a separate language. I have been told that this is still spoken by a few families.

Kafiristan.—And now comes a vast block of mountainous country, imperfectly explored, imperfectly converted to Mahometanism. It is bounded by the Belut Tagh districts on the west. On the east it touches Chinese Turkistan and Little Tibet. To the south lies Afghanistan, and to the north Kokan or Fergana, where the population is Tshagatai Turk. It is eminently, pre-eminently, a Cohistan, or country of mountains; for the Hindukush and the Belut Tagh, along with other ranges more mysterious, still belong to it. It is a land of gorges and valleys; of short streams and of long rivers. These, as we expect, belong to different drainages. They will, probably, be our best landmarks in the perplexed geography of these parts.

Some of them are carried into the Indus. Of these one series is received by the Caubul river; another by the Shayuk.

The best measure of the inaccessibility of the country is to be found in the name of one of its districts, Kafiristan. What this means we have already seen. Is it not the land of the Kafir, Giaour, or Infidel, whereunto Mahometanism, triumphant elsewhere, has failed to penetrate? If such spots exist in western Asia, they must be few and far between. They must be defended by either the most impracticable conditions of nature, or the most fanatic obstinacy of man. Be this as it may, there is within a day's journey of Shiite Persia, of Sunnite Turkistan, of Buddhist Tibet, and of Brahminic India, a true Kafiristan, whither no Mahometan can with safety penetrate.

Kafiristan and Kafir are of course Mahometan designations; a name which is, at one and the same time, native and general, being wanting. Other names there are, Afghan and Mahometan also, though not impossibly native as well, as, Siaposh, Speen (white) Siaposh, and Tor (black) Siaposh.

The following "are the names of some of their tribes.

"1. Traiguma, Gimeer, Kuttaur, Bairagullee, Chainaish, Dimdeau, Waillee Wauee, Cauma, Cooshteea, Dhaing, and Wauee, called Puneeta by the Mussulmauns.

"2. Caumojee, Kistojee (whose chief town is Muncheeashee), Moondeegul, Camtoze (half of whom are towards Budukhshaun, and half towards Lughmaun), Puroonee (whose capital is Kishtokee), Tewnee, Poonooz, Ushkong

Umshee, Sunnoo, Koolumee Roose Turkuma (to whom belong Kataur and Guinbeer), Nisha, Chumga, Wauee, Khoollum, Deemish, Eerait, &c., &c.

"3. Wauee Daiwuzee, Gumbeer, Kuttaur, Pundect, Khoostoze, Caumozee Divine, Tsokooee, Hurunseea, and Chooneea."

Again :

"The common names at Caumdaish were Chundloo, Deemoo, Hazaur Meeruk, Bustee, and Budeel. The names of certain men at Tsokooee were Gurrumbaus, Azaur, Doorunaus Pranchoolla, Gemeeruk, Kootoke, Oodoor, Kummur, and Zore. Those of certain women were Meeankee, Junailee, Maulee Daileree Jeenoke, Zoree Puckhoke, Malkee, and Azauree. The names of four men at Kuttaur were Toti, Hota, Gospura, and Huzaur, and of one woman Kurmee."

The Caumdaish call their chief god Imra ; the Tsukooe Kafirs call him Dagun. Their Paradise is Burry Le Bula ; their hell, Burry Duggur Bula. Buggish is the god of the waters. Mauni expelled Yúsh, or the Evil Principle. Seven brothers bore the name Paradik. Their bodies were of gold. So were those of the seven brothers named Purron. One or more of their gods was called Shee Mahadeo.

They have idols of stone and wood, male and female, mounted or on foot. One in particular is mentioned as having been erected by a Kafir magnate during his own lifetime. He purchased the privilege of doing so by giving a series of feasts to the village. Fire is used at their sacrifices ; blood also ; the blood of cows as well as of other animals.

The Koh-i-ghar Kafirs shave the head ; but when they kill an enemy allow a lock to grow. The Koh-i-kaf and Koh-i-loh tribes reverse this process. The hair grows naturally, but has a lock taken away from it when a Mussulman has been slain. Hence, whilst the Koh-i-ghar heroes rejoice in long locks, those of the Koh-i-kaf and Koh-i-loh may be bald shavelings. A party of Bhuri, with some Kafir girls for sale, had one of extraordinary beauty; the price asked for her being about half an ounce of silver. This tells us the state of the frontier. The Mahometans steal the Kafir women; the Kafirs kill the Mahometan marauders. The country is one which suggests legends and superstitions of all kinds. Sometimes the torrent disappears in some mysterious chasm leading to vast caves. Sometimes the caves themselves bear signs of human occupancy, excavated in labyrinthine windings, intricate, sculptured, and carven into pillars, the pillars themselves being figured.

In some of the chasms it is customary to consecrate certain medicinal herbs. Down one, near the Ziárat of Abba Shah, it is customary to hang a sort of gentian, and to leave it suspended for a month. After which it serves as a panacea.

Then there are the ruins of old cities; some of the monuments of which apparently bear inscriptions. About a mile and a half north of Esh, a Kafir district, bare and barren, is a colossal horse in pitchstone, measuring fifty-five feet from ear to hoof, forty-two from chest to tail. Nor is it the only one. Two others—like the first, in ruins—lie on the other two sides of the town.

The basaltic rocks, as is their habit in similar countries, assume fantastic shapes; sometimes that of a man, or man-like being. When this is the case, the Mussulman of the neighbourhood sees a petrified Kafir; and if asked who effected the petrifaction, answers Abraham. One of these, the Babo Bulan, is about twenty-five feet high, with red eyes, and an aquiline nose. Art has here, most probably, assisted nature. The Babo Bulan is an object of mysterious awe.

The fort of Ustam is said to have been built by Rustum, whose name is that of the great Persian hero. However, the legend makes him a son of Timur. Such are the elements of the Kafir fictions, and such their mixture. Half the inhabitants of the parts about Ustam are Mahometan, half Akaa. The foundations of the fort are Cyclopean, *i. e.* they consist of vast blocks of more than twenty feet in length.

Of the Akaa, the most Mahometan tribe is that of the Ujuem. Elsewhere the belief in the Koran is but slight. The men are short, stout, hardy, and clothed in skin; the women plain.

The Keiaz tribe seem to be among the rudest. The caves of the highest peaks are their occupancies. They hunt, eat raw flesh (which is unlikely), and are said to be cannibals, which is more unlikely still. Their women are handsome. When a Keiaz lover wishes to marry, he lays his bow at the foot of the fair one. If she take it up, kiss, and return it, the knot is tied, and she is his wedded wife. By varying this practice she can divorce herself, *i. e.* by taking her husband's bow and flinging it on the ground before him. Thirdly—she may make the offer herself, by unslinging one from the shoulder of the man she selects. On the other hand, their husband can sell them. He can also make them over to his visitor; who, if he be a Hindu devotee, may have the choice of the whole Keiaz wifedom; for the credulous mountaineers venerate these impostors, and believe that such progeny as their wives or daughters may bear to them are more or less divine.

The ruins of Mahu are in the Akaa country; the Turks of the neighbourhood being of the Kibi tribe.

Ma and Hu were twin brothers, descendants of Toth, Emperor of the East. Ma was a righteous prince; but Hu was wicked. Hu murdered Ma by burying him alive.

Before his death, however, Ma invoked the same fate on Hu. So the mountain tumbled down upon him and his. This is the account of the origin of the vast excavated tumulus of Ma-hu.

Such are the fragmentary notices of the northern Kafirs, and their congeners, the half-Mahometans, as taken from an appendix to Elphinstone's Caubul, and a paper of Dr. Gardiner's in the Asiatic Transactions of Bengal.

The following vocabularies for the parts nearest the Tibetan frontier are from Cunningham's Ladakh. The Khajunah of Hunz and Nagar is a very remarkable form of speech. All that can be said is that its nearest affinities are Paropamisan.

English.	Shina.	Arniya.	Khajunah.
Man	musha	rag	hir, er
Woman	grin	kamri	gus
Head	shis	sur	yetis
Eye	achhi	ghach	ilchin
Ear	kund	kad	iltumal
Nose	noto	naskar	gomoposh
Mouth	anzi	diran	gokhat
Tooth	duni	dond	gume
Hand	hath	hast	gurengga
Foot	pa	pang	goting
Blood	lohel	le	multan
Sky	agahi	asman	ayesh
Sun	suri	——	sa
Moon	yun	——	halans
Star	taro	satar	asi
Fire	agar	ingar	——
——	phu	——	phu
Water	wahi	augr	chil
River	sin	sin	sindha
Stone	bat	——	dhan

English.	Shina.	Arniya.	Khajunah.
Tree	tum	kan	——
Wood	katho	jin	gashil
One	ek	i	hin
Two	do	ju	altas
Three	che	triu	usko
Four	chhar	chod	walto
Five	push	punj	sundo
Six	shah	chui	mishando
Seven	sat	sut	talo
Eight	ast	ansh	altambo
Nine	no	neuhan	huncho
Ten	dahi	jash	tormo.

As far as their blood goes, some of the Little Tibetans may be Paropamisan. When I wrote my notice of Bultistan I had no reason to believe that this was the case. I have since, however, seen several casts of Bulti faces brought into this country by the brothers Schlagentweit. They are anything but Bhot. They are, on the contrary, more Persian than aught else. How far they may represent the average physiognomy is another question. Assume that they do so, and it becomes probable that, in the Mahometan districts of Tibet, the blood and language differ. If so, it is the Bhot tongue that has encroached. If so, the dialects which it has displaced are, in all probability, Paropamisan in the south, and Turk in the north; Turk in Kheris, Khapalu, and Chorbad. This, however, is a suggestion rather than a doctrine. Dard is the name for the Paropamisans of the valley of the Indus, and of the mountains on each side. Indeed, Cunningham uses the term in a generic sense, and calls his Shina, Armiya, and Khajuna vocabularies specimens of the Dard language. The term is convenient. It is also old. The Indian Puranas speak of the Daradas, the classical writers of the Daradæ. Whether it be sufficiently general is another question. The tribes, on the other hand, of Chitral and Gilghit are called Dunghers; Dungher being, also, a Hindu word. The Dangri vocabulary of Vigne represents the language of these Dunghers; word for word, the two names being the same.

That certain Paropamisans are, in the way of creed, either actual Hindus or Buddhists is specially stated by Gardiner; whose table I give as I find it. I hang a doubt, however, upon the last name of the list, Bhoti. What is the evidence that the Bhoti are not the ordinary Bhots of Tibet? The list, however, runs thus:—

Kafirs (Paropamisans) on the borders of Turkistan, Hindus or Buddhists.

Bu, or Buli,	calculated at	12,000
Kahuz, or Huhi	————	12,000
Phah, or Phagi	————	12,000
Aspah	————	12,000
Kúlis	————	12,000
Muklu	————	12,000
Maha	————	12,000
Kalesh, Malesh, Lesh	————	12,000
Beh, or Behel	————	12,000
Plahi, or Plaaghii	————	12,000
Bhoti	————	12,000

The last three divisions are subject to China. The numbers are, of course, only approximate.

CHAPTER IV.

The Brahúi.

WITH few populations is the consideration of their language of greater importance than with the Brahúi; and with few has its value been more utterly ignored. That it differed from that of the Biluches, and equally so from the Pushtu of the Afghans, was known to both Elphinstone and Pottinger—for both state the fact. Both, however, treat the Brahúi as Biluches with certain differential characteristics; neither asking how far some of these may be important enough to make them other than Biluch. This is because the political term Biluchistan has concealed one of the most important and interesting affinities in ethnology.

A short specimen of the Brahúi language in Leach's vocabularies commanded the attention of Lassen, who, after enlarging upon its difference from the Persian, Biluch, and Pushtu, drew attention to some notable similarities between the numerals and those of the South Indian dialects. Following up this suggestion, the present author satisfied himself, much to his surprise, that the Brahúi tongue was, in many respects, Tamul, an opinion which others have either recognized or been led to form from their own researches.

In the country, however, which they now occupy, the Brahúi consider themselves aboriginal; the Biluch admitting that they are themselves of foreign origin. The rugged and impracticable nature of the Brahúi mountains favours this view. Of any creed anterior to the introduction of Mahometanism no traces have been discovered, though, doubtless, discoverable. As Mahometans, they consider themselves favoured, inasmuch as the Prophet, mounted on a dove, paid them a visit one night, and left a number of saints behind him for their guidance. Forty of these lie buried under a mountain to the north of Kelaut, called *The Mountain of Forty Bodies*,* a place held sacred and visited not only by Mahometans other than Brahúi, but by the Hindus also. The particular form of the Brahúi Mahometans is the Sunnite, in which they agree with the Biluch.

They differ from the Biluch most in language, as has been stated already.

They differ from the Biluch also in physical form, and that notably. To this Pottinger speaks most decidedly: —"The contour of the people of these two classes is as unlike, in most instances, as their languages, provided they be the descendants of a regular succession of ancestors of either." He adds that the two populations intermarry. Again,—"It is impossible to mistake a man of one class for a member of the other. The Brahúi, instead of the tall figure, long visage, and raised features of their fellow-countrymen, have short, thick bones, with round faces and flat lineaments;—in fact, I may assert that I have not seen any other Asiatics to whom they bear any resemblance; for numbers of them have brown hair and beards." They are hardy; for they tolerate the scorching sun of Cutch Gundava equally with the cold frost of their own proper mountain-range. They are hardier, perhaps, than the Biluch. They are also more migratory than the Biluch, changing their pasturages several times in the year. They are harder workers; many of them in the plains to the south of Kelaut being

* Is not this the tale of page 150?

agricultural labourers. The product of their industry—which they dispose of to the occupants of the towns—along with the sale of a few coarse blankets and felts, forms the bulk of their traffic. Of their moral character I find a favourable account. They are less revengeful and less quarrelsome, though not less courageous, than the Biluches. Their chiefs have considerable power. Their women are but slightly, if at all, secluded. Their arms are the sword and the matchlock, in the use of which they excel, rather than the spear, for which they profess a kind of contempt. Their dress is the same for summer and winter. They are great eaters, especially of animal food. This they consume both fresh and dried. The drying is done by exposing the meat to the sun, after which it is smoked over a fire of green wood.

The division into tribes is Brahúi even as it is Biluch, Afghan, Turk, Arab, &c., the number of the tribual divisions being great. Pottinger gives the names of seventy-four; for fifty-two of which he gives the number of their fighting men. That of the Mingul, amounting to 10,500, is the highest. The lowest is that of the Jyanee, which is no more than sixty.

The list of Brahúi tribes could be doubled. "Were it answering my purpose I could enumerate twice as many more, but the foregoing list includes the principal ones in point of numbers, and will suffice to prove the multiplicity of the Brahooé, to say nothing of the absolutely innumerable *keils* into which they are subdivided." About one-fourth of the names end in *-zye*, as Jumul-*zyee*, Samo-*zyee*, &c.

The Kumburani tribe has two distinguishing characters. It only partially intermarries with the others, *i. e.* it receives wives from them, but not husbands, a common form of exclusiveness.

It is also divided into three distinct ranks,—(1) the Ahmedzyes, (2) the Khani, and (3) the Kumburani in the limited sense of the term.

English.	Brahúi.	Biluch.
Head	katumb	——
Hair	pishkou	phut
Eye	khan	tsham
Ear	khaff	——
Tongue	duvi	zawan
Tooth	dandan	dathan
Nose	bamús	phonz
Foot	nath	path
Sun	dey	——
Moon (*new*)	nokh	nokh
Star	istar	——
Fire	khakar	as
Water	dir	aph
Tree	darakht	darashk
Stone	khall	sing
I	I	ma
We	nan	mà
Thou	ni	thau
Ye	num	shumâ
One	asit	yak
Two	irat	do
Three	musit	shai
Four	tshar	tshyar
Five	pandzh	pantsh
Six	shash	shash
Seven	haft	hapt
Eight	hast	hast
Nine	nu	nu
Ten	dah	dah.

The following is a Brahúi legend.

" A frugal pair, who had been many years united in wedlock, had to regret that their union was unblessed by offspring. The afflicted wife repaired to a neighbouring holy man, and besought him to confer his benediction, that she might become fruitful. The sage rebuked her, affirming that he had not the power to grant what Heaven had denied. His son, afterwards the famed Hazrat Ghons, exclaimed that he felt convinced that he could satisfy the wife ; and casting forty pebbles into her lap, breathed a prayer over her, and dismissed her. In process of time she was delivered of forty babes, rather more than she wished, or knew how to provide for. In despair at the overflowing bounty of the superior powers, the husband exposed all the babes but one on the heights of Chehel Tau. Afterwards, touched by remorse, he sped his way to the hill, with the idea of collecting their bones, and of interring them. To his surprise he beheld them all living, and gambolling amongst the trees and rocks. He returned and told his wife the wondrous tale, who, now anxious to reclaim them, suggested that in the morning he should carry the babe they had preserved with him, and, by showing him, induce the return of his brethren. He did so, and placed the child on the ground to allure them. They came, but carried it off to the inaccessible haunts of the hill. The Bráhúis believe that the forty babes, yet in their infantile state, rove about the mysterious hill. Hazrat Ghous has left behind him a great fame, and is particularly revered as the patron saint of children. Many are the holidays observed by them to his honour, both in Balochistán and Sind. In the latter country, the eleventh day of every month is especially devoted as a juvenile festival, in commemoration of Hazrat Ghous."—*Masson's Journeys in Balochistán, Affghanistan, &c.* vol. ii. pp. 83—5.

The representative of the Brahúis, in the way of politics, is the Khan of Kelaut. The extent to which his dominions are Brahúi rather than Biluch will be considered in the sequel.

CHAPTER V.

Ancient History and Antiquities of Persia.—Relation of Persia to India. —The Religion of Ancient Persia.—The Parsis.

THE populations more or less akin to Persia, have now been enumerated in detail. The relations of Persia, however, as a preliminary to the ethnology of Hindostan, still stand over for notice. Of these two countries, the histories are inseparable. There were numerous Indians on the soil of Persia and Afghanistan, and there was scarcely a town of Caubul without its Hindus.

The literary language of India, allowance being made for a difference of dialect, is the inscriptional language of Persia.

Again,—Persian armies and Persian immigrants have, over and over again, occupied portions of India. They have done this so much, that even the strongest partisans of Indian autonomy and Indian self-development have admitted that, in analysing the ethnological elements of Hindostan, some part, at least, of Persia must be taken into account. But what do we gain by doing this, as long as Persia itself has been unsubmitted to analysis? What if, while Persia is an ingredient of India, Turkistan, Arabia, Armenia, Caucasus, and even parts of Europe, are ingredients of Persia? It is clear that an analysis is needed.

We have two instruments for effecting this, history and archæology. I begin with the first.

The general presumptions in favour of a Turk intrusion into the land of Persia have been already considered. They constitute the preliminaries to many questions in ethnology in general. To the particular ethnology of Persia they are a preliminary with which no ethnologist can dispense.

I consider that the ordinary notices of the once formidable Parthians suggest the belief that they were of the Turk stock, *i. e.* that they were what the classical writers would have called Asiatic Scythians; the Persians, Sacæ; the Mongols and Tibetans, Sok. If so, the Arsacidæ were what most of the Persian dynasts of the true historical period have been, foreigners to the soil over which they ruled, but not foreigners to the soil which, from the Caspian to the Paropamisus, lies parallel with that of Persia. Let Persia be called (as it is called at the beginning of its history), Iran, and let the parts beyond its frontier be called (as called they were) Turan, and the Arsacidæ were Turanians. Turanian, however, was scarcely the word for the Latins and the Greeks. They used, instead of it, Scythian. Few of them, however, paid much attention to language as an instrument in ethnological criticism. For this reason the special statement of Justin, that the speech of the Parthians "was midway between the Scythic and the Mede, and consisted of a mixture of the two," is valuable. Amongst modern writers Erskine unhesitatingly commits himself to the doctrine, that "the Parthians were a foreign race, who never fully assimilated with the native inhabitants." The Parthian coins have Greek legends. The particular Parthian province was Khorasàn.

I now submit the following inference from the similarity of the names *Parthia* and *Persia;* which are as much alike as the Greek words, πάρθω and πέρσω. I submit that, word for word, Parthia is Persia, and Persia Parthia; one being the name of a particular district, and, as such, implying a local conquest; the other being the name of a kingdom in general, and, as such, conveying the idea of a consolidation of power and a ruling dynasty. Just what is supposed to have taken place with these instances, has actually taken place with the word Frank. There is the particular Burgundian conquest of Franche Compté. There is the general French conquest of France. Both, however, were German; just as, *mutatis mutandis*, both Parthia and Persia are held to be Turanian. Let this be admitted, and the dynasty of Cyrus may have been Turanian, even as was that of the Arsacidæ. It was certainly other than Mede. The consideration, however, of the Mede and Macedonian dynasties stands over for the present.

Meanwhile, let those of Cyrus and the Arsacidæ bring us down to the epoch of the Sassanidæ. Word for word this seems to give us the Mongol title Zaisan. I do not, however, press this. I believe that current opinion is in favour of the Sassanidæ having been foreign dynasts.

They are succeeded by the Caliphs; out and out Arabian. But before the ninth century is over, the disturbances of the Turkish guards (the Turanian prætorians to an Arab court) have broken out, and Bagdad is in their hands. The Caliphat is shaken. The Taherites are nominally subordinate, practically independent. They govern in Khorasan, and they have come from the other side of the Oxus. This, however, is only a presumption in favour of their being Turanian. The Soffarids, who only reign from A.D. 872 to A.D. 902, may, not improbably, be Persians. The Samanids, who succeed them, like the Taherites, are from the north. They "passed the Oxus with 10,000 horse; so poor that their stirrups were made of wood, so brave that they vanquished the Soffarian army, eight times more numerous than their own." * The Bowids (from 933 to 1055) are said to have introduced the title of Sultan, a Turk term.

From the Bowid period to the present time, every king of either Persia, or any part of Persia, who consolidates a power with any pretension to stability, is either a Turk or a Mongol. Sebectegin, Mahmúd of Ghizni, Togrul Beg, Malek Shah, Alp Arslan, are all Turks. The Temuginian conquerors are Mongols; the Timurian, Turks.

It must be admitted, then, that the presumptions are in favour of the negative, and, therefore, hazardous, statement that the soil of Persia has never been permanently ruled by a native dynasty.

That a Turanian dynasty interposed between that of the Macedonians in Bactria, and the Arsacidæ, is shown by coin after coin, illustrative of the parts on the drainage of the Oxus during the first and second centuries of the Christian era.

Such is the *primâ facie* evidence (independent of that of the arrow-headed inscriptions which will be noticed hereafter) in favour of an influx of influential Turanians into Persia, beginning early and ending late. Such, too, the notice of the influences from Arabia. The Caliphat gave them. But Arabia is not the only Semite country which has told on Persia. Assyria has done the same. So has Media. So also Macedonia.

As the notice of both Assyria and Media involves a special line of criticism, it is only Macedonia which now arrests our attention. Alexander's army, so far as we see in it a civilizing influence and a vehicle for the thought

* Gibbon, chap. lii.

and learning of Eastern Europe, was an army of Greeks. Its captain was a reader of Homer. One, at least, of its generals was a historian. A geographer accompanied it. A philosopher or two might be found among its court elements. If we look at it, however, as a mere material force (and in this light the physical historian ought to view it), it was a Macedonian medley of half-barbaric Hellenes, Thessalians, and Illyrians. It may have had in its ranks Getæ and Thracians. Should any of its members be, at the present moment, represented by any of the mysterious tribes of the Paropamisus, the chances are against their being Greeks. Skipetar blood is more likely to be found amongst the Kafirs and Wakhanis than Hellenic. This, however, is but a speculation. Nevertheless, it is one which illustrates the case out of which it grows. Materially speaking, the Macedonians were, to a great extent, other than Hellenes. Morally and intellectually, they were Greeks. It was in north-eastern Persia that their power and language lasted longest. Soon after the death of Alexander it took root. By the end of the first century it was shaken by the Turanians.

The general import of the arrow-headed, or cuneiform, inscriptions is now pretty widely known. They represent three forms of speech. One of these, akin to the literary language of India, will be noticed ere long. The other two find their place here. Of these one is Semitic, and one Turanian. The simple existence of the Semitic record tells us this much, viz. that in the reign of Darius, as well as earlier and later, there was a sufficient amount of Assyrian blood within the limits of the Persian empire, to make it either necessary or convenient for public inscriptions to be written in the Assyrian tongue. The details tell us much more. This, however, is enough for the present question; which merely asks whether the foreign influences that have acted on Persia are great or small, new or old, homogeneous or composite. Our answer is, that they are both multiform and ancient. They are not only Semite as well as Turanian and Greek, &c., but they are Semite in two ways. Arabia gave the Koran; but one thousand years before the birth of Mahomet, Chaldea gave something else. There have been the older and the newer elements. And, in the time of the Sassanians there is evidence to an intermediate series of influences.

Respecting the Turanian inscriptions Mr. Norriss, whose opinion I am fully prepared to adopt, has laid down the following doctrine. They are not Turk; as we may possibly expect *à priori*. They are not Mongol. They are rather Ugrian or Fin. If so, we must suppose that, just as certain southern members of the great Fin family penetrated into Hungary in the tenth century, so did certain of their congeners, some fifteen hundred years earlier, penetrate into Persia. Be this as it may, the elements of the ethnology of Persia were, in the time of Darius, as well as before and after, sufficiently complicated to require two languages other than native for the rock inscriptions of royalty.

Roughly speaking, the arrow-headed inscriptions represent the times of Darius and his successors.

To one who holds that Persia was in the same category with Parthia and that Parthia was Turanian, the language of the inscriptions, which is other than Turanian, and, at the same time, not Semite, is more likely to be Mede than aught else—Mede rather than Persian.

Meanwhile the only remaining dynasty, the last in the order of notice, but the first in time, calls us; the dynasty of Deioces, Phraortes, Cyaxares, and Astyages. Now Deioces was a Mede, a Mede of a nation to which the Bysæ, the Parêtakæni, the Strukhates, the Arizanti, the Budii, and the Magi belonged, as opposed to that of the Persians, who were, according to their γένεα, Pasargadæ, Maraphii, Maspii, Panthialæi, Derusiæi, Germanii (a Turk gloss), Dai, Mardi (a Ugrian gloss), Dropiki, and Sagartii. That there were actions and re-actions of the kind suggested by the previous remarks in the time of Deioces, is evident from the text of Herodotus. The Assyrians had held the Medes in subjection. The Medes had not only been successful in throwing off the yoke from themselves, but had reduced the Persians. The Scythians and Cimmerians were overrunning not only Media and Persia, but Syria and Palestine as well. Let the history, then, of Persia speak to the great extent to which that country is the land of a mixed population.

It is Mede; it is Persian proper; it is Turanian.

More than this, the Cimmerii were Europeans; so that it has not been from Asia alone that its foreign elements have been derived.

The Cimmerii were Europeans. And so, in one sense, were the Scythians mentioned by Herodotus. They were the Skoloti of the southern parts of Russia rather than the Sakæ of independent Turkistan. They entered Media by the way of Caucasus. The Parthians, though equally Turk, entered Persia from the parts between the Caspian and the Paropamisus.

More unequivocally European than either the Scythians or the Cimmerii were the Thracians. It is impossible to study the campaign of Darius on the Danube without admitting that, notwithstanding all our tendencies to draw broad and trenchant lines of demarcation between the east and west, the early history of the Thracians, the Getæ, and the south-eastern Sarmatians is, to a great extent, that of Media—of Media rather than Persia. I am far from thinking that the Danubian principalities of the Great King were mere outlying possessions. I think that, of Media as opposed to Persia, they were central and integral parts, and that Macedonia was Persian quite as much because it was Thracian, as because it was Greek.

The influence that Greece exerted upon not only Persia in general, but that part of Persia in particular which lay nearest to India, is a matter of ordinary history. The influence of Rome is less distinctly seen. By Rome I mean the Rome of the west; Latin Rome; Rome proper rather than Greek Rome, Byzantine Rome, Constantinopolitan Rome. From the time of Lucullus to that of Julian there were either Roman proconsuls, or kings protected by Rome along the whole of the north-western frontier. There were Roman wars against the Seleucidæ, and Roman wars against the Arsacidæ. In after times there was Rome at second-hand from Constantinople.

It is chiefly through their early Christianity that Syria and Armenia (the former more especially) have acted on Persia. Persian Christianity, however, was short-lived. Yet it passed across the land so as to reach Turkistan, India, and even China.

The preceding analysis has been given because it is only when we undervalue the relations betwen Persia and Europe on one side and the relations between India and Persia on the other, that the phenomena presented by the ancient language and the ancient literature of Hindostan become mysterious; for mysterious they must be in the eyes of those who maintain that the Vedas are three thousand years old, and that the undeniable affinities between the Sanskrit and the languages of the west are explained by deducing the Russian, the German, the Latin, and the Greek from Asia. Any two points may be isolated by ignoring the interjacent area. The archæology of Persia is, to a great extent, the archæology of Hindostan. Persia has acted both morally and materially on India. Turkistan, Arabia, and Europe have similarly acted on Persia. Something was found on the land; something was brought into it; something was given off from it. This is the ordinary procedure when populations act and re-act on each, or where one acts on a second and the second on a third. What has been brought into Persia is, in some cases, extremely clear. It is clear, for instance, that one, at least, of the languages of the cuneiform inscriptions was an importation. So was Mahometanism. So were a great many other things.

The religion of the ancient Persians may or may not have originated on the soil of Persia. It is certain that it was from Persia that it more especially spread itself. It is also certain that, if foreign, the date of its introduction was early. Fire-worship, however, may have been Median rather than Persian proper, inasmuch as Media was (and is) a land where inflammable gases issue in mysterious currents in several localities. One, especially, near the city of Baku, is an object of devotion to the Guebres, who make pilgrimages to the spot, where "a blue flame, in colour and gentleness not unlike a lamp that burns with spirits," rises from the earth, and is supposed to be eternal. It may also, if we look at it on its sidereal, rather than its igneous aspect, have been Chaldaic or Arabian; for Sabæanism, as it is called, or the worship of the stars and planets, is pre-emimently Semitic.

I shall call the creed under notice Parsiism or Zoroastrianism indifferently. The chief *data* for its investigation are of three kinds:—the evidence of ancient authors other than Persian; the Parsi scriptures themselves; the practices and belief of the present fire-worshippers.

The Persians, writes Herodotus, think it foolish to

build temples. Yet they sacrifice. They sacrifice on the higher mountains. They sacrifice to the sun, the moon, the earth, to fire, to the winds. They have learned, of late, from the Assyrians and Arabians, to worship the deity called Mylitta by the former, Alytta by the latter, Mithra by themselves. The priest, girt with a wreath of myrtle, divides the victim, lays the parts on herbs, of which the trefoil is the chief, sings a hymn, and prays for all the Persians and the King of Persia. Lepers and white pigeons are not allowed to be near the sacrifice. He may not defile a river by even washing his hands in it. A Magus officiates. The bodies of the dead are first torn by dogs and birds, then interred. Previous to interment the body is smeared with wax. A Magus kills no animals except for the purpose of sacrificing. White is the colour of the sacred horses, of Nisæan breed. When Cyrus crossed the Gyndes one of the white horses plunged into the stream, whereon the king swore that from that time forward the river should not wet even the knees of a woman. So he turned off the main stream into 180 channels. Xerxes flogged the Hellespont, and threw fetters into it. Again, at sunrise he poured a libation from a golden cup into it, and prayed. Having finished the prayer he threw into the waves a golden cup and a scimetar. He also sacrifices white horses to the Strymon. Again,—" the Persians look upon fire as a god, and think it wrong to burn a dead man in a divine flame." Again, Xerxes sacrificed to the winds. Again, Darius wished to have his statue placed on the temple of the Ægyptian Vulcan, and Xerxes sacrificed to the Trojan Minerva. Dates forbade the fleet to approach Delos because it was the birth-place of Apollo and Diana. Xerxes buried certain boys and girls in honour of the god underground. The Magi, a γένος of Media, interpreted dreams, prophesied, and performed incantations. Ctesias makes Darius Hystaspes build an altar to the God of the firmament. Xenophon kills bulls, horses, and other victims according to the direction of the Magi. Strabo makes it unlawful to breathe on fire, according to whom the Cappadocians kept up a perpetual fire.

All this is the worship of the elements; especially is it fire-worship and sun-worship. It is not, however, Zoroastrianism in full. It is not the religion of the two principles. Of this, however, Xenophon gives an inkling. "I have two souls," says Araspes to Cyrus, "for a single soul cannot be bad and good at the same time," &c. Plutarch, from Theopompus, gives us Oromazes and Areimanius opposite and antagonistic to each other, the former of whom makes benevolence, truth, equity, wisdom, and joy; the latter their opponents. The former, too, makes the stars, and appoints Sirius guardian. He also makes twenty-four gods, and puts them in an egg, when Areimanius makes twenty-four others, who crack the egg, and out comes good and bad mixed. The heresy of Manes is stated by more than one of the early ecclesiastic writers to be Zoroastrian.

This gives us the great Dualism, along with a host of minor deities, who are, more or less, abstractions.

The next testimonies are those of the early Syrian and Armenian Christians. These give us a picture of fire-worship as it existed under the Sassanians. Elisæus in his History of the Religious Wars of the Persians and Armenians (as translated by Neumann) gives us the following proclamations and notices:—

"All peoples and tongues throughout my dominions must abandon their heresies, worship the sun, bring to him their offerings, and call him god; they shall feed the holy fire, and fulfil all the other ordinances of the Magi."

Again—

"Mihrnerseh, Grand Vizier of Iran and Daniran, to the Armenians abundant greeting:

"Know, that all men who dwell under heaven and hold not the belief of the Mastesens, are deaf and blind, and betrayed by the devil-serpent; for, before the heavens and the earth were, the great god Zruan prayed a thousand years, and said: 'If I, perhaps, should have a son, named Vormist, who will make the heavens and the earth.' And he conceived two in his body, one by reason of his prayer, and the other because he said *perhaps*. When he knew that there were two in his body, he said: 'Whichever shall come first, to him will I give over my sovereignty.' He who had been conceived in doubt passed through his body and went forth. To him spake Zruan: 'Who art thou?' He said: 'I am thy son Vormist.' To him said Zruan: 'My son is light and fragrant breathing; thou art dark and of evil disposition.' As this appeared to his son exceeding harsh, he gave him the empire for a thousand years.

"When the other son was born to him, he called him Vormist. He then took the empire from Ahrmen, gave it to Vormist, and said to him: 'Till now I have prayed to thee; now thou must pray to me.' And Vormist made heaven and earth; Ahrmen, on the contrary, brought forth evil; and thus they divided themselves among creatures; the angels are of Vormist and the devils of Ahrmen: All good, in heaven and here below, is from Vormist; all evil, which is done here and there, is produced by Ahrmen. And thus, whatever is good on this earth, this has Vormist made; and whatever is not good, that has Ahrmen made: as, for example, Vormist has made men; Ahrmen has made sorrows, sufferings, and death; all misfortunes and mournful events which occur, as also lamentable wars, are the work of the evil being; as fortunate events, riches, fame, honour, and health of body, beauty of countenance, eloquence in speech, and length of years, all have their being from good; but all which is not so is the corrupt working of evil."

Again—

"The Persian troops which had been in the land of the Huns are marching hither, with many other troops which had been placed at the gates. Besides these, they are accompanied by three hundred learned Magi, who are to disperse themselves throughout the land, convert every one, pull down the churches, and force all to conform to the king's command. These Magi say: If you receive our faith of your own free will, then shall you receive from the king honours and presents, from the court also a remission in the taxes; but if you receive it not freely, we have orders to construct fire-temples in the boroughs and cities, to kindle the fire Behram, and to appoint Magi and Mogheds learned in the law throughout the land. Should any one attempt resistance, he will suffer death, and his wife and children will be regarded as aliens, and banished."

The following gives us an insight into some of the more serious absurdities of the creed.

"Again, the Magi assign the following cause for the origin of light—they overturn what has just been said, and give another ground for the creation of the sun. They say: 'Ahrmen invited Vormist to a banquet. Vormist came, but would not partake of the meal till their children had fought against each other. Now after the son of Ahrmen had overthrown the son of Vormist, and they required an umpire and could find none, then they created the sun, that he might be the umpire between them.' Now they infer from this that Ahrmen is omnipotent even with regard to the sun, and contend that he took part in the creation of light. But was there, in reality, no other umpire present?—could they not have gone to the Father, or to Him to whom the Father and Son, according to their mythology, had addressed their prayers?

"And wherefore, then, were they in enmity against each other, Vormist and Ahrmen, who had been confined in one womb, who were about to banquet together, and who, by mutual co-operation, created the sun and set him up as umpire? But one Ssaratashd teaches the following disgraceful doctrine, that the Sun and the Light were made in maternal and sisterly embraces, and taught the nation that they might perpetrate the same atrocity: and to veil this disgrace it was given out that they (the Sun and the Light) were created for the office of umpire: for as their doctrines of belief are not contained in books, they sometimes say this, and at others they say that, and mislead the ignorant by it. But if Vormist was God, he was in a situation to create the sun, as well as the heavens and the earth, out of nothing, and not through a crime, or because there was no umpire at hand."

This is from Esnik, who is the chief evidence to the doctrine that both Ormuz and Ahriman are only secondary creations, the primary entity being Zeruan Akerane, *i. e.* Time Increate.

"Before yet anything was made, either the heavens or the earth, or any creature whatsoever which liveth in the heavens or on the earth, was one named *Zeruan*, a word signifying the same with *destiny* or *fame*. A thousand years he offered sacrifice that he might obtain a son, who should have the name Ormisd, and should create heaven and earth and all things in them. After a thousand years of sacrifice he began to reflect, and said, 'The sacrifice which I have performed, does it conduce to the end, and shall a son, Ormisd, be born to me, or do I strive in vain?' While he thought thus, Ormisd and Ahrmen were conceived in the body of their mother. Ormisd was the offspring of the sacrifice, and Ahrmen of the doubt. Zeruan knew this, and said,—'Two sons are in the mother's womb: he who shall first come forth to me will I make the king.' Ormisd knew his father's thought, imparted it to Ahrmen, and said, 'Our father Zeruan intends to make him king who shall first come to him;' and Ahrmen, hearing this, pierced through the body of his mother, and stood before his father. Zeruan, looking on him, said, 'Who art thou?' And he said, 'I am thy son.' Then Zeruan spoke to him: 'My son is of odoriferous breath and resplendent appearance, but thou art dark and of an evil odour.' While they were thus speaking together, Ormisd was born at his proper time, and he was bright-shining and sweet-breathing. He went forth and came before Zeruan: and when Zeruan looked upon him, he knew that this was his son Ormisd, for whom he had offered sacrifice. He took the vessel which he had in his hand, and wherewith he had sacrificed, gave it to Ormisd, and said, 'Hitherto I have sacrificed for thee, now and henceforward thou mayest sacrifice for me:' and hereupon Zeruan gave his vessel to Ormisd, and blessed him. Ahrmen saw this and said to Zeruan, 'Hast thou not taken an oath, whichsoever of the two sons shall first come to me, him will I make king?' Zeruan, that he might not break his oath, said to Ahrmen, 'O thou false and evil-doer! to thee be dominion given for nine thousand years; but I appoint Ormisd lord over thee. After the nine thousand years Ormisd shall rule, and what he wishes that shall he bring to pass.'"

The Mahometan writers were all subsequent to the time of the Sassanidæ. For this reason their evidence is not noticed. That of the Syrians is less full than that of the Armenians. Hence it is believed that the preceding notices, though anything but exhaustive, give a fair and sufficient notion of Zoroastrianism as a living creed at its zenith.

As a living creed at the present moment, Zoroastrianism is held by a few Parsis in Kirman, a few in Khorasan, and a great many more (the bulk of the faith) in Guzerat. In respect to its scriptures—

The Vendidad is a dialogue between Oromasdes and Zoroaster. The Yashna and Vispared are liturgies. The Khurdavesta is also a liturgy. The Yasts are minor and more fragmentary compositions.

There are, of course, in the Persian language several works which treat of Zoroastrianism, and which increase the bulk of the Parsi literature. Others, of which the Bundehesh is the chief, are in what is called Pehlevi. The language, however, of the religion of real life is the Gujerati, in which the Parsiism of India embodies its teaching, and conducts its controversies; for there are, at least, two sects—that of the Khadimi and that of the Rasami—who differ on a question analogous to that of the old and new styles in England. One admits, the other denies, the intercalation of a month. There are other elements of controversy besides, as will soon be seen.

The Parsiism of the present time has much that reminds us of Judaism. It makes few proselytes. It is not a religion for a poor man. Its adherents are chiefly mercantile. It differs, however, from Judaism in having never developed itself into any other religion; so that the creed which should stand in the same relation to the Zendavesta that Christianity does to the Old Testament is non-existent. This isolates Parsiism even more than Judaism is isolated.

The doctrines themselves are taken from the Zendavesta, and it cannot be said that the contents of the Zendavesta itself are unexceptionable. The apparent purity of a simple elementary worship, with a matter so suggestive of spirituality as fire for its main object, excited the imagination of the first investigators of the religion of the ancient Persians. The Parsi scriptures themselves, though not without better things, are full of angels and observances, of impossible epochs and absurd developments. That these are not taken *verbatim et literatim* speaks well for the present state of thought amongst the Parsis. The extent to which a freedom of interpretation existed (provided that it did exist, and was not evolved by the occasion) might not have been known had not the creed come within the sphere of the activity of the Bombay missionaries. These having got into controversy with the Parsis, found them ready to take their own part. I know the arguments of their defence only through the work of their arch-antagonist, the Rev. John Wilson, of the Scottish Church, which puts them in the light of eclectic critics rather than servile bibliolaters. They explain away their angels by making them abstractions, and excuse their ceremonies by reducing them to symbols. In short, they rationalize.

Thus—it is objected that they worship Feruher or Angels.

Answer by Dosabháí. "*Faruhar* means *johar*. They call that *johar*, which is in English called *Essence*. It is a *mantak*, or logical word. In Arabic, they apply *johar* to an article which is composed of its own substance; and they apply the word *araz* to an object which is composed of another object. Take for example the sun and sunshine:—The *johar* is the sun and the sunshine is *araz*. Take another example, of wood, and a chair:—the wood is *johar* and the chair is *araz*, for the chair is made from wood, and if there were no wood, there would be no chair."

Whether the trains of reasoning hereby suggested are strictly Zoroastrian or not is unimportant. Let them be ever so opposed to the original doctrine, Parsiism is still a creed, of which all that can be said is that its modern form differs from its ancient. In the fifth century, Zoroastrianism persecuted. In the nineteenth, it rationalizes.

CHAPTER VI.

The Ancient Languages of Persia and India.—The Persepolitan of the Cuneiform Inscriptions.—The Caubul Coins.—The Pali Inscriptions. —The Sanskrit and Pali of Literature.

THE next step in the ethnology of Persia and India is the consideration of those languages of which we have the oldest specimens, and of which the influence has been greatest. They all belong to one and the same class.

The language of this class that has commanded the greatest attention is, undoubtedly, the Sanskrit. Sanskrit, however, is by no means the most convenient name for the class; nor is the Sanskrit language the most convenient to begin with. The most convenient form of speech to begin with is what may be called

The Persepolitan.—The following is a sample at large from an inscription on the tomb of Darius at Naksh-i-Rustam, according to the text and translation of Sir H. Rawlinson :—

1 Baga wazarka Auramazdá, hya im
2 ám bumim adá, hya awam asm
3 ánam adá, hya martiyam adá, h
4 ya shiyâtim adá martiyahyá,
5 hyá Dár(a)yavum khsháyathiyam ak
6 unaush, aivam paruwanám khsháyath
7 iyam, aivam paruwanám framáta
8 ram.

The Great God Ormazd, (he it was) who gave this earth, who gave that heaven, who gave mankind, who gave life (?) to mankind, who made Darius King, as well the King of the people, as the lawgiver of the people.

Many inscriptions in the same language are found elsewhere, *e.g.* at Behistun, at Hamadan, and at Van. As a general rule, they occur in conjunction with two others in different languages. Whenever they do this, they take what may be called the place of honour, *i. e.* when the columns are arranged horizontally they stand at the left hand, so as to be read first, and, where there is a grouping round a centre, it is in the centre that the present language finds its place. Again, on a Persepolitan monument it stands alone. It is with good reason, then, that Sir H. Rawlinson considers that this is the primary language of the Achæmenian dynasty—a language of which the other members of the trilingual inscriptions are translations. Whether it be Persian rather than Mede is another question. It is safe to call it the language of the first inscriptions. It is safe, too, as well as convenient, to call it Persepolitan, inasmuch as, in Persepolis, it is found by itself.

In respect to its matter, it is the edicts of the Achæmenian kings which this language more especially embodies; the most important of which is that of the Behistun inscription. In respect to its structure it is closely akin to the oldest Sanskrit. There is no evidence, however, to it having ever been spoken in India, nor yet in the east of Persia. It is on the Kurd frontier, and in Fars, that samples of it most abound. It is only in inscriptions, and only in the cuneiform characters that it is found. Whether the Persepolitan inscriptions give us the oldest compositions in the class of languages to which they belong is uncertain. Most Sanskrit scholars would say that they do not. It is certain, however, that they are the oldest compositions that bear a date. Next to these come

The legends of the Caubul coins.—The kingdom which,

after the death of Alexander the Great, was founded in the north-east of Persia is better known through its coins than its historians. Of the former, some thousands have been deciphered. They show that the nearest successors of Alexander ruled as Greeks, their names being Greek and the legends on their coins being Greek. Letters and legends, however, other than Hellenic soon appear, and a series of coins, some bearing native, some bilingual, inscriptions follows. The mintage then degenerates, the names become barbarous, and the signs of a fresh dynasty of conquerors from Scythia show themselves. All, however, that is not Greek in the way of legend, belongs to the same class as the Persepolitan inscriptions on the one side and the literary Indian on the other. The fullest history of the dynasties in question is that of Professor Wilson, in the Ariana Antiqua. He calls the alphabet Arian.

The Pali of the oldest inscriptions.—Cotemporary with the earlier but older than the later Caubul coins, are certain inscriptions on pillars at Dauli and Girnar, known most especially through the papers of Prinsep; one of which gives us what will be noticed more fully in the sequel, the famous edict of Priyadasi, prominent and conspicuous in the real or supposed history of Buddhism. The language is a form of the Pali; the date of the inscription the reign of Sandracottus, or Chandragupta, the cotemporary of Seleucus.

Whether the inscriptions of the last two alphabets give us the oldest forms of the language to which they belong is uncertain. Most Sanskrit scholars would say that they do not. It is certain, however, that, next to the Persepolitan, they are the oldest compositions that bear a date.

Whether they give us the oldest alphabets is also uncertain. It is only certain that they give us the oldest documents on which an Indian alphabet appears.

The language of the Sassanian coins, &c.—The coins and inscriptions of the Sassanian kings exhibit a language of which it is unsafe to say much. It has affinities with the ones preceding. But it has also prominent Semite elements. The coins themselves are, of course, politically speaking, Persian. The alphabet, however, is Semitic. It contains no vowels, and only eighteen consonants. The legends which it embodies have, of course, a definite date. They range over the fifth, sixth, and seventh centuries.

Now come the compositions which, whether older or newer than the ones which have preceded, have no dates.

These fall into three great divisions:—(1) the Sanskrit, (2) the Pali, and (3) the Zend of the written literatures as opposed to the language of the inscriptions.

1. *The Sanskrit.*—The language of those numerous, long, and important compositions, of some of which further notice will be taken when we treat of the Brahminic literature of India, is the Sanskrit; the Sanskrit with its Devanagari alphabet, its fuller forms, and (along with other characteristics) its dual number, as opposed to the Pali. Of the Sanskrit, some forms are older than those of the literary language in general and some newer. Some present archaisms, some degenerations.

The Sanskrit of the Vedas is older than that of the great mass of the Sanskrit literature. How much is another question.

A Pracrit is a form of speech which, to explain *obscurum per obscurius*, bears the same analogy to the Sanskrit that the Lingua Rustica of ancient Rome may have borne to the pure Latin of Cicero. Or it may be compared to the Megarian dialect in the Acharnenses. Or it may be compared to the Gascon French in Molière; or to the Bolognese, and other dialects, introduced upon the Italian stage side by side with the purer Tuscan. It is in the Hindu dramas where the Pracrits are to be found; and it is women and servants who chiefly speak it.

The Kawi will be noticed when the influence of India upon Java, and

The Fan, when the influence of India upon China, is considered.

2. *The Pali.*—The scriptures of Tibet, Mongolia, Pegu, Ava, Siam, Kambojia, and Cochinchina, so far as they are composed in the learned or holy language of the Buddhist creed rather than in the vernacular of the several countries, are not in Sanskrit, but in Pali—Pali, the language of the Buddhism of the south of India. How far it was the language of Buddhism altogether, especially of the Buddhism of the north, is another question.

3. *The Zend,* or *language of the Parsi scriptures.*—This is a form of speech which requires more criticism than it has found. The matter which it exhibits is supposed to be older than the time of the Sassanidæ; the form only in which it appears being attributed to that dynasty. Under the Arsacidæ learning and religion had declined. There was a general knowledge of Zoroaster and his doctrines; but the Zoroastrian scriptures were wanting. So the old men with the long memories were looked up, and the Zendavesta, with its congeners, was constructed from their dictation. The result of this is a book discovered in India, in the seventeenth century, in a language different from that of the Sassanian coins, but akin to the Persepolitan and the Sanskrit. The alphabet, however, is not Indian—or rather it is and it is not. The letters are the letters of the Sassanian

legends adapted to writing; but the principles upon which they are applied are those of the Indian alphabet. They have eight or nine vowels—additions. In other words, the alphabet of the Sassanian coins consists of eighteen, the alphabet of the Parsi scriptures of forty-two characters.

The language of the glosses to the Zendavesta.—In the same letters as the Zend, *i. e.* in letters which represent the Sassanian inscriptions in a cursive form, are to be found certain glosses to the Zendavesta, which are neither Sassanian nor Persian proper, nor yet Gujerati, nor yet, exactly

The language of the Bundehesh (a work on the mythology of the Zendavesta), though closely akin to it, and written in the same characters.

That the preceding forms belong to the same class has already been stated. It should now be added that the Sanskrit and Pali are Indian rather than Persian; the Persepolitan Persian rather than Indian; the rest Persian in some respects, Indian in others, *e. g.* the Caubul legends are Pracrit in the way of language; whilst their alphabet is, in some respect at least, Semitic. On the other hand, the Zend alphabet is, in some respects, Indian, while the language itself is Persepolitan, rather than either Sanskrit or Pali. More, however, will be said on this head when the alphabets of India, &c., come under notice. More, too, when the origin of the present Persian and the modern dialects of India is considered.

CHAPTER VII.

On the Languages akin to the Tamul.—The Telinga.—The Tamul proper. —The Canarese.—The Cúrgi.—The Malayalam.—The Tulu, or Tulava. —The Ghond.—The Khond.—The Eastern Kol.—The Rajmahal.— The Tamul elements of the Brahúi.

THE languages which form the subject of the present chapter are the languages akin to the Tamul. Between these and the languages akin to the Sanskrit there is a strong contrast. The further we go into the ethnology of India, the clearer this will be seen. The languages of the last chapter were dead; the languages of the present are living.

The earlier writers (and *early* in Indian ethnology means the writers of the beginning of the present century) certainly undervalued them. The habit, too, of speaking of them as the languages of Southern India is inconvenient; for, in ordinary parlance, few of us make Southern India to begin at the Ganges. Mysore and the Carnatic, the Madras Presidency and the Canara country are southern in every sense of the word. Bombay, too, is in the southern half of India, if we begin with Cashmir. Yet the Rajmahal hills are north of Bombay, and the Rajmahali form of speech is Tamul—the word, of course, being taken in a general sense. Add to all this the Tamul elements of the Brahúi, and the reasons against localizing the great family to which that name applies increase. So far from being South Indian, it is not exclusively Indian.

It is Persian as well. The origin of the Brahúi has nothing to do with this view. We are simply looking to the actual distribution of the Tamul tongues in space, as they exist at the present moment. We are simply guarding against the influence of certain expressions which may lead us to under-estimate its extent.

The reasons for giving prominence to the forms of speech now coming into view are less manifest; indeed, the practice of doing so is anything but general. Yet nothing is clearer than the geographical contact between the languages of India and those akin to the Tibetan along the whole range of the Himalayas. Along the whole range of the Himalayas, from Cashmir to the end of Asam, the two groups touch each other definitely and directly; no intermediate language intervening. All that is not Tibetan, Nepaulese, or Burmese, is Hindu; all that is not Hindu is Burmese, Nepaulese, or Tibetan. Such the general character of the frontier. In its details we may fairly presume there has been a difference. What if the Tibetan or Nepaulese tongues have once extended further south, so that the Hindu dialects have encroached upon them? Nepaul, at the present moment, is Bhot. May not the parts south of Nepaul once have been the same? What if the history of the Hindus in the north of Hindostan be that of the English in England, the Nepaulese and Tibetans representing the Welsh of Wales? In such a case the whole valley of the Ganges may once have been, more or less, Bhot. More than this. There may have been a time when (for the eastern half of India at least) the southern frontier of the Tibetan, and the northern frontier of the Tamul, areas touched each other. What if the Ganges separated them, even as the Rhine separated Gaul from Germany? I do not, at present, say that this was the case; I only point out the bearings of the Tibetan tongues upon the ethnology of India. I add, too, that in one point, at the present moment, the distance between the two extremities of the two areas is not more than sixty miles as the crow flies. In the parts to the north and north-east of Calcutta the monosyllabic languages of the Garo hills are spoken to within a short distance of the northern bank of the Ganges. In the parts west of Calcutta the Rajmahal hills actually abut upon the river from the south. Yet the Rajmahal area is Tamul. Again—the original language of Kooch Bahar has its southern frontier a little to the north of Agra; to the south of which populations reasonably believed to belong to the Tamul family make their appearance.

The Telugu, Teloogoo, Telaga, Telunga, or *Telinga,* is spoken from Chicacole on the north to Pulicat on the south, extending in the interior as far as the eastern boundaries of the Mahratta districts; so as to be the vernacular language for upwards of fourteen millions of individuals in the northern Circars, and in parts of Hyderabad, Nagpúr, and Gondwana. The drainages of the Kistnah and Pennaur rivers are within the Telinga area. The great stream of the Godavery has Telinga districts on each side of it. A third or more of the eastern Ghauts is Telinga. Then there are the Telinga populations of the parts beyond the proper Telinga area, chiefly in the Tamul districts—Naiks, Reddies, &c. Of these there may be a million; yet it is doubtful whether the Telinga populations are either the most enterprizing or the most civilized of their class. With a smaller population there is, at the present moment, more activity amongst the speakers of

The Tamul.—Whether this was always the case is another question. The energy of the latter population is measured by the extent to which Tamul servants, Tamul labourers, Tamul tradesmen, are to be found beyond the proper boundaries of their language, working hard, pushing their fortunes, making money. This is considerable. As the parts on each side of the Godavery are Telinga, the districts which the Cavery waters are Tamul. Madras is Tamul, Pondicherry is Tamul, Tranquebar is Tamul, Negapatam is Tamul, the Carnatic is Tamul. In fact, the Tamul language succeeds and replaces the Telinga about Pulicat, a little to the north of Madras, and is spoken all along the coast of Coromandel to Cape Comorin. It then turns to the north, and constitutes the vernacular of the southern part of the Rajahship of Travancore, giving way to the Malayalim in the parts about Trevandrum. Inland, it extends to the Ghauts and Nilgherries—say to the parts about Coimbatúr. It is the language of a vast plain; contrasted in this respect with the Telinga, which is spoken over a varied surface, sometimes level, oftener broken.

Ten millions is the number given to the speakers of the Tamul tongue. They are not, however, confined to the district just indicated. There are Tamul settlers in Ceylon, especially in the north-western parts of the island. The coolies of the coffee plantations are generally Tamul all over the island. There are numerous Tamul merchants in the capital; and "ere long," writes Mr. Caldwell, "the Tamilians will have excluded the Singalese from almost every office of profit or trust in their own island." The majority of the domestic servants and camp-followers, even in the Telinga portions of the Presidency of Madras, are Tamul, and whatever may be the vernacular dialect, the Tamul is current in all the military cantonments of Southern India. Cannanore is in the Malayalim, Bangalore in the Canarese, Bellary in the Telugu, Secunderab in the Hindostani, countries; nevertheless, the language which (if not heard oftenest) is, at least, thoroughly understood, is the Tamul. Then there are the Klings in Pegu, in Penang, and in Sincapore. These, as a general rule, are Tamul. So are the emigrants to the Mauritius. Of course they have been compared to the Scotch, also to the Greeks. They may or may not be like them. If they were not active and energetic the comparison would never have been made.

The Tamul, being a language long cultivated, is known in two forms—an ancient or literary, a modern or colloquial.

The literary Tamul is called the Shen Tamul.

The colloquial Tamul is called the Kodun Tamul.

West of the Telinga, west of the Tamul, and in the central table-land of Southern India, is spoken the vernacular language of Seringapatam and Mysore.

The Canarese, Kannadi, or *Karnataka.*—Mysore is its centre. Yet it touches the coast in the district of Canara between Goa and Mangalore, a district to which it is scarcely indigenous, but one in which it has succeeded the Tulava, a language that will soon come under notice. On the east it nowhere even approaches the sea. Nor is it the only language of Canara. Beside it there is the Tulava. Beside it is the Malayalam of the southern frontier. Beside it is the Konkani of the northern frontier—the Konkani, which is a dialect of the Mahratta, and, as such, strongly contrasted with the other three forms of speech. In the Nizam's country it reaches as far north as Beder, the frontier between it and the Mahratta being, in many districts, eminently irregular.

There are two stages, or forms, of the Canarese, even as there were two forms, or stages, of the Tamul. The ancient or literary dialect exhibits a difference of inflection in several notable details—a difference of inflection, not merely of words.

The Coorgi, or language of Coorg and Wynaad, is a dialect of the Canarese.

Including the Coorgis, the number of individuals who speak the Canarese may amount to 5,000,000.

The Malayalam, if we allowed ourselves to refine upon its affinities, would possibly find its place immediately in contact with the Tamul. It is the Tamul with which it comes in the closest geographical contact. Like the Tamul it is a language of the extreme south. It has been imagined to be of special Tamul origin. It is, however, a separate substantive language, possibly more akin to the Tamul than its other congeners—but no Tamul dialect.

The Malayalam is the language of the western side of the coast of Malabar. On its east lies the Canarese; on its north the Tulava; on its south the Tamul. The Tamul succeeds it at Trevandrum, the Tulava and Canarese of Canara, about Mangalore. It stretches over about six degrees of latitude, but only in a narrow strip between the Ghauts and the sea. It is the vernacular of Cochin, and the northern and middle parts of Travancore.

The Tulu, Tuluva, or *Tulava* is spoken by no more than 150,000 souls. It succeeds the Malayalam about Mangalore, and reaches, northwards, the Mahratta frontier about Goa. Like the Malayalam, it covers but a strip between the Ghauts and the ocean. It is said to resemble both the Malayalam and the Canarese, the latter most.

The following are, according to Caldwell, the writer from whose Dravirian Grammar the preceding details are exclusively taken, the statistics of the above-mentioned languages.

1. Tamul is spoken by	. .	10,000,000
2. Telinga	,, . .	14,000,000
3. Canarese	,, . .	5,000,000
4. Malayalam	,, . .	2,500,000
5. Tulu	,, . .	150,000
		31,650,000

The previous forms of speech constitute a natural group —a natural group, and not a very large one. They all belong to the Dekhan. They are all spoken by populations more or less Hindu. They are all the languages of the civilized Indian. Their area is continuous; in other words, they are all in contact with each other, and their frontiers join. There is nothing between the Telinga and the Tamul, the Tamul and the Canarese, the Tamul and the Malayalim. Their area is continuous.

The forms of speech that now come under notice, though in all essentials closely allied to the preceding, in some respects form a contrast rather than a counterpart to them. They are spoken by the ruder, rather than the more civilized, sections of the Indian family. They are spoken beyond the Dekhan as well as within it. They are spoken in the hill and jungle rather than in the town and village. They are spoken by either actual pagans or imperfect Hindus. For the purposes of literature they have been wholly neglected. There is not a native alphabet amongst them. Finally, their area is, in many places, either actually discontinuous or very irregular, *i. e.* they are separated, or nearly separated, from each other by languages of either a different family or a different branch of the same. The level country is Hindu both in creed and language. The mountain which it encompasses is other than Hindu in language, and pagan in the way of creed.

The Gond.—This is the language of that portion of India which is marked in the maps as Gondwana; or, if not in the white district, of its hillier and more impracticable portions. Like most of the localities which preserve, in fragments, the older populations of a country, it is a watershed. The northern feeders of the Godavery, and the south-eastern of the Nerbudda, take their origin in the Gond country, of which, the greater part lies considerably to the north of the most northern portion of Telinga area, and of which the northern frontier, is (in the way of language), Hindu, the western and south-western Mahratta. As the region, however, to the south and south-east of Gondwana has been but imperfectly explored, I am unable to say whether it is absolutely isolated. It may or may not touch certain parts of Telingana. Again, it may or may not, touch the western portions of the

Sour, Kond, and *Kol areas.*—Word for word, Sour is Sairea, a name which will appear in the notice of Bundelcund and elsewhere. It is no native term, but one by which certain Hindus designated certain populations different from themselves. It indicates, then, a negative character; from which it follows that the populations to which it applies may or may not be allied; the affinity or the difference being, in each instance, determined by the special circumstances of the case. It is necessary to be familiar with the distinction, in order that we may not be misled by names.

Word for word, Kond is Gond, a name which has already appeared. It is no native term, but one by which certain Hindus designated certain populations different from themselves.

Word for word, Kol is Kúli, a name which will appear in the notice of Gujerat or elsewhere. It is no native term, but one by which certain Hindus designated certain populations different from themselves.

The Sours, Konds, and Kols are the Orissa analogues of the Gonds of Gondwana. They occupy the fastnesses of the eastern Ghauts rather than the more complicated ranges of the centre. They run in a rough kind of parallelism to the sea; their direction being vertical, *i. e.* from north to south rather than horizontal, *i. e.* from east to west. At the same time they run sufficiently inland to touch parts of Gondwana; so that the distinction between the present group and the preceding is, probably, artificial; Gondwana, for the most part, having been approached from the west, the Kond country from the east; Gondwana having been treated as an eastern district of the Mahratta country, the Kond region as a western portion of Orissa.

It is the Kond section that is best known; both in respect to its proper ethnology and its geography. It is this last alone which now lies under notice. The Konds are found as far north as 20° N. L., and as far east as the sea-coast. This brings them to the parts about Ganjam, about Kuttak, Juggernauth, and the Chilka Lake. Southwards they extend below Chicacole; portions of the Vizagapatam district being Kond. This is within the Telinga area.

The Sours (wholly within Telingana) extend from the southern frontier of the Konds to the Godavery.

The Sours to the south—the Konds in the centre—the Kols to the north—this is the distribution northwards.

The Rajmahali mountaineers.—These are the occupants of the Rajmahal hills in the neighbourhood of Bogilpur. How far their area is continuous with that of the northern Kols is uncertain. It is only certain that the numerous dialects of the Gonds, Konds, Kols, Sours, and Rajmahalis, are, at one and the same time, connected with each other, and connected with the Telinga, the Canarese, the Tulava, the Malayalim, and the Tamul.

The Brahúi.—The Tamul elements of the Brahúi have already been noticed. The details of the Brahúi occupancy will be noticed in the sequel.

CHAPTER VIII.

Relations of the languages akin to the Tamul.—Relations of the languages akin to the Sanskrit.

The languages akin to the Tamul.—The affinity of these is the one suggested by their geography. Their nearest congeners are the Tibetan and Burmese. The Tamul forms of speech, however, are in a higher stage of development. They are what is called agglutinate; *i. e.* they exhibit inflections; but those inflections can, for the most part, be reduced to separate words incorporated with the main term. Doing this, they stand in the same relation to the languages of the so-called monosyllabic class on the south, that the Turk, Mongol, Tungús, and Ugrians stand on the north and west. Whatever relation they may have with these last is indirect. In agreeing with them in structure, *i. e.* in their stage of development, they are their analogues, not their congeners. Whether there may not be direct (but intrusive) Turanian elements in India is another question.

The languages akin to the Sanskrit.—These are all truly inflectional rather than agglutinate, *i. e.* they are in the condition of the Latin and the Greek with their cases and tenses, rather than in that of the English or French with their prepositions and auxiliary verbs which have replaced them, or that of the Burmese and Tibetan wherein they have yet to be fully developed.

The Sanskrit, then, and its congeners are inflectional, after the manner of the languages of Europe, and, being this, stand in strong contrast to all the Tamul dialects, which are (as aforesaid), after the fashion of the Turk and Fin, agglutinate.

There is, then, a contrast here. There is another and a stronger one when we pass over to the field of the monosyllabic tongues. With the Tibetan, with all the Nepaulese dialects, and with the Burmese, the Sanskrit differs more decidedly than with the Tamul. Both these contrasts are important. They make us ask the following question:—If the Sanskrit be unlike its neighbours on the south, if it be more unlike its neighbours on the north, and if it be equally foreign to the frontier languages on the east, what is it like? What is it like, and where are its congeners? They are not to be found on the frontier of India; so that the Sanskrit comes from the north and west rather than from the south and east.

The Sanskrit language.—Westwards lie the Persian localities; the localities for the language of the cuneiform inscriptions, and perhaps of the Zend. Can these be in what we may term their proper *situs*, *i. e.* in geographical contact with the languages next akin? One of these is the Arabic, which is as little like the Sanskrit as are the Turk and Mongol. Another is the Armenian, which is somewhat more like, and another, the Iron, which is decidedly like the modern Persian. None, however, are the nearest congeners to either the Sanskrit or the Zend. To find these we must go westward, beyond the Black Sea and the Hellespont; beyond the Don. We must enter Europe. The nearest congeners to the Sanskrit are the languages of the Russian empire; then those of Rome and Greece; then those of Germany. Changing the phrase, the Sanskrit belóngs to the same class with the Sarmatian, the classical, and the German tongues; a class to which some (perhaps most) philologues add the Keltic. The ordinary (but exceptionable) name for this group is Indo-Germanic (or Indo-European); the languages which belong to it being spoken in Germany (or Europe) and in Hindostan. Its most eastern division is the Sarmatian, which falls into two branches—the Slavonic and the Lithuanic, the latter lying east of the former. Now, without doubt, the affinities of the Sanskrit are closer with the Lithuanic than with any other language on the face of the earth. It is not what we expect *à priori*. Still, it is the case.

I should add, however, that this is not the usual language of philologues; who, generally speaking, are satisfied with making the Sanskrit Indo-European, without deciding to which of the other members of the class it has the greatest affinity. I look upon this as the cause of much error; inasmuch as it is evident that to search for the origin of a language that is equally allied to half a dozen others (unless, indeed, it stand in the centre of them) is a waste of learning and acumen. Next to the Lithuanic, the Sanskrit is most like the old Slavonic; which is, again, the most eastern member of *its* class.

The Sanskrit is more closely allied to the Lithuanic than to aught else. In making the comparison, however, one very important fact must be remembered. The oldest specimen of the Lithuanic is no older than A.D. 1500. In Sanskrit there are compositions 2000 years old. The Sanskrit, in fact, is in the stage of the Latin and Greek. The Lithuanic, on the contrary, though not exactly in the modern condition of the Spanish or Italian, is, nevertheless, in an advanced stage. It has, doubtless, had inflections, which, like those of other languages, have existed and have died out—died out before the language was reduced to writing, and before their existence could be recorded. In some respects, then, the Latin and Greek are more like the Sanskrit than is the Lithuanic, inasmuch as they are in the same stage, the stage wherein inflections are numerous. Nevertheless, the real affinities are Lithuanic. Those with Germany are less close. Those with the Keltic tongues more remote still.

Here we pause for the present, and pass on to a new class of facts.

CHAPTER IX.

The languages akin to the Hindí.—The Cashmiri.—The Hindí.—The Gujerati.—The Bengali.—The Udiya.—The Mahratta.—Sectional and Intermediate Forms, &c.—Migratory Populations and Trades.—The Gypsies.—The Bhíl Dialects.—The Hindostani.

If the Sanskrit and the Pali be dead languages, and if the languages akin to the Tamul be limited to the areas which have been described (and they *are* so limited), what are the living forms of speech in those parts of India which lie north of the Dekhan and west of the Gond and Kond countries? What, indeed, are the forms of speech for certain tracts east of Gondwana? What is the language of Bengal? What is the language of the natives of Orissa itself, who are other than Kond? What is the language of Oud, of Delhi, of the Rajput country, of the Desert and the whole drainage of the Indus, of Gujerat, of the Mahratta country? It was not Sanskrit. Sanskrit, like Latin, has ceased to be spoken. It was not Telinga or Canarese. Canarese and Telinga belong to the Dekhan.

There is a class of languages which we may describe, as we have described the Pali, the Telinga, and their respective congeners. There is a class of languages the members of which may be said to be akin to the Hindí. Saying this we use a circumlocution. There are reasons, however, for doing so. That they are akin to the Hindí and to each other no one denies. That they belong to *one* of the two groups which have preceded no one denies either. That they are Tamul rather than Sanskrit many deny. That they are Sanskrit rather than

Tamul some deny, some doubt. It is best, then, to describe them as Hindí, or akin to the Hindí.

So much for the term. The group itself is dealt with as a separate class, not because it belongs to neither of the preceding, but because it is doubtful to which of the two it should be referred.

At the same time the group is, from a certain point of view, a natural one. All the languages it contains agree in giving the following contrasts. As compared with the Sanskrit they are poor in inflections; even as the Italian, when compared with the Latin, shows poor. As compared with the Tamul tongues, they abound and over-abound in words of Sanskrit origin; even, as compared with the Dutch or the Danish, the English abounds in Latinisms. It is unnecessary to say to what difference of opinion these conditions may give rise. There is the claim for the Sanskrit, and there is the claim for the Tamul, origin of the languages of northern India, with authorities and arguments on both sides. The highest authorities, and the greatest number of advocates, are for the Sanskrit. Whether the best arguments are in the same predicament is another question.

The dialects of the present group are numerous, and some of them will be noticed as we go on. At present it is convenient to enumerate the following six languages—for separate substantive languages they are usually considered to be.

1. The Cashmirian of Cashmir.

2. The Brij Basha, or Hindí.

3. The Gujerati, or Gujerathi, of Gujerat.

4. The Bengali of the lower Ganges, the *valley* of Asam, and parts of Sylhet and Chittagong.

5. The Udiya of Orissa.

6. The Mahratta or Marathi of Aurungabad, &c.

I give these divisions as I find them, adding that, though convenient, they are, by no means, unexceptionable. In the first place, the difference between a language and a dialect has never been satisfactorily explained: so that neither term has yet been defined. It will be seen, ere long, that there are several other forms of Indian speech, of each of which, though we may say with truth that it is more Hindí, more Bengali, or more Marathi than aught else, we cannot say that it is a Marathi, a Bengali, or a Hindí dialect. For this reason it is inexpedient to give the numbers of individuals by which each tongue is spoken. And it is also inconvenient to say whether such and such languages are mutually unintelligible. It is only certain that whatever difference may exist between any two is exaggerated rather than softened down when they are written. This is because the alphabets, though all of Sanskrit origin, differ from each other in detail.

Of the six languages under notice, the Cashmiri, the Gujerati, and the Udiya, are spoken not only over the smallest areas, but by the fewest individuals; the largest areas being those of the Marathi and Hindí, the largest mass of speakers being those of the Bengali language. It is the Bengali which has the greatest tendency to extend itself beyond the frontiers of India; the Bengali of Asam and Chittagong being the form of speech which is more especially encroaching upon the Tibetan and Burmese areas.

The languages that lie in the closest contact with the members of the Tamul group are the Marathi and Udiya. The affinities of the Cashmirian with the Dard tongues are decided.

I guard against the notion that the difference between the six tongues of the foregoing list is greater than it really is. A little more Sanskrit or a little less; a little more Persian or a little less; a Telinga or a Canarese element more or less; an alphabet of more or less detail —in these points and the like of them consist the chief differences of the languages akin to the Hindí.

I guard, too, against the notion that the preceding list is exhaustive. Before Hindostan has been traversed we shall hear of such sectional and intermediate forms as the Jutki, the Sindi, the Punjabi, the Haruti, the Marwari, the Konkani, and others; of all whereof thus much may be said—

1. That they are allied to each other and to the Hindí.

2. That they are not akin to the Sanskrit in the manifest and unequivocal way in which the Sanskrit, Pali, and Persepolitan are akin to each other.

3. That they are not Tamul or Telinga in the way that the Canarese, the Kond, &c., are Canarese, Tamul, and Telinga.

Necdum finitus Orestes.—There are certain populations which drive trades that require movement from one part of the country to another, trades like those of the drovers, knife-grinders, and the like, in England. Most of these have a mode of speech more or less peculiar. They will be noticed hereafter. Meanwhile, it may be laid down, as a general rule, that their dialect is that of the country to which they more especially belong, *i. e.* more Hindí than Tamul in the Marathi, &c., more Tamul than Hindí in the Canarese, &c., countries.

The Gypsy language.—That this is Indian is well known. What are its affinities, Tamul or Hindí? Hindí. Hence it belongs to the present group.

The Bhíl, &c., dialects.—In habits the Bhíls, the Wáráli, the Kols of Gujerat, and other allied tribes, are, on the western side of Gondwana, what the Sours, the Konds, and the Kols of Bengal are on the eastern. All are believed, on good grounds, to be of the same blood. At the same time, the language of the first is akin to the Hindí; just as the Cornish is English, though the blood of the Cornishman is Welsh. The Welshman, however, has preserved what the Cornishman has lost, *i. e.* the characteristic of language. *Mutatis mutandis*, this is what is believed, on reasonable grounds, to be done by the Konds and Bhíls, &c. On the eastern side of India the language and blood coincide. On the western the blood is southern, the language northern—the language Marathi, the blood more or less Canarese and Telinga.

The only form of speech that now stands over for notice is

The Hindostani.—This is the language of the Mahometans of Hindostan. It is essentially and fundamentally Hindí, but it comprises more Persian and more Arabic words than any of the true vernaculars. It is written, moreover, in Arabic characters.

CHAPTER X.

India as an influence.—Its action upon Tibet, Ava, &c.—Upon the islands of the Indian Archipelago.—Brahminism and Buddhism.

IMPORTANT as are the great polytheist mythologies of Greece and Rome in the history of art and literature, they have been but little influential in the history of the world at large. They may safely be ignored in the present chapter, which is devoted to a short notice of what may be called the six great creeds of mankind, viz. Judaism, Christianity, Mahometanism, Parsiism, Brahminism, and Buddhism. All these agree in being the religions of a lettered language; so that their doctrines can be expounded, their canons embodied, and their controversies conducted by means of writings more or less permanent, more or less capable of both multiplication and diffusion. When this is the case, creeds both increase in stability and become susceptible of development. They become measures of the multiplicity of ways in which the human mind can employ itself upon transcendental subjects, and they also grow into historical influences and determine the moralities or immoralities of nations. The division, then, between the lettered and unlettered religions is natural. As for the unwritten superstitions of the ruder varieties of mankind, it is convenient to denote them by the general name of paganism. It is also convenient to call the paganism of Asia and Europe shamanism; that of Africa fetichism. It is convenient to do this. I do not say that it is strictly scientific.

That the six great lettered religions fall into groups is manifest. The first three are in decided and palpable relations to each other, connected by their common monotheism, connected by their common recognition of several prophets and patriarchs. They belong to the west rather than the east, to those parts of the world where northern Africa and western Asia come in contact. The languages of the countries in which they arose were Semitic; and Semitic is the language of two of their scriptures, the Old Testament and the Koran.

In like manner Buddhism and Brahminism are connected; connected both in the doctrines which they convey and the language in which those doctrines are embodied. They belong to the east rather than the west, and they originated in those districts where Persia, Central Asia, and India join. The languages in which they are embodied are closely allied; indeed, they are a dialect of one language rather than separate forms of speech. The alphabets which represent them differ. So do the Arabic and the Hebrew. So do the Hebrew and Samaritan. This agreement in speech, combined with a difference of expression, is a common phenomenon in the history of religions.

What Brahminism and Buddhism are in the matter of language that is Parsiism also. Whether Zend or Pehlevi, the speech of the fire-worshippers was akin to that of the Indian rituals. The Zend and Pehlevi alphabets, however, are other than Indian. That there are Parsi elements in the Indian mythology is well known. It is well known, too, that from actions and reactions between the creeds of Judæa and Chaldæa, there is something Parsi (the word is used in its widest sense) in Judaism, something Judaic in Parsi.

As a religious influence, Parsiism is either stationary or retrograde. It is not dead like classical polytheism. It is only deficient in development. Its history, however, I believe to have been important; for I believe that in Turkistan, in Mongolia, in parts even of China and Siberia, not to mention many districts of Caucasus, there was, before the diffusion of the present Buddhist and Mahometan theologies, a more or less imperfect fire-worship.

Of the western religions, Judaism, of the eastern, Brahminism, are what may be called passive, *i. e.* they care little to propagate themselves abroad. What is Brahminism out of India? Who are Jews except the children of Israel? The religions for the Gentiles are the remaining three.

I have not made these remarks solely and wholly for the sake of either suggesting analogies or exhibiting the sketch of a classification. I have rather made them as preliminaries to a special fact connected with India as an influence on the history of the world. India, beyond the area of Hindostan, is chiefly a great religious influence so far as it is Buddhist; just as the western or Semite religions are chiefly forces so far as they are either Christian or Mahometan. Yet India, at the present moment, is no Buddhist country at all. Neither are Palestine and Asia Minor Christian. Yet it was in them that Christianity arose. The country that propagates a creed is not always the country that retains it.

The country that propagates a creed is not always the country that originates it. Neither Greek nor Latin Christianity originated in either Greece or Rome.

There is no Buddhism, *eo nomine*, in continental India at the present moment; though there is plenty of it in the island of Ceylon, and remains of it, as well as existing modifications, on the mainland.

There is no Buddhism, *eo nomine*, in continental India, at the present moment.

Is Buddhism, then, Indian in its origin? It is not safe to affirm even this. Fair reasons (to say the least of them) can be given for believing that, originally, Buddhism was foreign to the soil of Hindostan.

What, then, is its connection with India? It developed itself on the soil of that country and from that country it diffused itself.

It spread from two points, from the north and from the south. Of the Buddhism of the north, the Sanskrit rather than the Pali was the vehicle, and the route by which it diffused itself was Nepaul, Tibet, Western China, Mongolia, and Japan.

With the Buddhism of the south, the island of Ceylon is more especially connected. Its vehicle was the Pali rather than the Sanskrit, and the countries over which it spread were Pegu, Burma, Siam, and Kambojia.

With the creed went the alphabet and with the alphabet the civilization.

Hence, it is India to which nine-tenths of the civilization of the eastern part of continental Asia is due.

Indian also is the earliest civilization of the more civilized parts of the Indian Archipelago; though, at the present moment, the details of their older creeds and literatures are obscure. Mahometanism, except in a few places, has superseded the religion introduced from India. The island of Bali, however, is at this moment Indian. So is a small district in Java. Amongst the Battas of Sumatra; amongst the Philippine islanders; amongst the rude tribes of the interior of the Malayan peninsula; amongst even the Dyaks of Borneo the paganism is, by no means, pure and unmixed. On the contrary, it always exhibits Indian elements. Perhaps it may be styled a degraded Hinduism.

I am not prepared to say how far this peculiar offset

of the Indian religion is Buddhist rather than Brahminic, or Brahminic rather than Buddhist. It is sufficient for it to be Indian. Being this, it helps us to the measure of the influence of India as a civilizing power.

As such, India is what she is, only so far as she is either Buddhist or Brahminic. How far are Buddhism and Brahminism the indigenous growths of the Indian soil?

Whatever may be the best manner of exhibiting a series of recognized and undoubted historical details, it is manifest that for the purposes of *investigation*, the right points to begin with are those that are well defined, whether in time or place. In geography we look for accurate latitudes or longitudes; in archæology for ascertained dates.

Upon this principle, in attempting a sketch of the early history of the two great religions of India, I shall begin as I began with the Sanskrit and Pali records; *i. e.* with the facts that bear dates.

The notice of Herodotus can scarcely be called the notice of a religion. It is rather the account of an abominable social practice. Still, as it has its religious aspect, I give it.

The notice of Herodotus, to all appearance, rests upon the accounts given to the author by certain informants in either Persia or Babylonia.

It is to the effect that the land of the Indians was wide in extent, and heterogeneous in respect to its occupants; that a multitude of tongues was spoken within its boundaries; that some of the Indians were nomads, some Ikhthyophagi; that these last dwelt in the marshy swamps of the Delta of Indus; that they ate their fish raw. In all this there is rudeness and barbarism. So there is in the following account of the Padæi. They dwelt to the east of the Ikhthyophagi, and were eaters of flesh. This, however, was raw. When any one was sick, the men of his acquaintance would kill him, provided he were a man. If she were a woman, the females would do the same. This they did in order to enjoy a feast; for all that were killed were also eaten; and, as the ailment spoilt the quality of the flesh, it was in vain that the future victim protested against being treated as a patient. He was killed and eaten, say what he might about being in health.

The Kalatii, we are told in another part of the Herodotean account, ate their parents. Whether these were the same people as the Padæi is uncertain. It is only certain that they shrunk with horror from the idea of burning their dead.

Another tribe (name unknown) abstained from the slaughter of animals, and fed only upon vegetables. The sick they carried to some lone spot in the wilderness and left to die. They showed their rudeness in other matters as well. They kept themselves, however, independent. They "dwelt at a distance from the Persians, towards the south, and never obeyed Darius." Meanwhile the northern part of the Persian frontier gave signs of civilization. A city named Kaspatyros* was near the Paktyan land (Πακτϋικῆ χωρῆ) and not far from the districts which yielded gold. The men that held it were the most warlike of the Indians, and their manners were like those of the Bactrians.

That, word for word, Padæi is Batta,† has long been surmised. That, tribe for tribe, the Batta are the descendants of the Padæi is by no means certain. All that can fairly be inferred from the name is that certain Indians called certain tribes of their frontier by that name. Word for word, Vaddah is the same as Batta. A rude

* Also written *Kaspapyros*.

† The name of a population in Sumatra.

tribe in contact with an Indian population—this (and no more) is what comes of the roots *P-d*, *B-t*, or *V-d*.

Word for word, Kaspatyrus may or not be Cashmir. Place for place, the two localities certainly coincide.

The next notices represent the knowledge derived from the Macedonian conquest. They make it clear that, when that event took place, there were asceticism and philosophy in India. Before the Macedonian conquest there were, *iis nominibus*, Brachmani, Sarmani, and Gymnosophistæ. These observed practices, more or less, Buddhist and Brahminic (either or both), practices out of which either Buddhism or Brahmanism might evolve itself; practices which either the Buddhist or the Brahmin may claim as evidence to the antiquity of his creed. Brahminism, however, and Buddhism are one thing, practices out of which either or both may be developed are another. At the same time, or but a little later, we find evidence to a tenderness for animal life and to a difference between Brahmins and non-Brahmins.

Laws of the Brahmins which are in India.—Again, among the Indians, the Brahmins, among whom there are many thousands and tens of thousands, have a law that they should not kill at all, and not revere idols, and not commit fornication, and not eat flesh, and not drink wine, and among them not one of these things takes place. And there are thousands of years to these men, lo! since they govern themselves by this law which they have made for themselves.

Another law which is in India.—And there is another law in India, and in the same clime, belonging to those, which are not of the family of the Brahmins, nor of their doctrine: that they should serve idols, and commit fornication, and kill, and do other abominable things, which do not please the Brahmins. And in the same clime of India there are men that by custom eat the flesh of men, in the same manner as the rest of the nations eat the flesh of animals. But the evil stars have not forced the Brahmins to do evil and abominable things; nor have the good stars persuaded the rest of the Hindoos to abstain from evil things; nor have those stars which are well arranged in their places which it is proper for them, and in the signs of Zodiac which relate to humanity, persuaded those who eat the flesh of men to abstain from using this abominable and odious food.

This is from Bardesanes. Whether the facts just given constitute Brahminism is another question. It is certain that they fail to give us much that is Brahminic, *e.g.* Suttí, and the Brahminic system of incarnations, &c.

I should add that the Caubul coins exhibit certain signs or symbols of both (? either) Brahminism or Buddhism.

What Brahminism really is in full is to be found only in the practices and literature of the creed. The Brahminism, however, of the present time, and the Brahminism of the oldest works in the Sanskrit language, are different things. The oldest works in the Sanskrit are—

The Vedas.—The Vedas are hymns that formed either the part or the whole of an actual or possible ritual, the deities which they invoked being what is called elemental, *i. e.* personifications of earth, fire, water, the meteorological forces, and the like. Indra, for instance, (or the firmament,) conquers the Vrita, (or vapours,) with the Maruts, (or winds,) as allies.

An Ashtaka is a book; a Sukta is a hymn. Out of the 121 Suktas of the third Ashtaka, forty-four are addressed to Agni. Word for word, Agni is the Latin *ignis*, the Slavonic *ogon;* its meaning being *fire;* fire, however, personified, spiritualized, deified. Sometimes the attributes are obscure, and the language mystical; sometimes, instead of a series of epithets, we have a legend or an allusion to one. Sometimes it is Agni alone that is addressed; sometimes it is Agni in conjunction with some other personification.

1. I glorify Agni, the high priest of the sacrifice, the divine, the ministrant, who presents the oblation (to the gods), and is the possessor of great wealth.

2. May that Agni, who is to be celebrated by both ancient and modern sages, conduct the gods hither.

3. Through Agni the worshipper obtains that affluence, which increases day by day, which is the source of fame and the multiplier of mankind.

4. Agni, the unobstructed sacrifice of which thou art on every side the protector, assuredly reaches the gods.

5. May Agni, the presenter of oblations, the attainer of knowledge; he who is true, renowned, and divine, come hither with the gods!

This is a fair sample of the simpler style of invocation. The following supplies a contrast by being more mystical:—

1. I, Agni, am by birth endowed with knowledge of all that exists; clarified butter is my eye; ambrosia is my mouth; I am the living breath of threefold nature, the measure of the firmament, eternal warmth; I am also the oblation.

2. Agni, thoroughly comprehending the light that is to be understood by the heart, has purified himself (by the three) purifying (forms), he has made himself most excellent treasurer by (these) self-manifestations, and has thence contemplated heaven and earth.

Large as is Agni's share of the invocations of the third Ashtaka, that of Indra is larger; forty-eight Suktas being addressed to Indra, or the firmament, either singly or conjointly:—

1. Come, Indra, and be regaled with all viands and libations, and thence, mighty in strength, be victorious (over thy foes)!

2. The libation being prepared, present the exhilarating and efficacious (draught) to the rejoicing Indra, the accomplisher of all things.

3. Indra, with the handsome chin, be pleased with these animating praises: do thou, who art to be reverenced by all mankind, (come) to these rites (with) the gods.

4. I have addressed to thee, Indra, the showerer (of blessings), the protector (of thy worshippers), praises which have reached thee, and of which thou hast approved!

5. Place before us, Indra, precious and multiform riches, for enough, and more than enough, are assuredly thine!

6. Opulent Indra, encourage us in this rite for the acquirement of wealth, for we are diligent and renowned!

7. Grant us, Indra, wealth beyond measure or calculation, inexhaustible, the source of cattle, of food, of all life.

8. Indra, grant us great renown and wealth acquired in a thousand ways, and those (articles) of food (which are brought from the field) in carts!

9. We invoke, for the preservation of our property, Indra, the lord of wealth, the object of sacred verses, the repairer (to the place of sacrifice), praising him with our praises!

In the fourth Ashtaka there is somewhat less of a monopoly, though the shares of both are large.

The Maruts are the winds, and, next to Indra and Agni, they have the most hymns addressed to them.

1. The Maruts who are going forth decorate themselves like females: they are (gliders through the air), the sons of Rudra, and the doers of good works, by which they promote the welfare of earth and heaven: heroes, who grind (the solid rocks), they delight in sacrifices!

2. They, inaugurated by the gods, have attained majesty, the sons of Rudra have established their dwelling above the sky: glorifying him (Indra) who merits to be glorified, they have inspired him with vigour! the sons of Prisni have acquired dominion!

3. When the sons of the earth embellish themselves with ornaments, they shine resplendent in their persons with (brilliant) decorations; they keep aloof every adversary: the waters follow their path!

4. They who are worthily worshipped shine with various weapons: incapable of being overthrown, they are the overthrowers (of mountains): Maruts, swift as thought, intrusted with the duty of sending rain, yoke the spotted deer to your cars!

5. When Maruts, urging on the cloud, for the sake of (providing) food, you have yoked the deer to your chariots, the drops fall from the radiant (sun), and moisten the earth, like a hide, with water!

6. Let your quick-paced smooth-gliding coursers bear you (hither), and, moving swiftly, come with your hands filled with good things: sit, Maruts, upon the broad seat of sacred grass, and regale yourselves with the sweet sacrificial food!

7. Confiding in their own strength, they have increased in (power); they have attained heaven by their greatness, and have made (for themselves) a spacious abode: may they, for whom Vishnu defends (the sacrifice) that bestows all desires and confers delight, come (quickly) like birds, and sit down upon the pleasant and sacred grass!

8. Like heroes, like combatants, like men anxious for food, the swift-moving (Maruts) have engaged in battles: all beings fear the Maruts, who are the leaders (of the rain), and awful of aspect, like princes!

9. Indra wields the well-made, golden, many-bladed thunderbolt, which the skilful Twashtri has framed for him, that he may achieve great exploits in war. He has slain Vritra, and sent forth an ocean of water!

10. By their power, they bore the well aloft, and clove asunder the mountain that obstructed their path: the munificent Maruts, blowing upon their pipe, have conferred, when exhilarated by the soma juice, desirable (gifts upon the sacrificer)!

11. They brought the crooked well to the place (where the Muni was) and sprinkled the water upon the thirsty Gotama: the variously-radiant, (Maruts) come to his succour, gratifying the desire of the sage with life-sustaining waters!

12. Whatever blessings (are diffused) through the three worlds, and are in your gift, do you bestow upon the donor (of the libation), who addresses you with praise; bestow them, also, Maruts, upon us, and grant us, bestowers of all good, riches, whence springs prosperity!

Then there are the Aswins, or the inferior suns; Ushas or the dawn: Varani, which is, word for word, Uranus; Mithras, and other deities of greater and less importance, the majority of which are elemental, meteorological, or telluric. Yupa, the post to which the sacrificial victim is bound, has also a hymn:—

1. Vanaspati, the devout, anoint thee with sacred butter at the sacrifice; and whether thou standest erect, or thine abode be on the lap of this thy mother (earth), grant us riches.

2. Standing on the east of the kindled (fire), dispensing food (as the source) of undecaying (health) and excellent progeny, keeping off our enemy at a distance, stand up for great auspiciousness.

3. Be exalted, Vanaspati, upon this sacred spot of earth, being measured with careful measurement, and bestow food upon the offerer of the sacrifice.

4. Well clad and hung with wreaths comes the youthful (pillar); most excellent it is as soon as generated; steadfast and wise venerators of the gods, meditating piously in their minds, raise it up.

5. Born (in the forest), and beautified in the sacrifice celebrated by men, it is (again) engendered for the sanctification of the days (of sacred rites); steadfast, active, and intelligent (priests) consecrate it with intelligence, and devout worshipper recites its praise.

6. May those (posts) which devout men have cut down, or which, Vanaspati, the axe has trimmed, may they, standing resplendent with all their parts (entire), bestow upon us wealth with progeny.

7. May those posts which have been cut down upon the earth, and which have been fabricated by the priests, those which are the accomplishers of the sacrifice, convey our acceptable (offering) to the gods.

Of the mass of the Vedas an idea may be formed from the following *data*. A single hymn is called a *sukta*. So many suktas make an *anuvaka*, so many anuvakas an *adhyáya*; so many adhyáyas an *astaka*, ogdoad, or book, forming an eighth of the whole Rigveda. The third volume of Wilson's translation comes to the middle of the whole, so that the Rigveda alone gives six volumes of hymns. But the Rig is only one out of four Vedas; for besides it there is the Sama-veda; there is the Yagur-veda; and there is the Athava-veda—four in all. The Rig-veda, however, is the chief, containing nearly all the important matter of the rest; the Athava-veda being later in date than the other three, to which it forms a sort of supplement. These four compositions form the *Sanhita*, or text. The Sanhita itself, with the hymns it embodies, forms the *mantra*, or ritual, a ritual upon which there are notes and supplements.

Without being a Veda, in the strict sense of the term, the *Brahmyanas* are Vedaic. So that here we have another series of works; themselves incomplete without *Vedangas* (in which the grammar of the Vedas is explained) and *Upanishads*, which are a sort of supplement.

Few works are less metaphysical than the Vedaic hymns. This, however, does not prevent the existence of a *Vedanta* philosophy. The connection, however, lies chiefly in the name. Wherever there is tendency to rationalism anything can be rationalized.

It is not for nothing that this list of works, more or less Vedaic, has been given. That the Vedas are a root out of which much has grown is a fact of great importance in our criticism. Dates they have none. Failing these, what can we have recourse to? We must take a measure of the extent to which the original hymns have developed a system, and then ask at what rate such developments proceed.

The Institutes of Menu.—Later than the Vedas, and in many respects different from them, are the Institutes of Menu. These give us the legal, social, and political, rather than the poetical and religious, aspects of Brahminism. The Brahminism, too, is of a more advanced growth; containing much for which the Vedas have been appealed to in vain. It contains, for instance, the doctrine of cast.

Sir Graves Haughton's Translation.

1. For the sake of preserving this universe, the Being, supremely glorious, allotted separate duties to those who sprang respectively from his mouth, his arm, his thigh, and his foot.

2. To Brahmins he assigned the duties of reading the Veda, of teaching it, of sacrificing, of assisting others to sacrifice, of giving alms, if they be rich, and, if indigent, of receiving gifts.

3. To defend the people, to give alms, to sacrifice, to read the Veda, to shun the allurements of sensual gratification, are, in a few words, the duties of a Cshatriya.

4. To keep herds of cattle, to bestow largesses, to sacrifice, to read the scripture, to carry on trade, to lend at interest, and to cultivate land, are prescribed or permitted to a Vaisya.

5. One principle duty the Supreme Ruler assigns to a Súdra; namely, to serve the before-mentioned classes, without depreciating their worth.

6. Man is declared purer above the navel; but the Self-Creating Power declared the purest part of him to be his mouth.

7. Since the Brahmin sprang from the most excellent part, since he was the first-born, and since he possesses the Veda, he is by right the chief of this whole creation.

8. Him, the Being, who exists of himself, produced in the beginning, from his own mouth, that having performed holy rites, he might present clarified butter to the gods, and cakes of rice to the progenitors of mankind, for the preservation of this world.

9. What created being then can surpass Him, with whose mouth the gods of the firmament continually feast on clarified butter, and the manes of ancestors, on hallowed cakes?

10. Of created things, the most excellent are those which are animated; of the animated, those which subsist by intelligence; of the intelligent mankind; and of men the sacerdotal class.

11. Of priests those eminent in learning; of the learned, those who know their duty; of those who know it, such as perform it virtuously; and of the virtuous, those who seek beatitude from a perfect acquaintance with scriptural doctrine.

12. The very birth of Brahmins is a constant incarnation of Dherma, God of Justice; for the Brahmin is born to promote justice, and to procure ultimate happiness.

13. When a Brahmin springs to light, he is borne above the world, the

chief of all creatures, assigned to guard the treasury of duties, religious and civil.

14. Whatever exists in the universe, is all in effect, though not in form, the wealth of the Brahmin; since the Brahmin is entitled to it all by his primogeniture and eminence of birth.

15. The Brahmin eats but his own food; wears but his own apparel; and bestows but his own in alms: through the benevolence of the Brahmin, indeed, other mortals enjoy life.

16. To declare the sacerdotal duties, and those of the other classes in due order, the sage Menu, sprung from the self-existing, promulged this code of laws.

17. A code which must be studied with extreme care by every learned Brahmin, and fully explained to his disciples, but must be taught by no other man of an inferior class.

18. The Brahmin who studies this book, having performed sacred rites, is perpetually free from offence in thought, in word, and in deed.

19. He confers purity on his living family, on his ancestors, and on his descendants, as far as the seventh person; and He alone deserves to possess this whole earth.

The Epics.—A nearer approach is made to the existing form of Brahminism in the Ramayana and the Mahabharata; the Ramayana being the name of a poem which gives us the exploits of Rama, whilst the Mahabharata is a narrative of the Great War.

That both are later than the Vedas is evident from not only the general character of the details, but from the fact of both the Vedas and the Vedangas being mentioned by name in their text. The more a man knows of them the wiser and better he is represented to be. The hero of the Ramayana is Rama, who is Vishnu incarnate. The scene lies in Oud. The subject is the conquest of such parts of India as, at the time when the poem was written, belonged to Brahminic India; of Lanka, or Ceylon, most especially. That an island in the south is reduced at an earlier period than the interjacent portions of the continent to its north is remarkable. It suggests the idea of ships and sailors.

The following is the opening of the Ramayana as translated by Wilkins:—

I salute Kama, the beautiful, the elder brother of Bukshmuna, the illustrious Kughoo, the husband of Seeta, the descendant of Kukootstha, full of clemency, a sea of excellencies, the friend of Brahmans, the virtuous one, the sovereign, devoted to truth, the son of Dusharutha, him whose body is blue, the benign, the delight of the universe, the glory of Kughoo's race, Kaghava, the enemy of Kavuna.

Victory to Kama, the glory of Kughoo's race, the increase of Koushulya's happiness, the destroyer of the ten-headed, to Dusharutha, whose eye is like the water lily.

I salute Valmecki, the kokila, who, mounted on the branch of poesy, sounds the delightful note kama, kama, Kama. Salutation to the lord of the Moonis, the blessed, the Tupushee, the abode of all knowledge. To this Valmeeki salutation.

Valmeeki, the chief of the Moonis, devoted to sacred austerities, and the perusal of the Veda, the incessant Tupushee, pre-eminent among the learned, earnestly inquired of Naruda, Who in the universe is transcendent in excellence, versed in all the duties of life, grateful, attached to truth, steady in his course, exuberant in virtues, delighting in the good of all beings? Who is heroic, eloquent, lovely, of subdued anger, truly great? Who is patient, free from malice, at whose excited wrath the gods tremble? Who is great, mighty in preserving the three worlds? Who devoted to the welfare of men? The ocean of virtue and wealth. In whom has Hukshmee, the complete, the beautiful, chosen her abode? Who is the equal of Urida, Unula, Soorya, Indoo, Shukra, and Oopendra? From you, O Naruda! I would hear this. You are able, O divine Sage, to describe the man. Naruda, acquainted with the present, the past, and the future, hearing the words of Valmeeki, replied to the sage: Attend: the numerous and rare qualities enumerated by you, can with difficulty be found throughout the three worlds; not even among the Devtas have I seen any one possessed of all these. Hear: he who possesses these, and virtues far beyond, a full-orbed moon, a mine of excellence, is of Ishwakoo's race, and named Kama; of regulated mind, temperate, magnanimous, patient, illustrious, self-subdued, wise, eminent in royal duties, eloquent, fortunate, fatal to his foes, of ample shoulders, brawny arms, with neck shell-formed, and rising cheeks, eminent in archery, of mighty energy, subduing his enemies, with arms extending to the knee, manly, of fine-formed head and open front, of mighty prowess, whose body is exact in symmetry, of hyacinthine hue, who is full of courage, with eyes elongated, his cest circular and full, who is fortunate, imprinted with auspicious marks, versed in the duties of life, philanthropic, steadily pursuing rectitude, sapient, pure and humble, contemplative, equal to Prujapati, illustrious, supporting, the world, subduing his passions, the helper of all, the protector of virtue, skilled in the Vedas and Vedangas, deep in all the Shastras, strong, acquainted with the secrets of nature, practising every duty, penetrating, amiable to all, upright, ample in knowledge, of noble mind, ever attended by the good, as the ocean by the rivers, the companion of truth, social, the only lovely one, Kama, the seat of every virtue, the increaser of Koushulya's joy, profound like the deep, immovable as Heemaluya, heroic as Vishnoo, grateful to the sight as the full-orbed moon, in anger dreadful as the conflagration, in patience like the gentle earth, generous as Dhanude, in verity ever unequalled. By these his matchless virtues he conferred felicity on his subjects, and therefore is known by the name Kama.

The Mahabharata is the Great War waged between the Yadava and the Pandava dynasties; the scene being laid in the parts about Ujein. The uniformity of style and composition is said to be less in the Mahabharata than in the Ramayana; so that some parts of the former poem are older or newer than others. The fictions in both are supernatural, impossible, outrageous. In both the chief deity is Vishnu.

The Puranas.—The Puranas are compositions in the form of dialogue, between certain enquirers and Brahma, upon points of cosmogony and early history—also upon the attributes and actions of the three great deities; of Siva and Vishnu most especially, both incarnate. They (I follow Wilson almost *verbatim*) are derived from the same system as the Epics. They represent, however, modifications of opinion and feeling. They repeat and expand the epic cosmogony. They give special importance to new divinities; Vishnu and Siva most particularly. They give new legends. They are possibly founded upon earlier compositions. The word *Purana* means *old.* A typical Purana is, according to the lexicon of Umura Sinha, *Pancha-lackshanam,* or that *which has five characteristic topics.* These are—

1. Cosmogony.
2. Secondary creation, or the destruction and renovation of worlds.
3. Genealogies of Gods and patriarchs.
4. Reigns of the Manus, or periods called Manwantaras.
5. History of the kings of the Solar and Lunar families.

The existing Puranas scarcely meet the conditions here implied. Yet they meet them, perhaps, half way.

The Puranas are eighteen in number. Of these the best known, as well as the most important, is the Vishnu Purana, accessible to English readers through the translation of Wilson. It is the great repertorium for the elements of Brahminism in its working form.

The Upa-puranas are minor compositions, akin to the full Puranas both in matter and in form. They may be as few as four, as many as eighteen.

The "Vishnú Puráná has kept very clear of any particulars from which an approximation to its date may be conjectured." Wilson refers it to the eleventh century.

Now comes the notice of the general character of the Sanskrit literature. The best preliminary to the classification of this is a general view of the literature of Greece. In some shape or other *every* form of Sanskrit literature has its equivalent in that of Greece. In some shape or other *most* forms of Greek literature have their correspondents in Sanskrit. Are there Epics in the language of Stesichorus? So are there in that of Parasara. Was there a New Comedy in Greece? There was something very like it in India. The nearest analogues of the Vedas (respect being had exclusively to the class of compositions to which they belong) are, perhaps, the Homeric and Orphic hymns, by no means the only hymns of Greece. The Greek equivalents to the laws of Menu, though they have not come down to us in their full form, have had a real existence on the soil of Greece. Subject for subject, the authors of the Puranas dealt with the same kind of questions that the Greek logographers investigated. *Mutatis mutandis*, the same applies to the grammarians and lexicographers. Both are conspicuous in India;

both in Greece—Alexandrian Greece, however, rather than Athenian. And where there were grammarians and lexicographers, there were there geometricians also; in Ægypt as in India, in India as in Ægypt. There was science in both countries. There was, also, in both, philosophy. The Vedanta philosophy of India has already been noticed. It has its counterpart in Platonism and Neo-platonism.

Buddhism.—Buddhism is one thing. Practices out of which Buddhism may be developed are another. It has been already suggested, that the ideas conveyed by the terms Sramanæ, and Gymnosophistæ are just as Brahminic as Buddhist, and, *vice versâ,* just as Buddhist as Brahminic.

The earliest dates of specific Buddhism are of the same age as the earliest dates of specific Brahminism.

Clemens of Alexandria mentions Buddhist pyramids, the Buddhist habit of depositing certain bones in them, the Buddhist practice of foretelling events; the Buddhist practice of continence; the Buddhist Semnai or holy virgins. This, however, may be but so much asceticism.

He mentions this and more. He supplies the name Bouta; Bouta being honoured as a god.

Porphyry tells us of an important point wherein the Brachmans and the Samanai differed. The former were born to the dignity; the latter elected. This shows that though both may have been in the same category as to their ascetism, there was a difference between them; a difference which exists at the present day.

Cyril of Alexandria states that there were Samans (whom we may now especially connect with the cultus of Bouta) in Bactria.

From Cyril of Jerusalem we learn that Samnaism was, more or less, Manichæan, Manichæanism being, more or less, Samanist. Terebinthus, the preceptor of Manes, took the name Baudas. In Epiphanius Terebinthus is the pupil of Scythianus. Suidas makes Terebinthus a pupil of Baudda, who pretended to be the son of a virgin. And here we may stop to remark, that the Mongol Tshingiz-khan is said to be virgin-born; that, word for word, Scythianus is Sak; that Sakya Muni (compare it with Manes) is a name of Buddha. Even so cautious a speculator as Professor Wilson admits that Buddha may be the gentile name Bhot. I think that he might have maintained that such was actually the case. Its *quasi-*synonym Sakya bears just the same relation to the word Sak or Sakæ. Be this as it may there was, before A.D. 300,

1. Action and reaction between Buddhism and Christianity.

2. Buddhist buildings.

3. The same cultus in both Bactria and India.

Whether this constitute Buddhism is another question. All this and more may have existed, and yet the cultus to which it belonged have been just as far from Buddhism in the ordinary acceptation of the word, as modern Judaism is from Christianity, or the doctrine of the Sadducees from modern Judaism.

The Buddhist records themselves are—

1. *Chinese.*—The most that can be got from the earliest Chinese accounts is that in (say) the sixth century there was Buddhism in both China and India. The following is a piece of Chinese grammar for the Sanskrit.

Chinese.	Sanskrit.	English.
Po'-po-ti	Bhavati	He is
Po'-po-pa	Bhavapa	They two are
Po'-fan-ti	Bhavanti	They are
Po'-po-sse	Bhavasi	Thou art
Po'-po-po	Bhavapa	You two are

Chinese.	Sanskrit.	English.
Po'-po-t'a	Bhavatha	You are
Po'-po-mi	Bhavami	I am
Po'-po-hoa	Bhavavak	We two are
Po'-po-mo	Bhavamah	We are.
	NOUN.	
Pu-lu-sha	Purushah	Man
Pu-lu-shao	Purushau	Two men
Pu-lu-sha-so	Purushâs	Men
Pu-lu-sha-tsie	Purushasya	Of a man
Pu-lu-sha-pien	Purushâbhyâm	Of two men
Pu-lu-sha-nan	Purushânâm	Of men.

2. *Northern.*—It has already been stated that the vehicle of the Buddhism of Nepal and Tibet was the Sanskrit rather than the Pali language. In like manner, *mutatis mutandis*, the vehicle of the

3. *Southern*, or Cingalese, Buddhism was the Pali rather than the Sanskrit.

4. *Monumental.*—There are

a. Architectural,
b. Sculptural,
c. Sepulchral,
d. Inscriptional.

The literary documents are, *of necessity*, valid for the time at which they were written, and no other. They are, *of necessity*, valid only so far as they are evidence. What they tell us of the times previous to their composition may, or may not, be true. How far they are so depends on the details of each particular case. The *onus probandi* lies with the supporter of their accuracy. They contain a doctrine, a discipline, a philosophy, and a history. They are the scriptures of Buddhism, and from them must the nature of Buddhism, as a whole, be ascertained. The doctrine, the discipline, and the philosophy are dateless. The historical portion gives us three Councils; the latest of which took place about B.C. 153. I take this date as I find it. It tells us thus much—that earlier than B.C. 153 the work from which it is deduced could not have been composed. Common sense tells us that it need not have been composed even then. Who could write about the third council before it had met? This date is got from the Sanskrit authorities.

What applies to the Sanskrit applies, *à fortiori*, to the Chinese. Say that in the sixth century there was a voluminous mass of Chinese translations from the Indian. *Mutatis mutandis*, there was the same in the Christian world. There were translations from the Greek in Syriac, in Armenian, and in German. Yet the works from which they are translated were, each and all, at the the very least, fifty years later than the birth of our Saviour.

When Buddhism has so much in common with Christianity, and the Indian literature so much in common with the Greek, the question as to the probability of there being borrowings and lendings must be worked out with special attention to dates. A century more or less may seriously affect our results.

What applies to the Sanskrit is believed on good grounds to apply, *à fortiori*, to the Pali. The evidence that the Buddhist scriptures in this last-named language are newer than those in Sanskrit is less conclusive than it was in the case of the Chinese. Still it is satisfactory; so that, upon the whole, we may commit ourselves to the doctrine that no canonical works in Buddhism are older than the scriptures of northern India. That these are not older, and may be much newer, than B.C. 153, has already been stated.

Of monuments the most important are the Viharas or monasteries, and the Sthupas, or topes. Now, it is one thing to be a temple, or a tumulus; another thing to be a

Buddhist tumulus, or a Buddhist temple. It is one thing to be a king, another thing to be King Lear. Of records that are, at one and the same time, monumental, Buddhist, and undoubted, none are older than A.D. 300. *Non meus hic sermo.* The criticism of the Pali scriptures, the Viharas, the topes, and the cave-temples, along with nine-tenths (or more) of the preceding facts, is Professor Wilson's.

And now comes the notice of the famous Priyadarsi memorials. Dhauli is in Kuttak. Girnar in Guzerat. Kapurdigiri in Caubul. In each of these localities is a long and well-known inscription. It is the same, in the way of language and contents, in all. The inscriptions themselves are ancient. They contain the name of Antiochus. They are admitted, even by Wilson, to be, more or less, Buddhist. Be it so. It only shows the germs of the creed, not the full creed itself. It is true that, by certain assumptions, more than this may be got out of them. In a Singalese work some centuries later it is stated that Priyadarsi was Asoka; Asoka being a great propagator of Buddhism according to the historians of several centuries after his time. What, however, is the warrant for the identification? To say that *Priyadarsi* means *Asoka* is certainly a statement which may possibly be true. But it is not the *planus literalis et grammaticalis sensus* of the word.

As the Brahminic, or Sanskrit, literature reminds us of Greece, so does Pali Buddhism suggest comparisons with Christianity. It has its monachism, its councils—both conspicuous—I had almost said characteristic. If these resemblances are spontaneous they are very remarkable phenomena. Are they so? Are the presumptions in favour of their being so?

I can only say, in answer to this, that if we claim an

inordinately high antiquity for either Buddhism or Brahminism we must assume something that, in the eyes of the cautious critic, is illegitimate. To few of the monuments can we assign a truly historic date. Their epoch, then, is assigned on the score of internal evidence. The language is much more archaic than that of the Institutes, and the mythology so much simpler; whilst the Institutes themselves are similarly circumstanced in respect to the Epics. Fixing these at about 200 B.C., we allow so many centuries for the archaisms of Menu, and so many more for those of the Vedas. For the whole, eleven hundred has not been thought too little; which places the Vedas in the fourteenth century B.C., and makes them the earliest, or nearly the earliest, records in the world.

It is clear that this is only an approximation. Now, although all inquirers admit that creeds, languages, and social conditions, present the phenomena of *growth*, the opinions as to the *rate* of such growths are varied—and none are of much value. This is because the particular induction required for the formation of anything better than a mere impression has yet to be undertaken—till when, one man's guess is as good as another's. The age of a tree may be reckoned from its concentric rings, but the age of a language, a doctrine, or a polity, has neither bark like wood, nor teeth like a horse, nor a register like a child.

CHAPTER XI.

The Alphabets of India.

THE alphabet of the very earliest specimen of the languages akin to the Sanskrit is cuneiform. It is found only in Persia. It belongs to the reigns of Darius and his successors.

The alphabet of the next earliest *dated* monuments is of the older Caubul coins; those of Eukrates and his successors. This is what is called by Wilson Arianian, or Arian. It is written from right to left, and, *pro tanto*, is Semitic. It is held (and that on reasonable grounds) to be an older form of what appears afterwards as Sassanian.

It is monumental, *i. e.* in capitals, and in a form adapted for coins and inscriptions rather than documents written *currente calamo*. It is monumental rather than cursive.

In a cursive form it comes out, later, as the Zend of the Parsi scriptures, &c. It has, however, taken additions—Indian in character. Still, it is so far Semitic as to run from right to left.

The alphabet of the oldest Pali monuments of the soil of India is that of the Dhauli and Girnar inscriptions. It has more than one character like those of the old Greek alphabet, and, like the old Greek alphabet, it is written from left to right. It appears, under modifications, in the coinage of the dynasties called Saurasthra, Gupta, and Rajput.

The alphabet of the oldest MSS. (which, it must be observed, are not Pali but Sanskrit) is called Devanagari. It is inscriptional rather than cursive, in so far as it consists of capitals. It is a modification of the inscriptional and monetary Pali. As such, it runs from left to right.

The alphabets of the written languages akin to the Hindí are all visibly and manifestly derived from the Devanagari.

The alphabets of the languages akin to the Tamul are derived from some form of some prototype of the Devanagari—scarcely from the actual Devanagari. They are rounded rather than angular, *i. e.* they are cursive rather than either inscriptional or capital.

The alphabets of the Indian archipelago will be noticed in their proper place.

On these facts two observations must be made:—

1. That the alphabets of the Greek type—for so we may call those that run from left to right—are of equal antiquity with those of the Semite type, or those that run from right to left.

2. That the alphabet of not only the oldest MSS., but that of the so-called oldest compositions in Sanskrit (the pre-eminently literary language of Brahminic India) is of Pali origin.

The details of the extent to which the right-to-left, or Arian, and the left-to-right, or Indian, alphabets are used concurrently are curious.

The legends of the oldest coins are Greek. Then comes the Arianian: then the Indian and Arianian concurrently.

The Girnar and Dhauli inscriptions are Indian. The

Kapur-di-giri inscription (which, in language and import, is the same as the other two) is Arianian.

The provisional hypothesis which best accounts for this concurrence runs thus :—

The left-to-right alphabet reached India *viâ* Asia Minor and Northern Persia.

The right-to-left reached it *viâ* Babylonia and Southern Persia.

CHAPTER XII.

The Frontiers of India and Persia.—The Paropamisans.—The Afghans.—The Caukers, &c.—The Brahúi and Biluch.

I AM satisfied that the chief details of immediate ethnological importance to India are the details of its frontier. These are Persian. But the frontier of Persia is Asia Minor, and the frontier of Asia Minor, Europe.

The Paropamisans.—Of the Paropamisan boundary, the *minutiæ* on the west are obscure. The Huzara country is a British dependency. It is divided amongst numerous petty chiefs, *e. g.* the Khan of Turnoul, the chief of the Dhúnds, the chiefs of the Gukkurs, and others. They are (I believe) Mahometans. West of these occupancies lies the valley of

Kaghan; and west of Kaghan, on the very crest of the hills, the country of

The Hussunzye; whose name, at least, is Afghan or Patan.

I cannot say what, in these parts, is Afghan, what Paropamisan, what Indian proper.

Afghanistan.—That the Afghans themselves are far more heterogeneous in the matter of blood than of language is patent from more signs of intermixture than one. In the first place, there are few points in the map of Afghanistan whereof it is not said that the occupants are, more or less, recent and intrusive. The Ghilzyes, for instance, are derived from the Ghor mountains. That certain Berduranis have moved from west to east is specially stated, whether truly or otherwise is of no importance. The present observations merely go to prove the fact of there being presumptions in favour of the Afghan blood being mixed. The men themselves have no general name for their own country; *i. e.* no name at once general and native, for Afghanistan is a Persian term. It is one thing for the mountains of Ghor to have contained Afghan settlements at an early period, another thing for them to have been the cradle of the race. Let it be admitted, for argument's sake, that the princes of Ghor belonged to the Afghan tribe of Suri, and that at so early a period that their dynasty was considered old even in the eleventh century. What does this show? Simply that there were Afghans in two districts; Afghans who, in the Ghor principalities, may as easily have been immigrants as indigenæ.

Add to this that the districts named Gour are no less than three in number. The king of one of them reduced "Raver and Kermessir, which separate Ghor from Hindustan." This is an extract from Herbelot, upon which the editor of the last edition of Elphinstone remarks that in *Raver* and *Kermessir*, names which, *totidem literis* and *totidem syllabis*, no longer exist, we may have the present appellations of the *Dawer* and *Gurmsir* districts. If so, Hindostan must have extended far westwards. Whether it did so or not, and whether (assuming it to have done so) the boundary was ethnological rather than political, is another question.

The Arabs call the Afghans Solimani. This I believe to mean the occupants of the parts about the Tukt-i-Soliman, who were probably neither more nor less than the first members of the group with whom the Mahometans came in contact. If so, India must have been entered on the south, *viâ* Biluchistan and Sind, rather than by the valley of the Caubul.

The locality, then, of the nucleus of the nation is still to be discovered. The language, I think, originated in the north-east, *i. e.* on the Paropamisan rather than the Carmanian frontier. The language, however, is purer than the blood. This is largely Tajik, not a little Mongol, largely (perhaps) Indian, very largely Turk. There are special statements that certain Afghan tribes, at a certain date, spoke Turkish. There is *garden* after *garden* named *bagh*, and more than one *hill* named *dagh*. There are the tribual names Othmankheil and Turcolaini, along with other terms less transparently Turk. The question, however, is suggested rather than exhausted. There is much blood in India which has come from Afghanistan, and much in Afghanistan which has come from Persia, Turkistan, and Mongolia.

The Caukers, &c.—I do not say that these are not Afghans. I only desiderate the evidence to their being such. They may be Persian, Biluch, Brahúi, Indian (wholly or partially), rather than truly Afghan.

Biluchistan.—As compared with the term Biluchistan, the term Afghanistan is clear and unambiguous. Afghanistan, whatever may be the details as to the descent of its occupants, is, at any rate, the region of the Pushtu language. *Mutatis mutandis*, Biluchistan should be the same. It is nothing, however, of the kind. It is pre-eminently a political designation. It means the country of the Biluches. But many of its occupants are Brahúis. Nor is this all. I know of no definite test which enables us to separate, in a thorough-going manner, the two populations. I hardly know which is the more important of the two. The four works that tell us most about them are those of Pottinger, Masson, Postans, and Burton. In the two last the view is taken from Sind, the conquest of which country is (apparently) attributed to the Biluch proper rather than to the Brahúis, the Kalora and Talpúr dynasties being simply called Biluch.

The inference from the notices of both Postans and Burton is, that, in Biluchistan, the Biluch family is the rule, the Brahúi the exception.

From this Masson, and, to a certain extent, Elphinstone suggest something very different. *Biluchistan* is, doubtless, the name of the country which Masson describes. Yet when he comes to detail, it is a *Brahúi* history that he investigates. The Sehrais, a Mahometan family from Sind, govern at Kelaut, until they are displaced by the Séwah (Hindus), who are, in their turn, expelled by the Brahúis.

Again, the Brahúi conquest is believed to have been effected under Kambar, of the Mirwari tribe. Now the *Mirwari* is the head tribe, the Khan-kheil as it would be called in Pustú; whilst Kamburani is the actual term for one of the primary divisions of the Brahúi name. From this we may infer, that Kambar (whether a real or hypothetical personage) was the hero of the dominant family. In accordance with this, it is fixed that the power of the descendants of Kambar should be supreme and hereditary, whilst from the two next tribes, the Raisani and the Zehri, Sirdars should be appointed, for Saharawan and Jhalawan respectively; these Sirdarships being, also, hereditary. Meanwhile, the Vizeers were to be Dehwaurs, or Tajiks. Time goes on until, at the beginning of the last century, Nazir Khan, the most energetic and intelligent of the Kelaut Khans, attempts (and that effectively) to introduce union and homogeneity into the Biluch community. The Rinds are settled in Saharawan, the Magazzi in Jhalawan. Kutch Gundawa is added to

Khanat. So is Shall. So is Mastung. So are Hurrund and Dajil. So are Kej and Punjghír. This is during the last days of the Kalhora dynasty in Sind. The history (it is Masson who gives it) is continued up to the present period; and throughout the whole of it the Khelat Khans are called Brahúis.

Again, in Ferishta, and doubtless, in other historians of India as well, there are numerous notices of a hostile nation called the Varahas; the particular portions of Hindostan which they attacked being the western States of Rajasthan.

All this gives to the Brahúi population of Biluchistan a much greater prominence than the name of their country suggests. The *name* suggests the predominance of the Biluches.

That the foregoing cautions against being misled by the name of the district are, by no means, unnecessary will soon become manifest. When Sind comes under notice we shall find it necessary to speak of, at least, one Biluch dynasty; that of the Talpurs. That the Talpurs were so far Biluch as to have come from Biluchistan may safely be asserted. Whether they were Biluches is another matter. What if they were Brahúis? I raise, rather than solve this question. The ethnological position of the tribes of Biluchistan must be determined by the circumstances of each individual case. I doubt whether it can always be determined at all. Physical appearance is something: but the physical appearance of both the Brahúis and the Biluches varies. Language, too, is something; but it is especially stated that the blood and the language by no means coincide. And here the Biluch tongue preponderates. I find no evidence of any Biluch tribes having unlearned their own tongue and adopted the Brahúi. I find decided evidence, however, of certain Brahúis being in the habit of speaking Biluch. The khans and sirdars of the Mingalls and Bizunjus do so. It would be vulgar to use the Brahúi.

I find, too, that this latter language is said to be peculiar to Jhalawan and Saharawan. Now, admitting that these are the chief Brahúi localities, we must be convinced that there is much Brahúi blood beyond them.

Again, it is probable that certain Brahúis may have adopted the Jutki and Sind dialects.

That certain Rinds (Biluches) have done so, is specially stated by Masson; who (along with others) tells us that their physical form is, more or less, Indian; at any rate, that it differs perceptibly from that of the Nharui tribes of the west. What, then, I ask, is the evidence that the Rinds are Biluch at all? Their form is Indian; their language Indian. They come, indeed, from Biluchistan —but so do some of the Brahúis and some of the Juts.

What is the evidence, &c.? I ask this for information. I do not say that it is wanting. I think it very likely that it can be adduced. I only suggest that it is wanting. At present the Rinds are Biluchistanis (*i. e.* men of a country named after the Biluches), rather than Biluches in the proper sense of the word.

The typical Biluches, then, are the Nharui tribes of the west; and the typical Brahúis certain tribes of Saharawan and Jhalawan. The others are, to all appearance, more or less, the exhibitors of mixed characteristics.

These characteristics may be derived from several quarters; from Central Asia, from Arabia, from Persia, from Caubul, from India.

Central Asiatic elements.—These may be either Turk or Mongol. Laying aside the doctrines suggested by the local names, especially Seistan (Segistan), (which is

Sakastene, or the country of the Sakæ) as well as those implied in the term Indoscythæ, let us look at Masson's list of the Brahúi, and Pottinger's of the Biluch, tribes. The first gives the names Sâka and Minghal; both referable to the Western Provinces. That Saka is Sakæ is suggested by Masson himself. Can Minghal be Mongol? Possibly. That Mekran is not beyond the confines of the Mongol world is shown in the following genealogy. The Numris of Luz trace their origin to Samar the founder of Samarkand, who had four sons—Nerpat, the father of the Numris and Jukias; Bopat, the father of the Bhats of Jessulmer; Gajpat, father of the Chura Rajputs; and Aspat, father of the Tshagatai—the Tshagatai being, of all the Turks, the most mixed-up with the Mongols. Indeed, to suppose that the two words are synonymous is as legitimate here as in India, where (as is well known) the empire founded by Baber, is called the empire of the Great Mogul, *i. e.* Mongol. Yet Baber was a Tshagatai Turk, and no Mongol at all.

Let, then, the Brahúi name *Mingall* be considered as a probable form of *Mongol*—word for word. Whether it stand for a Turk tribe or a tribe from Mongolia, in the strict sense of the term, is another question. The names of both Tshingiz-khan and Timur are known in the parts about Kelaut.

Arabian.—I lay but little stress upon the so-called tradition of the Biluches that they came from Arabia. I have elsewhere suggested that Arabia may mean the *Arabius fluvius*, and the promontory of *Arabat* in their own immediate neighbourhood. In this, too, it is possible that we may find the origin of the name of the *Arab* Gudur, a Luz tribe. On the other hand, the Arab conquest of Sind, and the parts to the west of the Indus, in the first century of the Hegira, is a historical fact, so that, over and above a certain amount of imaginary, there may, also, be some real, Arab blood in Biluchistan.

Persian.—The Nushirvanis of Kharan (it is Masson who speaks), along with the Rajputs of Udipur, trace their origin to Nushirvan. Such the doctrine. *Valeat quantum.* It shows, at least, Persian ways of thinking. In like manner the Shirwani Brahúis believe that their forefathers came from Shirwan, which they may easily have done, or have not done.

The Mehmasani bear a Kurd name. So do the Lari; though not one exclusively Kurd. So do the Kurds, *eo nomine* and *totidem literis.* The Kurds of Dasht Bedowlat, Merv, and part of Kutch Gundava, are divided into

The Made Zai	The Saltag Zai
—— Shudan Zai	—— Shadi Zai
—— Zirdad Zai	—— Massutari.

Word for word, *Zai* appears to be the Afghan *Zye.*

Caubul.—The Kaidrani of the hills about Khozdar appear in Masson's list as Brahúis.

I have found them, however, treated as Biluches, as Afghans, and as a population neither Afghan nor Biluch. There are two divisions of the name, the occupancies of which are separated from each other.

The Bizunji are, in like manner, called Brahúi, yet the name appears elsewhere, and that beyond the Brahúi area.

Indian.—That the Jatuks of Masson's Brahúi list are Juts is suggested by Masson himself. It is also suggested by Masson himself that the Kalmatti of his Brahúi list are Sindis.

Then there are the tribes that appear both as Biluch and Brahúi.

Also the Langhow tribe, the members of which are said

to be enfranchised slaves of the Rinds; a fact, however, which is not incompatible with their being Brahúi in blood.

And now, premising that I, by no means, consider that the above-named exceptions are conclusive, and that I have exhibited them chiefly for the sake of making out a case in favour of the blood of the Brahúi and Biluches being more or less mixed, and with the view of inducing others to go minutely into the analysis, I give the remainder of Masson's list.

In the Western Provinces.

Mirwari	Sanghur
Gitshki	Hallada
Homarari	Rodahi

Rakshani (?)

In Saharawan.

Raisani	Mahmudshahi
Sirperra	Bangul-zai
Ghazghi	Shekh Husseini
Samalari	Sunari.

In Jhalawan.

Zehri	Saholi

Lutiani.

So much for the details of the Brahúi name as opposed to the Biluch.

The details of the Biluch name, as opposed to the Brahúi, are as follows.

The first division is into the western and the eastern Biluches, the western Biluches being named Nharúi; the eastern, Mugsi and Rind.

The Nharúi.—The Nharúi list contains seven names, three of which may be other than Biluch.

1. *The Rukshani.*—In Masson the Rukshani are made Brahúi.

2. *The Mings.*—Word for word, this seems to be Mingul.

3. *Kurd.*—This is the name for the tribes of Bushkurd, Kohuki, and Mydani; tribes which are, probably, Kurd in blood as well as in name.

To the following four tribes no exception is taken. They are, probably, true Biluches.

The Sajadi	The Urbabi
—— Khasogi	—— Mullikah.

They lie to the south of Seistaun, between the Brahúi frontier and the Kurd districts; these last leading to the truly Persian province of Kirman.

By "true Biluches" I mean men whose language neither is nor has been either Brahúi or Jut, and who are, in other respects, Persian rather than Indian, and Biluch rather than either Afghan or Kurd.

I have already noticed the statement that the Rinds, to some extent at least, speak Jutki. To what extent? Burton writes that the Domki, Magasi (Magazzi Mugsi), Burphat (Bulfat), Kalpher (Kalpur), and many other smaller tribes, speak the hill language; the hill language meaning the Biluch. Meanwhile, the Rinds, Talpurs, Murris, Chandiya, Jemali, and Laghari speak "either Jatki or the hill-tongue; and their selection depends upon the district they inhabit." The Bulfat, however, are specially connected with the Numris, who are Sindi in speech. Again—the "Jataki is also called Siraiki from Siro, or Upper Sind, where it is commonly spoken by the people, and Belocki (Biluch) on account of its being used by several of the Biluch clans settled in the low country. The Langha or Sindhi bards seem to prefer it to their own language, and many well-educated natives, especially Belochis, have studied it critically and composed works in it." All this goes for the Rinds being Indian rather than Persian in speech. All goes to the suggestion of the following question—is there any better reason for making them Biluch than the fact of their coming from Biluchistan?

Be this as it may, there is a certain number of tribes that belong, or are supposed to have originally belonged, to the Khanat of Kelaut rather than to India proper, and who are other than Afghan as well as other than Brahúi in speech. Their manners and religion—predatory and Mahometan—are Biluch; their language and physiognomy more or less Indian. Their political importance is considerable, inasmuch as they lie along the whole of the Dera Ghazi Khan frontier, beginning where the Afghans end and extending into Sind.

The most northern of these, after the Khetrans, whose place is ambiguous, are—

The Khusranis, on the hills, and

The Mutkanis, on the plains. Then follow

The Bozdars, of whom there are, at least, the following sections—

The Seharni	The Jelalani
— Suwarni	— Chandiah
— Gulamani	— Shahani.

The Bozdars are both mountaineers and occupants of the lower country.

The Lúnds, and

The Khosahs, on the plains. Khosa is a Rajput name.

The Lagaris.

The Ghurkanis.—These occupy Hurrund and Darjil, falling into

The Lushari	The Durkhani, and

The Chakri.

The Drishuks, a peaceable, and

The Murri, a warlike, tribe;

The Mazaris, and

The Bugtis (both powerful), succeed; south of whom the Brahúi name appears.

All the preceding tribes belong to the British frontier; either on or within it.

Behind the frontier, especially in Kutch Gundava, lie

The Dumki	The Puzh
— Pugh	— Kullúi,

and others. These appear in both Masson and Pottinger, and, by both authors, they are especially stated to be Rind, *i. e.* Rind rather than Mugsi.

The Magazzi of Masson seem to be the Mugsis of Pottinger. Of the Magazzi, however, all that is said by the former author is that they are the inveterate enemies of the Rinds. Pottinger, on the other hand, gives the following list of their tribes:—

The Lashari	The Musari
— Matyhi	— Kukrani
— Burdi	— Isobani
— Unurs	— Jullani
— Nari	— Turbundzye
— Kullunderani	— Jekrani

The Jutki.

The Jekrani are probably Rind; the Jutki, Juts in the proper sense of the term. The Musari and the Lashari have already appeared. They were among the tribes of the frontier (Lusharis and Mazaris). Upon the whole, it seems that the Rind area is Kutch Gundava rather than the valley of the Indus, the Mugsi area the valley of the Indus rather than Kutch Gundava. The details, however, are very obscure.

But little has to be said concerning the archæology of the Brahúi country. It contains but few ruins, and none of any very great importance. Of coins, but few have been found within its limits; of inscriptions (I believe) none. That some, however, exist is specially stated. It should be remembered, however, that, with the exception of Pottinger and Masson, few Europeans have, at one and the same time, explored the country, and given an account of their explorations. Hence the statement that "of its Greek rulers we have no vestiges," is one which future discoveries may not improbably modify. A city was founded in Arachosia by Demetrius. Near Kelaut are the sites of three towns—of Sorra Bek, of Kuki, and of a third with an unknown name. These, however, seem to have belonged to the times of the Kalifat.

At Mehara, in the hills, to the east of Kelaut, are a few caves and cave-temples; also the remains of what is called a city of the infidels (Kafirs); also walls and parapets of stone—works of the infidels too. Hinglatz, in Luz, is a sacred spot, visited by both Hindu and Mahometan pilgrims. It is in the eyes of the latter, at least, the shrine of the Bíbí Nání = the Lady Mother. It is suggested by Wilson that, word for word, *Nani* is *Nanaia*, the name of a goddess, which appears on many of the Caubul coins.

Let us now assume, *provisionally*, that the Brahúis are Indian, and ask (such being the case) what are the western boundaries of India? Where does it begin?

If the Brahúis be as Indian as their language is believed to make them, and if the Gitshki and Minguls, and Rakshanis, be Brahúi, the Indian area must be carried as far north as Noshky, and as far west as Punghír and Kij. If so, half Mekran is Brahúi. Noshky touches the Baraich districts of Shorabuk, and all but touches Seistaun. It is watered by the river Kaiser. It is the occupancy of the Rakshanis, upon whom the Minguls from the parts about Kelaut have encroached. They reside in tents.

Panjghur, an agricultural district, is cultivated by the Gitshki; as is Kij—after which begins the territory of the Imaum of Muskat on the south, and Persia proper on the north.

That India, then, in some shape or other, has a great extension westward is manifest. It shows itself long before we get to the Indus. Indeed, it is by no means easy to say where India begins or Persia ends.

CHAPTER XIII.

Foreign influences in India.—Bacchic (?).—Assyrian (?).—Persian.—Turanian.—Macedonian.—Arab.—Afghan.—Turk (Tshagatai).

OF the invasions of India, the chief are

1. *The conquest by Bacchus.*—Whether this be so purely mythic as is generally believed will be considered in the sequel. Say, however, that it is ever so much so. The belief in its existence shows, at least, that Greece and India were contained in the same world of fiction. Now, where there is a community of fiction there are also other points of contact—direct or indirect.

2. *The conquest by Semiramis.*—This, if real, would introduce Assyrian influences.

3. *The Persian conquest.*—In order for any part of India to have become a part of the empire of Darius conquest from Persia must have been effected.

4. *Turanian conquest.*—If no conquest from Turania had been effected the term Indo-scythæ would be non-existent.

5. *The Macedonian conquest*, ending in a permanent occupation of Bactria, has already been noticed. This brought Greece upon the Indus.

6. *The Arab conquest.*—In the forty-fourth year of the Hejra, the Mahometans appear on the frontier of India—the Mahometans of the Kalifat, Arabs in language and nationality. Their impression, however, is but slight. They invade, and retire from, Multan ; but the occupancy

is partial, and the withdrawal early. They also invade Sind, but not, in the first instance, effectually.

A.D. 711.
A.H. 92.

Forty-eight years later, in the reign of Walid, begin what may be called the campaigns and conquests of Mohammed Casim, a brave, skilful, and successful general. They end in the reduction of Multan and Sind. How much further his arms penetrated is doubtful. There is a notice of his having begun a march toward Canuj, in which he succeeded in reaching a place which seems to have been Udipur. His actual conquests, however, we limit to the above-named countries, the countries most immediately on the Persian or Afghan frontier. I imagine that his army was largely recruited from Persia, it being expressly stated that it was raised at Shiraz.

The conquests of Casim were made over to his successor, in whose family they remained for about thirty-six years, when a native insurrection, of which we do not know the details, ended in the ejection of the Mahometans and the restoration of Sind and Multan to the Hindus. This state of things lasted 250 years—from 750 to 1000, there or thereabouts.

The Turk conquests.—The first undoubted Turk dynasty in India was founded A.D. 1000—say when Canute was King of England. Its founder's name was Mahmud. He was governor of Korasan under the Samanid successors of the Caliphs. His chief town was Ghuzni, so that he is called Mahmud of Ghuzni, or Mahmud the Ghuznivid, he and his descendants forming the Ghuznivid dynasty. His father was a Turk, Sebek-tegin (a Turk compound) by name. He was originally a slave, his patron and predecessor in the occupancy of Ghuzni having been a slave also; also a Turk.

Such the dynasty. The country from which India was

invaded, the kingdom of this dynasty, was Caubul. It was in the parts about Ghuzni that Alp-tegin first found the nucleus of his empire. One historian states that he had with him, when he first attempted his independence, 3000 Mamelukes; and a Mameluke, at this time, would be a Turk, not (what he is now) a Circassian, or something else of mixed blood and no definite extraction. He would, doubtless, too, have numerous additions from the Ghuzni district itself, and these would be chiefly Afghans. Let us say, then, that the bulk of what Mahmud of Ghuzni, or his father, Sebek-tegin, may have called the army of India, was Turk and Afghan, without going too minutely into the question as to how far the two terms mean the same thing. I imagine, too, there must have been in it Persians, Lughmanis, aud perhaps Biluches.

The hostilities that led to the Ghuznivid conquest of India began with Sebek-tegin, but the conquest itself was the work of Mahmud. The opponents to both were the Rajputs of western and northern Rajasthan.

The descendants of Sebek-tegin held India from the death of Mahmud, A.D. 1030, to that of Khusru Malik, A.D. 1186. They were all Turk on the father's side at least—probably on the mother's as well. The succeeding dynasties are all Turk.

Tamerlane retired from India A.D. 1399. For two months after Tamerlane's departure there was anarchy, then the rule of a chief named Ekbal, then the restoration of Mahmud; who is succeeded by another chief, Doulat Khan Lodi, who, at the end of fifteen months, is expelled by the governor of the Punjab. This takes place fourteen years after Tamerlane's departure; during, however, Tamerlane's lifetime.

It is as a subordinate to Tamerlane that the governor of the Punjab, who expels Doulat Khan Lodi, affects to govern. His name is Khizr Khan, and he is a native of India, probably an Indian rather than a Turk. If he has no Turk blood at all in his veins, he is the first ruler of India without it. He is, moreover, a Synd, *i. e.* a descendant of Mahomet, so that he and his three descendants constitute what is called the Synd dynasty. Soon after his seizure of Delhi, his original province, the Punjab, revolts, and his family has to struggle for it during the whole duration of the dominion.

The Synd dynasty ruled thirty-six years, *i. e.* from 1414 to 1450, when Ala-u-din, the fourth of the family, makes over his capital and titles to

An Afghan, Behlol Khan Lodi, the first ruler of the house of Lodi. The kings that this house gave to India were three in number—by name Behlol Lodi (already mentioned), Secander Lodi, and Ibrahim Lodi, under whose reign India was invaded by

The Tshagatai Turk, Baber, the founder of the empire of the Great Mogul. As a Tshagatai, Baber came from the Mongol frontier; the extent to which Mongol elements entered into his army being indicated by the name of the dynasty.

Since the time of Baber the foreign influences have been Portuguese, Dutch, French, and English.

CHAPTER XIV.

General view of the divisions of the populations of India.—Cast.

I now bid farewell to the numerous preliminaries by which the notice of the populations of India proper has been preceded, and I use the term India proper because, in the forthcoming chapter, no notice will be taken of the Paropamisans and the Brahúi. Ethnologically, indeed, they are Indian; geographically, they are Persian.

They ought not, perhaps, to be excluded. The objects, however, of the present work are mixed. If it were more purely scientific than it is, I should claim them for Hindostan. The Hindostan, however, of the forthcoming notices extends no further westwards than Cashmír, the Punjab, and Sind.

Qui bene dividet, bene docet. For our *primary* division the best basis is language, either actually existing or reasonably inferred. This gives us;

1. The populations whose languages, as now spoken, are Tamul rather than Hindí, along with such Bhils and Kols as are believed to have unlearnt their own tongue and to have adopted that of their neighbours. It also comprises (though the evidence to their belonging to this group is capable of great improvement) the Mairs, Minas, Moghis, and some others;

2. The populations whose languages are Hindí rather than Tamul, the chief of which are the Cashmírian, the Hindí itself, the Bengali, the Uriya, the Gujerathi, and the Marathi.

Are the forms of speech the best basis for our *minor* divisions? I think not. I think it better to take in more characteristics than one. I also think it better to form our groups by type rather than definition. If these views be right, the classification will explain itself.

1. In the extreme north-west, Cashmír stands by itself. It is largely Mahometan. It is Paropamisan as much as it is Indian. It is a land without (or with a *minimum* of) casts.

2. The next division is less simple. Like the first it is largely Mahometan. It is also Sikh. It is by no means sharply defined on its frontier. So far as it is Hindu (and it is so to a very great extent) it is Kshetriya rather than either Sudra or Brahminic. Its area is nearly, but not wholly, commensurate with the extension of the Rajput dynasties, present or past, patent or inferred.

3. The third contains the pre-eminently Brahminic districts along the Ganges, from Oud to Bengal inclusive. It also contains the area of the Uriya language.

4. The fourth contains the populations that occupy the southern slope of the Himalayas, in contact with the Bhots of Tibet, Nepal, Sikkim, Butan, and Asam.

5. The fifth gives us the Marattas, who are Sudras rather than either Kshetriyas or Brahmins.

And here we may notice the meaning of the word *cast*. When two sections of the same group, class, or division, refuse to intermarry, there is an approach to it. There is an approach to it when the intermarriage is other than reciprocal, *i.e.* when a man of one section may take his wife from another, though wives, similarly situated, may not take husbands.

There is an approach to it when individuals of different sections may not eat together; or when they will not eat food cooked or served by one another.

There is the same when mutual contact is eschewed.

There is the same when certain branches of the population are limited to the exercise of certain trades, crafts, or professions, and when (as, of necessity, must be the case) these trades, crafts, or professions become hereditary.

When one class is, in any one of these ways, separated from the other, an approach to cast is the result. When several principles of separation are united the approach becomes nearer.

Nearer still does it become when, in addition to these forms of mutual repulsion, the cohesion of the several members of the same class is strengthened by common ceremonies, legends, beliefs, prejudices, and genealogies, real or hypothetical.

Let all this take place, and let certain classes be held more honourable than others, cast becomes more decided. The higher classes avoid, despise, abhor the lower.

Let the number of classes be great, and the degrees of dignity will be numerous. There will be a highest and a lowest.

All this is cast, and of all this there is more in India than in any other part of the world. There are approaches to it, however, in most countries.

In most of the reports and memoirs upon Hindostan, lists may be found of the casts of the several districts. They are often long ones. They differ, too, from one another. In many cases they do this simply because the languages are different. In essentials they agree. They chiefly consist of the names of trades. There is the cast of cultivators, gardeners, fishers, porters, sweepers, and the like—some high, some low. The lists, however, are long, and the casts are numerous.

The lists are long and the casts are numerous when we

look at the realities of Indian life as it exists at the present moment. And, except that in a ruder condition of society, the division of employments was less, the lists of the earliest historical period are long also.

Theoretically, however, the number of casts is four.

1. There is the priestly cast, or that of the Brahmins.

2. There is the warrior cast, or that of the Kshetriyas.

3. There is the Vaisya class, or that of the merchants; and

4. There is the lowest class, or that of labourers—the Sudra class.

The outcasts are of no class at all. The commonest name for these is Pariah.

The origin of these is given in an extract from the Institutes of Menu, already laid before the reader.

I doubt, notwithstanding, whether this fourfold generality was ever an historical fact.

I think that priests, soldiers, merchants, and labourers were Brahmins, Kshetriyas, Vaisyas, and Sudras only in the way that apes, lions, horses, and hogs are Quadrumana, Carnivora, Solidungula, and Pachydermata. In ethnology, as in zoology, it is the species only which has a tangible definite existence. The genus lies in the mind of the contemplator.

In ethnology, however, as in zoology, the genus and species may coincide. In India this is done by the class of Brahmins. Whatever else a Brahmin may be, he is a member of a privileged order. Hence arises the observation of one of the classical authorities on India to the effect that India is the land, not of four, but of one superior, and many subordinate, casts. To a certain extent, the terms Rajput and Kshetriya coincide. The Vaisyas, however, are pure *entia rationis*.

The Mahratas are called Sudras. This can but mean

that they are neither Brahmins nor Rajputs; at any rate, no fact in history is more patent than their activity, courage, and success as soldiers.

The extent to which the rules of cast press upon individuals can never be laid down in generals. The details of each case regulate it. The most stringent restraints can be set aside by actual lawlessness. The Pindarris, for instance, who were armed robbers, but at the same time so numerous as to resemble an army rather than a banditti, found no difficulty in recruiting themselves from all classes. The Sikhs, again, and the several members of the casts which they left upon conversion, keep up both domestic and social arrangements, and marry and are given in marriage with each other. The view on the part of the Hindus of their neighbourhood (who, it should be remarked, are not of the strictest) is, that it is a political confederation of which their converted brothers have made themselves members. On the other hand, the cases are numerous where the violation of the laws of cast are unnaturally strict; and that without defeating themselves. They are so (for instance) in Nepal, as will be seen when that country comes under notice. Cast, then, is easily lost or easily regained as circumstances dispose.

Upon the origin of so peculiar an institution much speculation has been expended—some, perhaps, wasted. Many maintain that, wherever it occurs, there has been invasion and conquest. If so, it implies the juxtaposition of two hostile nations, and tells a tale of intrusion, resistance, subjugation, slavery, contempt. That this is a possible, and not an improbable, mode of developing such an institution as cast is clear. Whether it be the only one is doubtful. There is cast, in some degree or other, all over the world. Hereditary privileges are cast. Monopoly of employment, continued from father

R

to son, is cast. Social exclusiveness is cast. The tribe-system and the cast-system are often contrasted, and it is true that the circumstances under which the two are evolved are, for the most part, different. Yet there are tribes which assume a superiority over the rest, and refuse to intermarry with them. Again—the tribe and the municipality are contrasted. But what is the tribe whereof the members have certain occupations but cast?

Thus far we have considered cast as a condition and as an effect. But what is it as cause? Assuredly, it is a great ethnological force. Let the business of a jockey, on one side, or of a pugilist, on the other, become, even in England, hereditary, and it is clear that the one will give big, the other small, men. In like manner, though in a less degree, Brahminism must encourage one physiognomy, Sudraism another. We are justified, then, in taking cognizance of cast even where it may not coincide with original ethnological differences.

CHAPTER XV.

Populations whose languages are akin to the Hindí.—Cashmír.

Cashmir is a basin rather than a valley; the bottom of a lake rather than the holm of a river.

The physical form of its occupants is that of the Paropamisans.

On the side of Tibet, its frontier is decided and definite; by which I mean that the whole of Cashmír is Cashmírian. No fragments of any earlier occupancy have been discovered within its frontier. On the east, it stands contrasted with the more purely Hindu countries of Kistewah, and the Sub-himalayas in general. The difference, however, here is one of degree rather than kind.

On the west the details are obscure; the exact extent to which the parts interjacent to Cashmír and Swaut are Cashmírian, Afghan, or Dard being unknown.

The language is quite as much Paropamisan as Hindí. This, however, is the language of common life rather than the language of literature and polite society. The literary language is Persian. As far, however, as the Cashmírian is written, it is written in a character derived from the Devanagari.

Word for word, Cashmír is believed (and that on reasonable grounds) to be Caspatyrus, or Caspapyrus. So that the notices of the country are early.

Cashmírians beyond the limits of Cashmír are numerous, for the population is industrial and commercial.

They are also numerous in Tibet, where intercourse and intermarriage between the two populations are by no means uncommon.

In the way of politics, Cashmír is Sikh, having been so since 1831; in creed, however, it is Mahometan, the Mahometanism being mixed. To a certain extent, it is, like that of Persia, Shiite. To a certain extent, it is, like that of Afghanistan, Sunnite, for between the break-up of the Mogul and the rise of the Sikh power, Cashmír was a portion of the Durani dominion. That many of the converts have been forcibly made is stated by good authorities, and the fact seems likely. It is certain that, at the beginning of its history, Cashmír was one of the strongholds of Brahminism; at the same time the reign of the first Mahometan king belongs to the fourteenth century. His descendants and successors reign till (about) the end of the sixteenth century; when Cashmír, ceasing to be independent under kings of its own, becomes one of the *subahs* of the Mogul empire. As such, it is the least part of itself. Pukhli and Bajowr belong to it. So does Swaut. So do Caubul and Zabulistan. I mention this to show that, even in the way of politics, its connections have run westwards.

Description of Cashmir by Abulfazel.

The whole of the *subah* represents a garden in perpetual spring, and the fortifications with which Nature has furnished it are of an astonishing height, so that the grand and romantic appearance cannot fail of delighting those who are fond of variety, as well as they who take pleasure in retirement. The water is remarkably good, and the cataracts are enchantingly magnificent. It rains and snows here at the same seasons as in Tartary and Persia; and during the periodical rains in Hindostan, here also fall light showers. The soil is partly marshy, and the rest well-watered by rivers and lakes. Violets, roses, narcissuses, and innumerable other flowers, grow wild here. The spring and autumn display scenes delightfully astonishing. The houses, which are built of wood, are of four stories, and some higher, and they are entirely open, without any court yard. The roofs of the houses are planted with tulips, which produce a wonderful effect in the spring. In the lower apartments are kept the cattle and lumber; the family live in the second story; and the third and fourth stories are used for warehouses. Earthquakes are very frequent here, on which account they do not build their houses of brick or stone, but of wood, with which the country abounds. Here are, however, many ancient idolatrous temples, built of brick and stone, some of which are in perfect preservation, and others in ruins. Here are varions woollen manufactures, particularly of shawls, which are carried to all parts of the globe. Although Cashmir is populous and money scarce, yet a thief or a beggar is scarcely known amongst them. Excepting cherries and mulberries, they have plenty of excellent fruits, especially melons, apples, peaches, and apricots; grapes, although in abundance, are of few kinds, and those indifferent. In general they let the vines twist round the trunks of the mulberry trees. The mulberry trees are cultivated chiefly on account of the leaves for the silkworms, little of the fruit being eaten. The silkworms' eggs are brought from Kelut and Little Tibet, but those of the first place are best. The inhabitants chiefly live upon rice, fish, fresh and dried, and vegetables, and they drink wine. They boil the rice over night, and set it by for use for the next day. They dry vegetables, to serve in the winter. They have rice in plenty, but not remarkably fine. Their wheat, which is black and small, is scarce, and *mowng*, barley, and *nakhud* are prodnced, but in small quantity. They have a species of sheep, which they call *Hundoo*, resembling those of Persia, the flesh of which is exceedingly delicious and wholesome. The inhabitants wear chiefly woollen clothes, an upper garment of which will last several years. Their horses are small, but hardy and sure-footed, and they are very cheap. They breed neither elephants nor camels. Their cows are black and ugly, but yield plenty of milk, of which is made good butter. Every town in this *soobah* has as many handicraftsmen as are found in the large cities of other countries. They have no fairs, all their goods being sold at regular shops. In their cities and towns there are neither snakes, scorpions, nor other venomous reptiles. Here is a mountain called Mahades, and every place from whence it can be seen is free from snakes, but the country in general abounds with flies, gnats, bugs, and lice. Sparrows are very scarce, on account of the general use of pellet bows. The inhabitants go upon the lakes in small boats to enjoy the diversion of hawking. They have partridges; the elk is also found here, and they train leopards to hunt them. Most of the trade of this country is carried on by water, but men also transport great burdens upon their shoulders. Watermen and carpenters are professions in great repute here. Here dwell a great number of Brahmins.

Cashmír is the only portion of Hindostan of which there is a native history. When Akbar "led his victorious standards into the region of perpetual spring, the natives presented him with a book called Raj Turungi, written in the Sanskrit language, and containing the history of the princes of Cashmeer for 4000 years back." Akbar ordered it to be translated into Persian. The original text has since been procured, and as it is "the only Sanskrit composition yet discovered to which the title of history can with any propriety be applied," it has commanded no little attention. An elaborate essay upon it by Professor Wilson* gives us a clear view of its general character. It gives us, too, not a few of its details. It gives us, too, a view of the authorship. At any rate, it gives us the names and approximate dates of four authors. The first of these is Calhana, who quotes as predecessors Suvrata, Narendra, Hela Raja, Padma Mihiri, and Sri Ch'havillacára, along with Nila Muni, a purana. The history of Calhana begins with the fabulous ages, and comes down to A.D. 1027. The author himself is believed to have lived about the middle of the following century. Then follows

Jonah Raja, author of the Rájávali, who begins where Calhana ends, and, himself, ends A.D. 1410; followed by

Sri Várá, whose Sri Jaina Rájá Taringíní continues the Rájávali down to A.D. 1477.

The fourth part was added by the order of Akbar. It brings the work down to the time of that monarch.

It is the history of Cashmír as an independent Mahometan kingdom, that this latter part of the work, more especially, delivers. It is a domestic history; *i. e.* its range is a narrow one. The political horizon, a single mountain-basin, must needs be limited. It comprises Tibet, Kashgar (or the Paropamisan countries), Budukshun, and part of Caubul. Of Indian principalities, the little rajahship of Kistewah is Cashmír's nearest neighbour, and it is into Kistewah that the Cashmírian

* In the Transactions of the Asiatic Society, vol. xv.

captains are most particularly in the habit of retreating when defeated. Of external enemies the most formidable are the Turks, by whom invasion after invasion is effected; the way lying over the Baramula pass. Of internal movements the chief are made by the Chuk, Reigna, and Magrey—names which I give as the names of either actual tribes or of something more or less tribual. The Chuks are probably, word for word, the Gukkers.

Mahometanism was introduced as early as A.D. 1341. It took root, however, but slowly and imperfectly, until the end of the century, when Ali, a Syud, who had incurred the anger of Timur, fled from his native city of Hamadan (A.D. 1388), and, attended, it is said, by 700 others, settled in Cashmír. His son, a fugitive also, introduced 300 more. And now the zeal for making proselytes burned bright and hot, and shrines multiplied, and persecution set-in. The Hindu temples were either burnt or thrown down. The Hindu devotees were forced to abjure their religion. Industry, however, was encouraged, and Cashmír became, under its independent princes, what Abulfazel described it. The Rishis, a set of Mahometan ascetics, numbered, in the reign of Akbar, about 2000. They have since either simply decreased, or become wholly extinct. So much for the times described by the last three authors of the chronicles of Cashmír.

The work of Calhana may or may not be trustworthy for the times immediately preceding those of the author. The mass of his statements is fabulous.

Most of the kings bear Indian names. Some, however, are specially stated to be Turks; whilst, in one of the very oldest and most decidedly fabulous dynasties, the title of each and all of the kings is the Turk adjunct, *khan*. One of these Turanian kiugs introduced Buddhism. Eventually, however, Brahminism prevailed.

Older, however, than either of the great Hindu creeds, was the worship of Nagas or snake Gods. Abulfazel relates that he found carvings of snakes in seven hundred places—these being objects of respect.

"Whether," writes Wilson, "the Cashmirian worship of snakes was mystical, at least in the earliest ages, may be questioned. There is likewise reason to suppose that this worship was diffused throughout the whole of India, as besides the numerous fables and traditions relating to the *Nagas*, or snake gods, scattered through the Puránas, vestiges of it still remain in the actual observances of the Hindus. It seems not improbable that the destruction of the whole serpent race by Janaméjaya, the son of Paricshit, recorded in the Puránas as a historical fact, may in reality imply the subversion of the local and original superstition, and the erection of the system of the Vedas upon its ruins." The *cultus* itself was old. A strange passage in Strabo tells, that "Abisarus fed two serpents (δράκοντας); one of which was 80, the other 140 cubits long." Again, Taxiles showed Alexander an enormous snake, which he reverenced as the symbol of Dionysus.

These notices (from Wilson) are not given for nothing. Like so many other phenomena, they point westwards. Stories connected with snakes appear twice in Gardiner's account of the Kafirs. Stories connected with snakes appear more than once in the mythology of Persia: prominent amongst which is that of Iblis and Zohauk—Iblis tempts Zohauk, a youth who, until the time of his temptation, is well disposed and virtuous, to the committal of gross crimes, and to the indulgence of an epicurean sensuality. Taste after taste is gratified. Every day something newer and more delicate than the luxuries of the day before appears at table; and that with the promise that "to-morrow there shall be something more delicious still." Pampered and corrupted, Zohauk now asks Iblis how he can show his gratitude. "By allowing me to kiss your naked shoulder." So Zohauk stripped, and Iblis kissed, and from the spot between the shoulder-blades, which he touched with his venomous and deceptive mouth, sprang two black snakes. Some time after this happened, Iblis, in the garb of a physician, visited Zohauk, and prescribed as the only means of preventing him from being gnawed into nothing by the serpents, a daily meal of human brains. So Zohauk fed the snakes; even as did Taxiles.

Now Zohauk was a usurper, the true king being Jamshid, for some time a fugitive in Zabulistan; for some time a wanderer in Caubul — in both places a drinker of wine.

Of Jamshid's family is the famous champion Rustam, who fights against (*inter alios*) the great Turanian champion Afrasiab, in Caubul, in Segistan, in Zabulistan and elsewhere.

There is nothing new in the notice of these numerous fictions. It is well known that they constitute the basis of the great poem of Firdausi—the Shah Nameh; wherein the stories of Jamshid, Feridun, Kavah the blacksmith, Zohrab, and others form a cycle. There is nothing new in the notice of them. There is no reason for mentioning them on their own account. The fact that claims attention is that of their localization in the Paropamisus—on the Paropamisus itself and on each side of it, in Cashmír as well as in Afghanistan, in Afghanistan as well as in Cashmír.

In both countries Jamshid is a real name. It was borne by one of the kings of Cashmír. It is borne, at the present time, by one of the tribes of the Hazarehs, or Afghans. Suhauk, too (word for word Zohauk), is the name of another of them. Forts, of which the building is attributed to Rustam, are common over the whole district. Finally, either Chitral or Kafiristan is the so-called wine-cellar of Afrasiab.

In the notice of Hwantsian, Cashmír stands prominent. His account contains a long story of a serpent that lay in the middle of the lake. Of the draining of the lake the following legend is native.

The country was entirely covered with water, in the midst of which a demon, Jaladeo, resided, who preyed upon mankind, and seized upon every thing and person he could meet with in the neighbouring regions. It happened, at length, that Cashef, the son of Marichi, and according to some accounts, the grandson of Brahmá, visited this country, and having spent some time in pious abstraction on mount Sumar, turned his attention to the desolated appearance of the earth, and inquired its cause: the people told him of the abode of Jaladeo in Sati Sar, and his predatory incursions upon them. The heart of Cashef was moved to compassion, and he took up his residence in Noubadan, near Hirapur, for a thousand years, employing that period in religious austerities; in consequence of which Maháideo appeared to him, and assented to his prayers for the extirpation of Jaladeo; Maháideo accordingly sent his servants Vishnu and Brahmá to expel the demon. Vishnu was engaged in the conflict one hundred years, when finding that the mud and water afforded a secure retreat to the Deo, he at last made the chasm at Baramouleh, by which the waters were drained off, the demon exposed, taken, and slain, and the country recovered and rendered habitable; being thence called Cashef-Sir, or the Mountain of Cashef.—*Asiatic Researches*, vol. xv. p. 94.

The first of the following tables gives us the comparison between the Cashmírian and the Paropamisan forms of speech: the second the words common to the two chief Paropamisan dialects, the Cashmírian, and the Hindí.

(1.)

English.	Cashmíri.	Arniya.	Khajunah.
Man	manu	rag	hir
——	——	moash	er
Woman	zanana	kamri	gus
——	——	kamedi	——
Head	kalah	sur	yetes
Eye	akh	ghakh	ilchin

English.	Cashmiri.	Arniya.	Khajunah.
Ear	kan	kad	iltumal
Nose	nast	naskar	gomoposh
Mouth	aso	diran	gokhat
Tooth	dand	dond	gume
Hand	atha	hast	gurengghar
Foot	khor	pang	goting
Blood	rath	le	multan
Sky	nab	asman	ayesh
Sun	aftab, suraj	——	sa
Moon	tsandar	——	halans
Star	tarah	satar	aso
Fire	nar, agan	ag, ingar	phu
Water	ab, pani	auqr	chíl
River	bulwit	sin	sindha
Stone	khain	——	dhan
Tree	kulu	kan	——
Wood	zun	jin	gashil
One	ak	i	han
Two	zih	juh	altas
Three	trah	trui	usko
Four	tsor	chod	walto
Five	panz	push	sundo
Six	shah	chui	mi-shando
Seven	sat	sut	talo
Eight	ath	ansht	altambo
Nine	noh	neuhan	huncho
Ten	dah	jash	tormo.

(2.)

English.	Cashmíri.	Shina.	Arniya.	Punjab, &c.
Air	hawe	——	hawa	hawa
Arrow	kan	kon	——	kaneru
Blood	——	lohel	——	lohu
Daughter	——	dhi	——	dhi
Ear	kan	kund	——	kan
Earth	——	birde	——	prither
——	——	——	bhum	bhumi
Eye	ach	achhi	ach	akh
Fire	agan	agar	ag	ag
Foot	——	pa	pang	pan
Grass	ghaso	kats	——	ghas
Hair	wal	——	balo	bal
——	——	——	sur	sar

English.	Cashmiri.	Shina.	Arniya.	Punjab, &c.
Honey	manch	macchhe	——	makhir
Leaf	——	patta	——	patta
Milk	dod	dudh	——	dudh
Moon	tsandar	yun	——	jun
Mouth	aso	asi	——	——
Name	——	noma	——	nam
Night	rat	rat	——	rat
Nose	——	——	naskar	nasika
Snow	shin	hin	him	him
Son	——	pucha	——	putr
Star	tarah	taro	satar	tara
Stone	——	bat	——	patthar
Sun	——	suri	——	suraj
Tooth	dand	dhuni	dond	dand
Wood	——	katho	——	kath
Right hand	dachin	dachin	——	dakhin
Red	——	lolo	——	lal
Behind	pat	pato	——	pit
Strait	synd	suntho	——	sidha
Dry	hok	sukho	——	sukha
Hard	——	koro	——	karha
Hot	tat	tatto	——	tatta
Large	bod	baro	——	bara
Ripe	——	pakko	——	pakka
Thick	——	tulo	——	tula.

That the Khajunah is the least Indian of the Paropamisan forms of speech has already been stated.

CHAPTER XVI.

Populations whose language is akin to the Hindí.—The Rajput and Jut division.—The Sikhs.

THE second division is, in the way of creed, Sikh, Hindu, and Mahometan.

In the way of cast, its noblest tribes are Kshetriya rather than either Brahminic or Sudra; though, of course, in the Sikh and Mahometan districts, the spirit of cast is abated.

The chief form of speech is the Hindí, of which the dialects are numerous—the Hindí, rather than the Bengali, Uriya, or Marathi.

Its area is bounded by Cashmír, Afghanistan, Biluchistan, the Ocean, and the Vindya mountains—there or thereabouts. In the north, it approaches the Himalayas, in the east and north-east the Jumna—sometimes touching it. In the east its boundaries are obscure. They lie beyond the Chumbul, beyond the Sind, and, in some cases, beyond the Betwa.

This contains—

1. The valley of the Indus.
2. The Desert.
3. The hilly districts of the Aravulli range, and the drainage of the south-western feeders of the Jumna.
4. The drainage of the rivers that fall into the gulfs of Kutch and Cambay.

5. The Peninsula of Gujerat.

Politically speaking, it contains the Punjab, Sind, the proper Rajput country, Gujerat, and other districts of less importance and prominence.

On the east it is Hindu; on the west, Sikh and Mahometan.

As this difference of creed is attended with a difference of nomenclature, it is necessary to be on our guard against being misled by terms. As a general rule, a Rajput is a Hindu. As a general rule, a Jut is a Mahometan. As a general rule, a Jut is a peaceable cultivator. For all this the Jut may be, in blood, neither more nor less than a converted Rajput; and, *vice versâ*, the Rajput may be but a Jut of the ancient faith. That other differences have been effected by this difference of creed is likely. The difference between arms and tillage as a profession, the difference between a haughty autonomy, and a submissive independence, are sure, in the course of time, to tell upon the temper and the features. That they have done this in the cases before us no one doubts. At the same time, it is safe to maintain that, before the introduction of Mahometanism, the difference between the Jut and the Rajput was but slight. That the Sikhs are, *mutato nomine*, and, *mutatâ fide*, with few exceptions, Juts is a matter of ordinary history.

The Punjab.—The notices of some of the populations of the valley of the Indus are well nigh as old as those of the river itself. This was crossed by Alexander: so that the kings who opposed him were Punjab sovereigns. Such were Porus and Taxiles.

Lower down the stream lay the dominions of kings whose names end in *-khan*—Musi*canus*, and Oxy*canus*.

Later in time comes the name Indoscythæ.

Memorials of the kingdom founded by the successors of Alexander, have been found on the eastern side of the Indus—though less abundantly than in the valley of the Caubul river.

Word for word, *Multan* is supposed to be the country of the *Malli*.

In the way of physical geography, the Punjab falls into the hill-country, and the low-country. The hill-country (the details of which are imperfectly known) belongs to the remnant of the Great Sikh Empire, rather than to Britain. It was left to Gulab Singh.

On the southern frontier of Cashmír lie what were once the petty independencies of Prúnch, Rajour, &c.; now parts of Gulab Singh's dominion. They are Mahometan rather than either Hindu or Sikh. The rajahship of Jumma, the original territory of Gulab Singh, is Sikh.

The parts marked in the map as the country of

The Bumbas is but little known. I cannot say in what respect the Bumbas differ from another population with whom, both geographically and ethnologically, they are connected, viz.,

The Kukkars.—Word for word, this is Cauker; and it is a name which occurs frequently in the Mahometan historians. It seems to be the general name for the mountaineers of the Salt range, and the ranges to the north. That occupants of districts like these are hard to conquer, is what we expect *à priori*. We find that it was their habit to harass the armies of most of the invaders from the west. The Kukkars and Bumbas form a natural division of the Punjab population. So do the inhabitants of the level country.

Essentially these are (Jits) Juts—*i. e.* they are Jut in blood, language, and physical form; though not, wholly, Juts *eo nomine*. They are Sikhs rather than Mahometans;

but, before they became Sikh, they were Jut in every sense of the word.

The Sikh sect came into existence in the latter half of the fifteenth century, its founder, Nanak Shah, having been born in the district of Lahore, A.D. 1469. He was both the founder of a sect himself, and the father of a founder, inasmuch as one of his two sons, Dherm Chand, took to asceticism and originated the sect named, at first, Udasi; but afterwards (and now) Nanak Putrah, or sons of Nanak. It is one of the existing Sikh sects. Nanak was a devotee, a philosopher, and a writer. The first of the Sikh scriptures, the Adi Grunt'h, was composed by him. He saw with equal pain the bigotry of the Mahometan, and the superstition of the Hindu. He wished to replace both by a pure and charitable monotheism. Yet his means were conciliatory. He dealt tenderly with absurdities of both belief and practice. He was a man of peace rather than war.

(2.) Guru Angaa succeeds him; himself succeeded by (3) Amera Das, succeeded, in his turn, by (4) Ram Das; who leaves his authority to

(5.) Arjunmal, who, adding to the chapters of the original Adi Grunt'h, puts the whole into form, and gives shape and consistency to what is now a definite and important creed—the creed of a sect which up to this time has comported itself quietly, mildly, inoffensively. But Arjunmal is murdered by the Mahometans; and

(6.) Har Govind succeeds him. But not as the head of a peaceable population. The anger of the Sikhs is awakened, and a long series of hostilities, destined, in the end, to overthrow all the Mahometanism of the Punjab, now commences. Every Sikh now wears steel. Every Sikh is a zealot, and a soldier. Har Govind, priest militant and prophet captain, wears two swords, "the one to revenge the death of his father, the other to destroy the miracles of Mahomet." He has converted a race of peaceable enthusiasts into an army of fiery soldiers. In 1644 his grandson

(7.) Har Ray succeeds him; succeeded by

(8.) Har Crishn, succeeded by

(9.) Tegh Behadur—These are the days when Aurungzeb is emperor; no good days for any new sect; least of all for one that has set itself against the Koran. The Sikh power is broken—partly by the strong hand of the emperor, partly by internal dissensions. In the days of Aurungzeb and Tegh Behadur, miracles are wrought by the Sikh *gurus* or priests, especially by Har Crishn, and Ram Ray. Tegh Behadur himself is murdered: even as Arjunmal was murdered. Like causes, like effects. Out of the blood of Arjunmal rose the awakened spirit of the Sikhs, under Har Govind. Out of the blood of Tegh Behadur rises the power of his son,

(10.) Guru Govind—When his father died he was a stripling; but he devoted himself to revenge. Like the Pindari and Mahratta chieftains, Guru Govind opened the ranks of his army and the gates of his faith to all comers. Nanak wished to abolish cast, and taught that before God all men were equal. It was a saying of Guru Govind's, that the four tribes of Hindus, the Brahmins, the Kshetriyas, the Vaisyas, and the Sudras, would, like lime, betel-nut, betel-leaf, and catechu, become all of one colour when chewed. The name Sikh he changed into Singh (Lion), a name first assumed by the Rajputs. He required that every man should bear arms, should wear a blue dress, should let his hair grow, and should use, as a part of his salutations, Glory to the Guru (spiritual leader). The Grunt'h, or book of the scriptures, was to be his law, his duty obedience to his chief, his pleasure war. It is Govind himself—priest, soldier, and poet—who writes the following :—

Cripál rages, wielding his mace: he crushed the skull of the fierce Hyat Khan. He made the blood spurt aloft, and scattered the brains of the chief, as Chrishna crushed the earthen vessel of butter. Then Nand Chand raged in dreadful ire, launching the spear and wielding the sword. He broke his keen scymitar, and drew his dagger, to support the honour of the Sondi race. Then my maternal uncle, Cripál, advanced in his rage, and exhibited the skilful war-feats of a true Cshatriya. The mighty warrior, though struck by an arrow, with another made a valiant Khan fall from his saddle; and Saheb Chund, of the Cshatriya race, strove in the battle's fury, and slew a blood-thirsty Khan, a warrior of Khorasan.

* * * * * * *

The blood-drinking spectres and ghosts yelled for carnage; the fierce Hetala, the chief of the spectres, laughed for joy and sternly prepared for his repast. The vultures hovered around, screaming for their prey. Hari Chund (a Hindu chief in the emperor's army), in his wrath, drawing his bow, first struck my steed with an arrow; aiming a second time, he discharged his arrow; but the deity preserved me, and it passed me, only grazed by my ear. His third arrow struck my breast; it tore open the mail and pierced the skin, leaving a slight scar: but the God whom I adore saved me. When I felt this hurt, my anger was kindled; I drew my bow and discharged an arrow; all my champions did the same, rushing onwards to the battle. Then I aimed at the young hero and struck him. Hari Chund perished, and many of his host; death devoured him who was called Rájá among a hundred thousand Rájás. Then all the host, struck with consternation, fled, deserting the field of combat. I obtained the victory through the favour of the Most High; and, victorious in the field, we raised aloud the song of triumph. Riches fell on us like rain, and all our warriors were glad.

Hero as he is, Govind finds it necessary to yield to the superior power of Aurungzeb; and becomes a fugitive, a wanderer, a madman. He had written to the emperor thus: "You make Hindus Mahometans, and are justified by your laws. I, on a principle of self-preservation, will make Mahometans Hindus. You may rest in fancied security. But beware, I will teach the sparrow to strike the eagle to the ground." The latter part of the vaunt was never realized. Many a Mahometan, however, was made a Hindu. The proselytes fall into four divisions, retaining, as Sikhs, the distinctive appellations as Mahometans. Two of these are founded on their pedigree, two on their country:—

Syud Singh	Mogul Singh
Sheikh Singh	Patan Singh.

The latter part of Govind's life is obscure. He was the last ruler of the Sikhs who was, at one and the same time, a religious chief, and universally acknowledged to be such. The number ten was fated, and Govind was the ninth from Nanak. He was the last head of a united Sikhdom. His friend, however, and follower, Banda, availed himself of the confusion which set-in after the death of Aurungzeb, plundered the country, and defeated some of the minor Mahometan chiefs, especially Foujdar Khan, governor of Sirhind, and murderer of the infant children of Govind. Quarter was neither asked nor given. The wife and children of the murderer were slaughtered. There was an indiscriminate massacre in Sirhind; there was the same, or sadder, bloodshed, when the province of Saharanpur was invaded. The buried dead are said to have been disinterred; the unburied were mutilated and exposed to wild beasts.

The power as well as the temper of these savage sectarians has become formidable; but it is broken. The following notice of the death of Banda and his followers is from a Mahometan, and an enemy:—"They not only behaved firmly during the execution, but would dispute and wrangle with each other, who should suffer first. Banda was at last produced, his son being seated on his lap. His father was ordered to cut his throat, which he did without uttering one word. Being then brought nearer to the magistrate's tribunal, the latter ordered his flesh to be torn off with red-hot pincers, and it was in those moments he expired; his black soul taking its flight by one of those wounds, towards the regions for which it was so well fitted." A proof that Banda, with all his authority and bravery, was no true religious chief to the whole Sikh sect is found in the fact of some writers having considered him a heretic. He departed from more than one of the institutions of Nanak, and he put to death some of Govind's most devoted followers for not doing as he did.

The extirpation of the Sikhs is now attempted. The remnant flies to the hills. Yet, thirty years afterwards, when Nadir Shah invades India, we find them descending upon the plains.

In 1805, the country, according to Sir T. Malcolm, who, being with the army under Lord Lake, describes what he saw and heard, was weak, distracted, disunited. There were different districts, and different chieftaincies in the country between the Beas and Ravi. "Runjít Sinh of Lahore, Futteh Sinh of Aliwal, and Jud'h Sinh of Ramgadia, are the principal chiefs."

How familiar are, at least, two of the names, now! The consolidation of the Sikh power under Runjít Singh, and its subsequent overthrow, are events that have taken place before our eyes.

The Punjab is a district wherein the traces of either anything Tamul from the south, or anything Bhot from the north, are at a *minimum*. We cannot, indeed, say that they exist at all. At the same time, we cannot say that they do not.

Of recent intrusion there has been abundance. The extent to which the valley of the main stream of the Indus is, more or less, Afghan and Biluch has already been noticed. Turk names (Hissar, &c.) of geographical localities are numerous. Upon the whole, however, the

Punjab has been a country to pass through rather than to settle in.

Bahawulpur (*Daudputra*).—This is one of the pre-eminent Biluch districts of India,—whatever that word may mean; the Biluch intrusion being recent. The creed is chiefly Mahometan, the older elements of the population Jut.

CHAPTER XVII.

Populations speaking either the Hindí or languages akin to it.—The Rajput and Jut divisions.—Sind.—Kutch.—Gujerat.

India, even when we take no account of the Brahúis, and limit ourselves to the prolongations of the Sind population, extends far into Mekran.

The special Sind tribes do this. So do

The Juts, Jits, Jauts.—Word for word, all these forms are the same; though they apply to populations between which there are some notable differences both in respect to habits and creed.

In the parts beyond the India frontier, in parts of Caubul and Biluchistan, a population more or less sporadic and gypsy-like, bears the name. Of this we take no notice.

In the Punjab the term is Jit; the Punjab being pre-eminently a Jit occupancy, and the blood of the Sikhs being (as aforesaid), for the most part, Jit.

Sind, along with a portion of the Desert, is the chief occupancy of the Mahometan Juts; the congeners of whom, with the same name, extend over the greater part of Rajputana; until at Bhurtpore and Dholpore we find an actual Jaut dynasty.

The Juts of Kutch Gundavá have already been noticed. The Juts of Sind are Mahometan cultivators—numerous and peaceable descendants of the first converts. They fall into divisions and subdivisions, called *khum*, a term which re-appears with a similar meaning in Burma. The camel is the chief animal of the Sind Juts, who live together in large communities, sometimes with fixed, sometimes with movable, dwellings. Sometimes they hire themselves to the Biluch landowners as agricultural labourers.

Sindis to the west of Sind.—As far within the limits of Mekran as Hormara, on the Kalamat creek, lives a small tribe which believes that it came originally from Sind. Whether this be true is uncertain. It is only certain that considerably to the west of Cape Monze a Sindi population is to be found.

The Med.—This is the name for the maritime and fishing tribes for the eastern coast of Mekran. The Meds fall into four divisions—

The Gazbur	The Jellar Zai
— Hormari	— Chelmar Zai.

These may or may not be in the same category with the Kalamatti tribes.

The Numri.—This name is sometimes spelt Lumri. It is that of the chief population of the small province of Luz, one of the numerous dependencies of the Khanate of Khelaut. The minute details of the Numri group differ. The most specific account, however, is the following.

		Fighting Men.
The Jamutri	division can muster	600
— Shuru	————	200
— Burah	————	300
— Shukh	————	100
— Warah	————	100
— Mungayah	————	300
		1600

The Arab Gudur tribe is, perhaps, other than Numri;

inasmuch as it professes to be, what its name suggests, Arabian in origin.

The Numri is the chief population of Luz. But it is not confined to the province. The Jokías and Jukrias of Sind differ from the Numri in their political relations only. The Numri are Mahometans.

The Chuta.—On the upper and middle part of the Hub river, which falls into the sea at Cape Monze, lies a rugged district occupied by the Chuta, whose origin is said to be Sumrah, whose dress is Brahúi, whose manners are pastoral, whose houses are huts. They are, probably, in the same category as the Numri.

They bring us to Sind proper.

The history of Sind gives the following periods :—

(1.) From the earliest times to the Mahometan conquest. —During this period the invasion of Alexander took place; one of the results of which was the descent of the Indus by Nearchus. But, before this, Turanian occupancies had been effected, and Indoscythæ is the name of one portion of the Sind population.

(2.) From the Mahometan conquest to the end of the Ghuznevid dynasty.—The Mahometan conquest was one of the conquests of the Kalifat. This means that the conquerors were Arabs rather than Persians or Afghans. Under Mahmud of Ghuzni the influence would be both Afghan and Turk.

Of the Sumrah and Summa dynasties which succeeded, the latter, at least, appears to have been Hindu. At the present time there are few or no Kshetriyas in Sind; consequently few or no Rajputs. The Summa chiefs, however, conquered Kutch. Now, Kutch is, to a great extent, Rajput. More than this, some of the Rajput families affect a Summa, or Sind, origin. Jam, a Bhot word, was the title of the Summas, who were overthrown by Shah Beg

Arzhun, prince of Candahar, A.D. 1519. Soon after which Mirza Isa Tirkhan, a military adventurer, raised his family to power. The prince of Candahar seems to have been an Afghan; Isa Tirkhan, a Turk. The next were—

The Kaloras and *Talpuras.*—Long before A.D. 1736 the power of the central Government had been diminished, and the protection of its distant States had become impossible to the descendants of Akbar and Aurungzeb. Meanwhile, the descendants of one Adam Shah, of the Kalora tribe, who, in the fifteenth century, had imbibed fanaticism from the teaching of a holy man, Mian Mahomed Mikidy, had become powerful, both in religious influence and in secular possessions. They had appropriated lands belonging to others, and had defended their appropriations by the sword. They were a set of fighting, formidable fakirs. In 1717 Mian Nur Mahomed had obtained from Mahomed Shah the title of the Friend of God, and the government of Sewestan. By '36, he was, to all intents and purposes, the ruler of Sind.

By A.D. 1768 the Kalora dynasty was overthrown by the Talpurs.

In '43 the British replaced the Talpurs.

At the present moment Sind is the least Indian part of India. The extent to which it has admitted foreign influences has been suggested by the preceding sketch of its history.

The Sindi form of speech falls into dialects and subdialects, each of which approaches the language of its neighbourhood. Thus the Siraiki of Upper Sind contains numerous Jutki words; whilst the Kutch dialect has Gujerati elements; and a third dialect, belonging to the Thull, or Desert, and spoken as far as Jessulmir, has borrowed from, or given to, the Marwar. It is the language of the Shikari (hunters) and Dedhs (tanners), who are said to have their own peculiar scriptures called Pali, written in a peculiar character. The Lar form of speech is the purest, Lar being Lower Sind.

English.	Sar.	Lar.	Punjabi.
Man	maru	——	manas
——	murs	——	——
Woman	zal	mihri	gharwali
Head	matho	sisi	sir
Hair	war	jhonto	bal
——	choti	——	——
Eye	ak	——	akh
Ear	kan	——	kan
Hand	hath	kar	hath
——	chambu	——	——
Foot	per	——	pao
Mouth	wat	——	mukh
Tooth	dand	dandan	dand
Tongue	jhibh	——	——
Day	dink	——	din
Night	rat	——	rât
Sun	sijj	adit	suraj
Moon	chandr	——	chand
Star	taro	——	tara
Fire	bar	jando	ag
——	——	jeru	——
Water	pani	——	pani
——	sandaro	——	——
Tree	wanper	——	rukh
Stone	rahan	——	hatar
——	khod	——	——

Among the subordinate populations of Sind are

The Moana or *Miani.*—A Miani is a boatman, a fisherman, and a Mahometan—strongly built and dark skinned. Many of the Miani, like the Chinese, live on the water, rather than by its side. When occupants of a town, the Miani have a separate quarter. Their women are lax and handsome; an inordinate portion of them being courtesans and dancing girls. The name re-appears in

Kutch. The Meyanna, however, of the Meyanné district in Kutch, are robbers by profession, and but half Mahometans in creed. A section of them called Munka neglects circumcision. When a Munka dies a bundle of burning grass is laid on his face previous to interment.

Arab families.—Syuds, or descendants of the Prophet, Kurayshi, or descendants of the ancient Koreish, Alawi and Abbasi, descendants of Ali and Abbas, are all to be found in Sind.

Meman.—The Memans, numerous about Hyderabad, Sehwan, and Kurraché, are industrious, well informed, and sharp bargainers. I do not know their special chaacteristics, or whence they get their name. They are Mahometans.

The Khwajo.—The Khwajo are heretics, holding the Ismaelite creed. They amount to some 300 families, and are believed to be of Persian origin.

The Sidi.—Under the Amírs there was a considerable importation of slaves from the eastern coast of Africa. The trade has now either ceased or decreased. The full-blood African is called Sidi; the half-blood, Gaddo; the Quadroon, Gambrari.

The Khosa fall into two divisions. The first contains those of Upper Sind, who are peaceable cultivators. The second is represented by a body of robbers, who, within the present century, left Sind, and betook themselves to the Desert, where they joined the Sodha in their forays, being numerous, bold, and well mounted.

Sind leads to

Kutch.—Of actual Juts, *eo nomine*, Kutch contains few or none. Their analogues, however, and perhaps their congeners, are

The Katti.—A Katti is a herdsman, occupant of the districts of Pawur, Puchur, and Parkur, or the parts on the north, rather than the south of Kutch, resembling in dress, habits, and dialect,

The Ahir, with whom, however, he does not intermarry.

The Rehberi.—Neither the Ahir nor the Rehberi, still less the Katti, refuse to eat with Mahometans. Their widows are free to form second marriages.

The Rajputs are either Jareyas or Waghelas. The Waghela Rajputs, or the Rajputs of the district of Wagur (the most eastern part of Kutch), are few in numbers, and unimportant in respect to their influence. A few families represent their original power; for powerful they were before the rise of the Jareyas. They resemble the Rajputs of Gujerat, except that they are somewhat less scrupulous. This is what we expect from their neighbourhood and relations; for the leading Rajputs of Kutch, the Jareyas, are half Mahometan. They eat food cooked by Mahometans, and swear by Allah.

Some, indeed, are stricter, and adhere to the *cultus* of Vishnu. The general character, however, of the Jareya Hinduism is lax. The more a Jareya venerates Vishnu the more he abstains from spirits and indulges in opium. The nearer he approaches the Mahometan the less he takes of opium, and the more of spirits. The two vices seem to stand in an inverse ratio to each other. In both of them few; in one almost all, indulge. Every village has its still, sometimes applied to sugar, sometimes to dates, sometimes to carrots. The Jareya wakes to drink and drinks to sleep. His bard, a musician (*bhat* or *lunga*), amuses him during the waking intervals with song or story. His wives intrigue. It is in vain that, after the strictest fashion of the Mahometans, they are secluded. They intrigue with high and low. They intrigue and do worse. In no part of India is female infanticide more general than in the Jareya districts. Sometimes it is effected by means of opium, sometimes by drowning the infant in milk, sometimes by smothering. The father hears that his wife has been delivered, and that the child is in heaven. So he bathes and asks no questions. Should the mother hesitate or delay, he declares his resolution not to enter her house as long as the child lives.

In respect to female infanticide but too many of the Mahometans act after the manner of the Rajputs; with whom they agree in blood, and differ only in creed.

To the north of the Waghela district lies Parkur, an oasis, and, in cases of attack, a place of refuge. Its one poor town, and its twenty poor villages, represent the power, such as it is, of the Sodha Rajputs, or the Rajputs of the Desert, between Kutch, Sind, and Jessulmir. Less Hindu than even the Jareya, the Sodhas are distinguished by their creed only from the Mahometans of their area and neighbourhood. They are herdsmen, poor and unlettered. They intermarry with the Rajputs around them, but not with each other. And they give their daughters, who are remarkable for their beauty, to the Mahometans. In doing this, they show themselves in a strong contrast to the Jareyas, with whom the birth of a girl child is not only a misfortune, but the cause of a crime. The Sodha practice, on the other hand, like that of the Circassians, makes capital out of the female part of the family. The Rajput father sells. The Mahometan husband buys.

A Sodha gives his daughter or sister one day in marriage, and has no scruple, the next, in driving-off the cattle of his bridegroom.

The Chawrah.—The geographical names Kurrir, Khori, and Kawra, appear in the parts to the north of Kutch, and I have little doubt as to their being connected with that of the population so-called, a population occupant of Kutch, reduced in power, and limited in numbers; a population, however, which has some imperfect Rajput rights, though practically subordinate to the Jareyas.

Kutch leads to

Gujerat.—The area of the Gujerathi language begins to the west of the Little Desert. This assumes that the language of the occupants of that district is either Kutchi or Sindi. If it be not, the Gujerathi extends somewhat further westward. In Kutch itself it is the language of business and literature, though not the vernacular of the people. To the east and north-east of the Run it is spoken on both sides of the lower Lúni, though to what extent inland is uncertain. In Marwar the dialect changes; and I presume (without being certain) that the language of the Bhíls of Sirohi is other than Gujerathi. In the Rewa Kanta the population is Kol, the exact details of the Kol philology being uninvestigated. Along the coast, however, the language is, to a certainty, Gujerathi. So it is on the neck of the peninsula. So it is on the neck of the peninsula of Kattiwar. So it is in Cambay, and a great portion of the Surat collectorate. Here, however, change begins. In Durhampur and Bundsla, petty States to the south-east of the town itself, the Marathi shows itself. Both languages, however, are in use. In Penth, still further to the south, (though at the same time to the north of the Damaun river,) the language is "Marathi with numerous Gujerathi words."

Between the Little Desert, Marwar, and the Gulf of Kutch, lies a mass of extremely small States.

Four of these are Mahometan, viz. Pahlunpúr, Radhunpúr, Warye, and Terwara.

Four are Rajpút, viz. Thurad (*cum* Morwara), Wao, Soeghaum, Deodur, and Suntulpúr (*cum* Charchut).

Two are Kol, or Kúli—Bhabhur and Kankruj.

In the north-eastern parts of Pahlunpúr the language approaches the Marwari. Again—though the larger portion of the area is Mahometan in respect to its dynasties, the decided majority of the population is Hindu; the Gujerati, rather than the Hindostani, being the language of even the Mahometan minority. In Suntulpur there is a Ahir population. Terwara and Deodur, though Rajput in the way of politics, are as thoroughly Kuli as Bhabhur and Kankruj. The Kols affect a Rajput origin, and explain their loss of cast by the fact of their ancestors having made marriages of disparagement. The Kols, too, where they come in contact with the Bhíls, look upon themselves as the superior people.

In Pahlunpúr the Mahometans are from either some other part or from Afghanistan, the ruling family itself being Patan. Of the other two divisions—the Sheiks and Synds—the former call themselves after the name of the country from which they came, and are Behari, Nagori, or Mundori Mussulmauns, according as they came from Behar, Nagore, or Mundore. Others, of Rajput origin, are Purmas, Chowras, and Rahtors. The Boraks speak Arabic. The Mehmans are descended from the Sind Lohanas.

Amongst the Hindus the Brahmins are—

1. Owdich Brahmins
2. Suhusra Owdich
3. Meywara Brahmins
4. Omewul Brahmins
5. Sirmali Brahmins.

To which add certain half-bloods, who have lost cast by marriages of disparagement.

The Kshatryas are either Rajputs or Banians.

The Rajputs are—

1. Purmar
2. Solunkhi
3. Gohil
4. Chowra
5. Waghela
6. Chowan
7. Rathor
8. Diol
9. Rana
10. Jhalla
11. Deora.

The Banians are—

1. Visa Sirmali
2. Uswal
3. Pirwal
4. Dussa Sirmali
5. Pancha
6. Wussawul Nagra
7. Dussawul Nagra.

Of the Sudras, the most important class is that of the Kúmbi, or cultivators, who fall into the Leora, the Arjuna, and the Kurwa divisions.

That the Kuli affect a Rajput origin has already been stated. Hence they take Rajput patronymics, and are—

1. Rathor Kúli
2. Waghela Kúli
3. Solunkhi Kúli
4. Songhurra Chowan
5. Dabi Kúli
6. Mukwana Kúli.

These details may serve as a sample of the complexities of Indian ethnology—in the parts under notice more complex than usual. Sind, Gujerathi, Bhíl, Kuli, Rajput, and Mahometan populations, meet in the parts between Marwar and Kattiwar; Kattiwar being the name for the country of the Katti, the peninsular portion of Gujerat.

For this, the newer occupants are Rajputs, the older Ahirs, Katti, and Babrias, *i. e.* what we have observed in Kutch repeats itself here. In Jhalawar the Rajputs are of the Jhala branch. They either take their name from, or give it to, the district. In Hallar they are Jareyas, guilty here, as elsewhere, of female infanticide. The Rajah of Purbunda in Soruth is a Jetwa Rajput. Gohilwar is the occupancy of the Gohillas, whose name is conspicuous in the history of Marwar. When the

Rahtors from Canuj invaded Marwar, they found the Gohillas in the land, and ejected them from it. The result was the settlement in Gohilwar. This may be a true history, or it may merely be a hypothesis founded upon the appearance of the name in two places.

In most, perhaps in all, of the districts of the peninsula there are Katti. Their chief locality, however, is, as the name suggests, the central district of

Kattiwar proper.—The Katti of Kattiwar proper consider themselves to be descended from Khat, who was produced by Kurrun. Kurrun struck his rod on the ground, and out came Khat. The function of Khat was to steal certain cattle from Berat or Dholka. He afterwards married the daughter of an Ahir in the district of Powar, between Sind and Kutch. He had eight sons. His descendants seek their fortune and join the Charun who are doing the same. They reach the town of Dhauk, the chief of which was Walla Rajput, who marries one of their women, and becomes a Katti. From Walla come the Shakayut, or chief nobles; the other division consisting of the Urtia (Ourteea) or inferiors. The Katti then went to Kutch, moving thence under a leader who saw the sun and took advice from it, in a dream. They, then, came into their present occupancy which was (till then) held by Ahirs and Babrias. They expelled

The Babrias, who still give their name to Babriawar, a district on the sea-coast, south of Kattiwar proper, in which they are the chief inhabitants; poor, rude, predatory; less predatory now, however, than they have been. The Babrias are said to be the offspring of an Ahir with a Kuli woman. They intermarry with the Ahirs.

The Sidi of Muzuferabad, or *Jafarabad.*—Muzuferabad is the fort of Babriawar. The governor is always a Sidi, *i. e.* an African in blood, and a slave in origin. The details of the history by which they became independent sailors are unknown.

The Mher pretend to be Rajputs, their claim being doubtful. In every village belonging to the Rana of Purbunder there is a certain number of Mhers, who are charged with its defence. They are supported by grants of land. They breed horses and camels; the males of which they give to the Rana. They were formerly exempted from paying taxes; their personal services being all that the State required. At present, however, they are taxed—though lightly.

A portion of the Purbunder army, the militia, consists of these Rebharis and Mhers. A portion consists of foreign mercenaries, chiefly from Arabia and Mekran. So that

Arab and *Mekrani* elements are to be considered in the ethnology of western Gujerat.

The Mian occupants of the fortified town of Mallia, are said to have been introduced into the district of Muchukund from Waghur, having originally come from Sind. This may be a historical fact, or it may be a mere inference from the name. The Mian under notice are predatory Mahometans.

Of the Ahir and Rebhari notice has already been taken.

The Isthmus is more Bhíl and Kol than the Peninsula, the petty States of Dunduka, Runpur, and Gogo, being more especially Bhíl. In Dholka there is a considerable amount of Mahometanism.

The parts between the Suburmuti and the Mahi contain Kulis; the fewest of which are in Neriad, the most in Bijapur.

The parts between the Mahi and the Nerbudda are Bhíl and Rajput; Bhíl and Rajput, but not without Mahometan elements. Some of the districts belong to the Company, some to the Guikowar, some to Sindia's territory. Some are independent. Some are mere village chieftaincies.

The parts between the Nerbudda and Tapti are Bhíl; Bhíl and Rajput, but not without Mahometan elements. Rajpípla, to the north-east of Surat, is, pre-eminently, a Bhíl area. So are the more impracticable districts of the collectorate of Surat, or the parts between the Tapti and the Damaun Gunga; in which, however, we pass (as already stated) from the Gujerathi to the Maratta area.

As a rule, Kandeish is Bhíl, so that its details will be given when that population comes under notice.

CHAPTER XVIII.

Populations speaking either Hindí or a language akin to it.—The Rajput and Jut divisions.—Rajputana, Rajwarra, or Rajasthan.

Tod, who takes the Rajput districts as he found them when he wrote, gives the following boundaries,—

1. To the north—the sandy desert beyond Bikanir.
2. To the south—the Nerbudda.
3. To the west—the Mahometan districts on the Indus.
4. To the east—the river Sind, a feeder, from the south of the Ganges.

This gives us Bikanir, Jessulmir, Marwar, Mewar, Ajmir, Jeypúr, Búndi, Kotah, and Malwa, and other districts of less importance; altogether a very considerable portion of India.

It also leads us to ask the import of the word Rajput in its stricter sense. In any other country but a country of casts, like India, Rajputana would be a land of tribes; one or more of which possessed (or claimed) a superiority over the others. In India it is this, with the phenomena of cast superadded.

The highest tribual division seems to be a *kula*, word for word, the Afghan *kheil*. A *kula* contains so many *sachas*; a *sacha* so many *gotras*. The races are thirty-six in number, some being of solar, some of lunar, descent. The Rajputs of Mewar, as they exist at the present moment, are Rajputs of the Sísodía division; Sísodía being the name of a *sacha*. The *kula* to which it belongs is the Gehlot, or Grahilot—Suryavansi (Solar or Sun-born) in blood, and attached to the Lord of Chitor. Silladitya, the last prince of Gujni, leaves a posthumous son named Grahaditya, whence Grahilot, or Gehlot. In the sixth century this name is replaced by Ahar; the Aharya dynasty ruling in Chitor. Chitor, however, they leave in the twelfth century, under two brothers, Rahup and Mahup. Rahup settles in Dongurpur, where, at the present moment, his descendants, the Aharya Rajputs, are to be found. Meanwhile, Mahup fixes himself in Sísodía. All this seems to be mere logography. What, however, are the real facts? Out of the twenty-four *sachas* into which the Gehlot *kula* is divided, eight are "almost extinct," eleven are "small and obscure." In Dongurpur there are some Aharyas; in the Desert some Mangulías; in Marwar some Piparras; in Mewar the proud and powerful Sísodías. The following legend shows how mythologies degenerate. Colonel Tod, our authority, is speaking of a part of Mewar.

In these wilds an ancient Rana of Cheetore had sat down to a *gote* (feast), consisting of the game slain in the chase; and being very hungry, he hastily swallowed a piece of meat to which a gad-fly adhered. The fly grievously tormented the Rana's stomach, and he sent for a physician. The wise man (*bèd*) secretly ordered an attendant to cut off the tip of a cow's ear, as the only means of saving the monarch's life. On obtaining this forbidden morsel, the bèd folded it in a piece of thin cloth, and attaching a string to it, made the royal patient swallow it. The gad-fly fastened on the bait, and was dragged to light. The physician was rewarded; but the curious Rana insisted on knowing by what means the cure was effected; and when he heard that a piece of sacred kine had passed his lips, he determined to expiate the enormity in a manner which its heinousness required, and to swallow boiling lead (seesa)! A vessel was put on the fire, and the metal soon melted; when, praying that his involuntary offence might be forgiven, he boldly drank it off; but lo! it passed through him like water. From that day the name of the tribe was changed from Aharya to Seesodia.

Such is the Gehlot *kula*. That of the Agnicula is more complex. Before falling into *sachas* it divides itself into four primary branches—

1. The Pramara, with thirty-five *sachas;*
2. The Purihana;
3. The Chaluk, or Solankhi;
4. The Chohan.

To the Purihanas belong—

a. The Sodha;

b. The Sumra;

c. The Omutwarra families; all real—the two former being found in (or on the frontier of) Sind, the latter in a district so-called.

The Yadu *kula* stands in contrast with the Gehlot in being of Lunar rather than Solar origin. It contains—

The Bhattis of Jessulmír, amongst whom is a belief that their ancestors came from Zabulistan, a Turk district;

The Jareyas of Kutch;

The Yadu of Kerowli, a small State on the Chumbul;

The Sumaicha of Sind converted to Mahometanism.

The Rahtor *kula* contains twenty-four *sachas*. Its original occupancy was Canúj. It is at present a real and important dynasty in Marwar.

The Kutshwaha *kula* holds Amber or Jeypúr.

The Chohans, already mentioned as Agniculas (twenty-four *sachas*), rule in Bundi and Kotah. They also occupy parts of the Desert.

The Chaluks held Bhagelkund.

The Chawura or Chaura are in Gujerat. They are neither Lunar nor Solar.

All these are real families, whose pedigrees and pretensions are, in the latter part of their so-called annals, historical. Others, however, are, evidently, either fictitious or false. There is a *kula* called *Hun*, of which all we know is that *Hun* is what it is called.

There is a *kula* called Jit. This, however, is neither more nor less than the denomination of that widely-spread group of tribes which has already been noticed.

Nearest to Sind and the Punjab lies

Jessulmír, a true Rajput district, the Rajputs being of the Bhat section. The cultivators, however, are, as is expected, Jut.

Bikanir, Jut and Rajput, differs from Jessulmír chiefly in the real or supposed origin of its nobles, the Rajputs of Bikanir being Rahtors from Marwar, who entered the country under a chief named Bika; whence the name Bikanír.

Bhutnair, on the northern frontier of Bikanír, is, probably, one of the more especially Turanian parts of India. It lies on the road from the Indus to the Ganges, and, as such, is likely to have been important in the eyes of the invaders. A little to the east stands Hissar, Turk in name. The opponent of the earlier Rajputs was Chugti (Tshagatai) Khan.

In the notices of the wars of the Jessulmír frontier the name Barahi continually occurs. Word for word, this is Brahúi.

The Pokurna Brahmins of these parts are of suspicious purity. The bridegroom buys his bride, Turk fashion. The horse has amongst the Pokurnas undue and un-Indian importance. The bridle is an object of real or feigned respect. So is a pickaxe; for the Pokurna Brahmins are said to have earned their rank by digging the great Pokurna reservoir.

Marwar.—From Bikanír Bhutnair—from Marwar Bikanír—this is the order of invasion. Bika was a Rahtor Rajput of Marwar. Like all the countries already mentioned, Marwar is, more or less, Jut. But this it may be without being other than Hindu. It is, however, something more than Jut. It is Maruwâr, Marústhan, or Marudesa—not the country of Death (as has been argued), but the country of the Mairs.

In the thirteenth century, *i. e.* A.D. 1212, eighteen years after leaving Canúj (mark the multiples of six), Seoji and Saitram, Rahtor Rajputs, invaded the country of the Gohillas and other Hindu populations, occupants of the valley of the Lúny; occupants, too, of the western skirts of the Aravulli, but not occupants of the range itself. There were Brahmins amongst them, *e. g.* the Palla Brahmins, who invoked the aid of the strangers against certain Mair tribes of the contiguous hills. The help was given. Land was appropriated. The original Brahmins were made uncomfortable in a land once their own. Others, too, besides them, got oppressed and ejected; so that, in the course of time, the district of Marwar became Rajput. Mundore first, and afterwards Jodpur, were founded as capitals.

The most numerous of the inhabitants of Marwar are the Juts. Colonel Tod considered that they formed about five-eighths of the population, the Rajputs forming two-eighths. The chief Brahmins are of the Sanchora class.

Amber or *Jeipur.*—Mewar, like Marwar, is Jut and Rajput. Mewar, like Marwar, is, more or less, other than Hindu. The Minas are to Mewar as the Mairs are to Marwar.

Beyond the Chumbul, the pure Rajput character is less prominent. Beyond the Chumbul, there has been contact with either the Gonds or a population akin to them. There has, also, been the Brahminism of the north bank of the Ganges. There has, also, been the subsequent intrusion of the Mahrattas. This excludes the parts about Gwalior (Sindia's territory), and Bundelcund, from the Rajputana of Tod, though, in many respects, they are truly Rajput.

Bhurtpur and *Dholpur* are Jaut.

Bhopal.—Partly on the drainage of the Ganges and partly on that of the Indus, Bhopal is, more or less, a watershed; and as it is in physical geography so is it in ethnology. It is Hindu and Gond; so much so, that I find the statement that the boundary between Gondwana and Malwa ran through the metropolis; one gate belonging to one district, the other to the other. Some part of the population of the hillier districts is Gond at this moment. The bulk is Hindu; but the Nawaub is a Mahometan of Afghan blood, and so are many of his subjects.

Rewas (*Bagelcund*).—That the Rajputs extended thus far is a matter of history. The soil, however, is essentially and originally Gond.

Malwa is Rajput in the north, Bhíl and Mahratta on the south.

CHAPTER XIX.

Populations speaking either Hindí, or a language akin to it.—Delhi, Allahabad, Bahar, Bengal, Orissa.

Bikanír and Bhutnair are Rajput. In the parts, however, to the north a change takes place,—a change both in way of ethnology and physical geography. The limits of the Sandy Desert are passed, and the distance between the drainages of the Ganges and the Sutlej decreases. The foot, too, of the Sub-himalayan hills is approached. The watershed, however, between the two great rivers is insignificant.

The political geography is complicated. To the south lies the frontier of the Rajput country; to the north the territory of the Raja of Bisahur; to the north-west the Sikh frontier; to the south-west Delhi; in the centre the small Rajaships of Puttiala, &c.

With the district in question begins Gangetic Hindostan, as opposed to the India of the Desert and the Indus. The distance from Afghanistan, Biluchistan, and the Paropamisus, has increased. Bahar and Bengal are approached.

The district is important in the way of history. It is the point towards which so many of the invaders of India made their way. It was at Paniput where the decisive battle between the Mahrattas and the Patans was fought. It was in the parts about Thanesar that the army of Mahmud of Ghuzni was met by the army of Anungpal of Jeypur.

The name Hissar points to a Turk, the name Hurriana to an Iranian, occupancy.

More than this, the two small, but famous rivers, the Sersúti and the Caggar, find their channels in the sands of Hurriana; the Sersúti being, word for word, the Seraswati, and the Caggar being identified with the Drishadwati; these in their turn being the rivers upon which the Institutes of Menu place the first occupancy of the Brahmins, or Brahmaverta. The sacro-sanctitude of rivers (impossible in the Desert and kept within moderate limits on the water-system of the Indus,) now becomes conspicuous. The Ganges throughout its course is holy. Its feeders to the north are holy also. They are holy in the eyes of both the Hindu and the Bhot. Was it not said, when the Kooch, Bodo, and Dhimal were under notice, that the Pantheon of those semi-pagan populations consisted in the deities of the streams and streamlets of their irriguous countries? And will it not be seen, when we come to Oud, that, at the present moment, both Mahometans and Hindus believe that to swear by a river is to take the most binding of oaths?

That a natural group begins in these parts is true. And it is also true that it is pre-eminently Brahminic. In no part of India do the members of the holy class bear so great a proportion to the rest of the population as in the districts about to be noticed. At the same time no decided line can be drawn. Still less can Rajput blood and Rajput modes of thought be excluded. In many respects Oud is one of the most Rajput countries of India. It is the seat of the great Solar and Lunar dynasties. What the Sersúti district is in Menu, that is Oud in the Ramayana.

Neither must a great amount of Mahometanism be

ignored. Though no portion of the present area be Mahometan after the fashion of Sind, the fact of Delhi having been the metropolis of the Great Mogul is important.

To recapitulate—

In the eyes of the author of the Institutes the parts about the Seraswati were the first occupancies of the Brahmin.

In the eyes of the military critic they are the parts for which a foreign army would, most especially, make its way.

In the eyes of the actual historian they are the localities of the first Turk and Mongol occupancies.

What all this points to is evident. The parts about the Sersúti are the terminus of the high road to India, and beyond the Sersúti the pre-eminently Indian parts of India begin.

The district, however, which first comes under notice is somewhat exceptional.

Rohilcund.—The name is Hindu, the area to which it applies Hindu and Afghan. Roh, in the Punjabi dialect, means a hilly district, and denotes the eastern frontier of the Biluch and Patan countries. The western boundary of Dera Ghazi Khan is called Roh. The Rohillas, then, of Rohilcund are Patans or Afghans. The settlement was made in the beginning of the last century. At the present time the majority of the population of Bareilly (and perhaps of the country round) is Mahometan rather than Brahminic.

Canúj.—Less important, at the present moment, than Delhi, Agra, Allahabad, and the other great cities of the Doab, Canúj claims attention from its antiquity, and from the name it gives to the chief division of the Brahminical cast. Before the Ghuznevid conquest, it was the metropolis of a large empire, which the Rahtor Rajputs believe to have belonged to their ancestors. The Canúj (Canacubya), Brahmins and the Ujein Rajputs are the noblest divisions of their respective classes.

Oud.—Brahminic, Rajput, and Mahometan, Oud, along its northern frontier, is Sub-himalayan, *i. e.* it touches Nepal. Whether there are Bhot elements in Oud will be considered in the sequel.

Bahar.—Bahar, or the kingdom of Magada, is the mother-country of the language of the Buddhist scriptures—the Pali. In (say) the seventh eentury, or the time when the Chinese traveller Hiouen Thsang visited India, Buddhism was, if not the dominant creed, at least, on a par with Brahminism. At the present time, Bahar is one of the least Buddhist parts of Hindostan.

In north Behar Bhot elements present themselves.

In Delhi, in Agra, and in Allahabad, the language is Hindí; being spoken in the greatest purity about Agra. In Bahar it changes character. Still it is Hindí rather than Bengali.

Bengal.—The Bengali form of speech belongs to the provinces from which it takes its name, from which it has extended itself both into Asam and Arakan; where it has encroached upon the Burmese and Tibetan. That it is bounded on the north by the Kooch, Bodo, Dhimal, Garo, Aka, Abor, Dofla, and other dialects, has already been suggested in the notice of those tribes. In Sylhet and Tippera the Bengali is similarly intrusive.

From the number of individuals by whom it is spoken, and from its geographical contiguity to the Indo-gangetic peninsula, the Bengali is, perhaps, the most important of Indian languages.

In the district of Midnapúr, it is succeeded by

The Uriya of Orissa, into which some of its dialects are believed to graduate. To the back of the Uriya area lie the Khond, to the south the Telinga, districts, the latter of which begins at Ganjam. At Baurwah, however, to the south of that town, the Uriya re-appears. At the same time, it is pronounced Telinga-fashion; in other words, *d* replaces *r*, and U*r*iya and Ge*r*h, become U*d*iya and Ga*d*da.

Of all the forms of speech akin to the Hindí the Uriya is most unimportant. It is spoken but by few individuals. It is but slightly cultivated. The work that has the most pretensions to originality is a poem on the conquest of Conjeveram. The rest of the literature consists of translations.

Of Bengal, Gour was the capital, and it is believed to have been the capital of an important empire; of an empire which spread itself, both towards the north and towards the east: towards the east most especially—Asam being conquered from Bengal. From Bengal, also, must have spread the Brahminism of Munipúr and Arakan.

Of Orissa the political influence has been but slight.

In the way of physical form, it may safely be said that the best features and the stoutest limbs are to be found within the area of the Hindí dialects. This means that the men of Oud, Allahabad, &c., are better-made than those of Bengal. Oud, however, and Allahabad, &c., lie higher up the river. That the muscular power of the Bengalis is but slight is generally, if not universally, stated; indeed, extreme effeminacy, both in the way of their *physique* and *morale*, is attributed to them. In the *turai* this attains its *maximum*. In the *turai*, however, there is a difference of blood. This may or may not exist in the sunderbunds; which are inhabited by but few occupants, and those unhealthy; sufferers from fever, sufferers from ague, sufferers from dysentery, sufferers from cutaneous disorders.

According to Stirling the men and women of Orissa are even inferior to the Bengalis.

Of both we may say, with safety, that the language is Indian. Of neither can we safely say that the blood and language coincide. The lower Ganges but just separates the northernmost members of the Tamul, from the southernmost members of the Bhot, stock. There are the Kols and Sontals in the Rajmahal hills. There are some miserable undersized Sontals in the jungles of Midnapúr. They are tribes denominated impure in Dinajpur, the district in which stood the ancient Gour metropolis. There is a tract in Purnía called Gondwara. In the Mechpara districts of Rungpur there are both Bodos and Garos. Surely, then, there is a mixture of blood in both Bengal and Orissa; and that mixture is three-fold.

In Bengal, too, and in Orissa, the military element (by which I mean that cast which has elsewhere been called Rajput and Kshetriya) notably decreases. There are Brahmins in both districts; and these numerous. There are Sudras; who are numerous also. There are mixed classes and impure classes—numerous as well. But the analogues to the Rajputs are few. The nearest approach to them is in what is called the militia of Orissa; wherein the landowners take the appearance of petty feudalists, aud can call into the field a certain number of armed followers. It is, however, specially stated, that the blood of these fighting-men is mixed; some being of Telinga, some of Mahratta, some of Afghan, some of Khond origin.

English.	Bengali.	Asam.	Uriya.
Man	manushya	manuh	minipo
Tooth	danta	dant	danto
Head	mastak	mur	motha
Hair	kesh	——	halo
——	chul	suli	——
Mouth	mukh	mukh	muho
Eye	chhakhyuh	soku	akhi
Ear	karna	kan	kan
Hand	hát	hát	hato
Foot	had	bhori	goro
Blood	rakta	tez	rokto
Day	din	din	dino
Night	ratri	rati	ratc
Sun	surjya	beli	surjiyo
Moon	chandra	jun	chando
Star	tara	tora	tora
Fire	agni	jui	nina
Water	pani	pani	pani
Stone	prastan	hil	pothoro
Tree	gachh	gosh	gochcho.

Bundelcund and *Sindia's country*.—Of the districts to the south of the Ganges, between the proper Rajput country on the west, Orissa and Bengal on the east, and Gondwana on the south, I say but little. Sindia's country and Bundelcund are the most important of them. Their ethnological character is mixed; the elements being what we expect from their geographical relations. To the north lie the southern portions of the Doab, Allahabad, and Bahar; to the south and east decided Gond districts; to the west a region as decidedly Rajput. Such being the case, it is safe to say thus much—that

1. The parts to the west of the Chumbul are chiefly Rajput with superinduced Mahratta elements;

2. The parts to the east of the Soane are chiefly Kol;

3. The actual valley of the Ganges is in the same category with the districts on the opposite side;

4. The Gondwana and Mahratta frontiers are, more or less, Mahratta and Gond.

The language is an outlying form of the Hindí: the creed Brahminic. The Jains, however, begin to show themselves; increasing in numbers and importance as we move towards the south and south-west; being numerous in Central India, numerous in the Mahratta countries, and pre-eminently numerous in the area of the Tulava language on the Mahratta and Canarese frontiers.

CHAPTER XX.

Populations whose language is either Hindí or akin to it.—The Sub-himalayans.

THIS division is, by no means, wholly natural. It contains the northern members of the two last sections. A Punjabi, on the edge of Tibet, is still, in most respects, a Punjabi. A Bengali on the frontier of Butan is, in most respects, still a Bengali. We cannot even say that the physical conditions of its area are uniform. That the range of the Himalaya is a mountain-range is true; but it is not true that the soil and climate of its slope are the same throughout. The high levels at the head-waters of the five rivers are one thing. The jungles of the parts above the lower Ganges are another.

The real character of the class lies in the nature of its ethnological frontier. From Cashmír to Upper Asam the populations with which the Hindu comes in juxtaposition, are Tibetan, Bhot, or Burmese. The phenomena of the line of contact justify the formation of the present class; a class which for the purposes of investigation is, to say the least of it, eminently convenient.

The general history of the populations under notice is, for the western portion of their area at least, just what we expect, *à priori*, from the face of the country. The face of the country is like that of Little Tibet—so many valleys—so many lords of the valley. We begin with a mass of petty Rajaships. By conquest or intermarriage they become confluent, and two or three smaller form one larger one. Eventually they get absorbed by the powers of their neighbourhood.

In the way, Kistewar, Hanur, &c., between Cashmír and the Sutlej, belong to Gulab Sing's dominion; whilst Gurwhal is divided between Great Britain and the Raja of Bisihur. Kumaon is wholly British; the parts to the east of Kumaon, Nepalese.

As a general rule, the blood of the Rajas and their descendants is either actually Rajput, or believed to be so. The creed, too, is, as a general rule, Brahminic. There is, however, something Sikh in the western and something Buddhist in the eastern districts.

Where both the physical conformation and the language are Bhot, we have, of course, an actual Tibetan or Nepalese. Where one only of these characteristics occurs, we have a possible one. Where, both being absent, we have Tibetan customs, Tibetan superstitions, or Tibetan names of plàces, we have the elements of an interesting investigation. That these *do* occur is a fact. I am unable, however, to give the details. Captain Cunningham finds Tibetan names beyond the limit of the existing Tibetan localities. Most writers have noticed instances of the Tibetan practice of polyandria in Kistewar, Sirmor, &c.

From Cashmír to the Sutlej, the frontier with which the Hindu area comes in contact is Ladaki—*i. e.* it is Ladakh, rather than Tibet proper, which overlies the hill-country belonging to Gholab Sing.

The Rajaship of Bisihur touches Kunawer and Hungrung.

Kumaon (which is British), and the forty-six Rajaships (which are Nepalese), underlie Tibet proper.

In eastern Nepal, in Sikkim, and in the parts beyond, lie,

between the Hindus and the Tibetans, an intermediate series of minor populations, Magar, Gurung, and the like. It is not necessary to give the details and order of these. It has been done already.

From Kumaon to Nepal proper, the language (a variety of the Hindí) is called *Khas*. In Nepal proper it is called *Parbatiya* or *Purbutti, i. e.* the *Highland* form of speech.

Kumaon.—Kumaon, being British, is known, in detail, through an elaborate report by Traill. In the northern districts the people are strong, but short, stout-built, and fair-skinned. In the south the colour is darker, the stature greater, the form more spare. In the intermediate districts the type is also intermediate.

Spirits, as a stimulus, are commoner in Gurwhal than in Kumaon. In both provinces tobacco is smoked by all but the high-class Brahmins, who substitute for it the inspissated juice of the hemp.

The Hinduism of Kumaon is of that imperfect kind, which leaves room for innumerable vestiges of the original paganism to show themselves. Every village has its own especial deity, and, humbler than the Hindu temples (but not less venerated) their shrines are found over the whole country. The region, too, of spirits is both wide and populous. The individual who has died a violent death may revisit the earth as a *Bhút*, to haunt his posterity through many generations, and to be appeased by sacrifices and offerings. The bachelor who, without getting married, dies at an advanced age, becomes a will-of-the-wisp, or *Tola*, whose society is shunned even by his brother spirits; for which reason he is only seen in lone places. The ghosts of men killed in hunting haunt the forests in which their deaths occurred, and these are *Airi*. To hear the voice of an Airi (and it may be heard hallooing to its dogs) is to become obnoxious to some future misfortune. The *Masán* are the ghosts of young children, buried instead of being burnt. The Masán haunt villages in the shape of wild animals. The Acheri are the ghosts of young children also; but of females. They it is who love the lonely mountain-top, better than the inhabited village—but only during the daytime. At dusk they descend to hold revel. To meet with a train of Acheri is death. Neither is it safe to cross the spots where the revels are usually held, even in the daytime, and when they are not there. The intruder may get molested; especially if she be a female, or wear any red in her dress; for red is the colour that the Acheri most especially dislike. Numerous optical phenomena that present themselves under certain atmospheric conditions, in mountainous countries, are attributed to the Acheri.

The village-gods are, in name at least, Hindu. Some of these are obnoxious to men, some to women, some to children, some to cattle. Ruma, one of them, moves from place to place riding on a rock, never molesting men, but by no means sparing females. Should he take a fancy to one her fate is fixed. She will be haunted by him in her dreams, pine and die.

The *Bogsa* is a sorcerer, endued with the property of becoming a wild beast at will. Lycanthropia, then, or its analogue, is a Kumaon superstition; as is the belief in the evil eye.

Kumaon, though now British, is an acquisition from Nepal; so that, in reference to its political history, it must be looked upon as a portion of the

Nepalese Empire.—This falls into two extremely natural divisions; a western and an eastern. The former, originally containing Kumaon, now contains what may be called the districts of the forty-six Rajaships.

I speak of forty-six Rajaships. The reader, however, will find more than forty-six names. This is because the exact details of the nomenclature are not known. The number, however, is forty-six.

I shall also speak of these forty-six petty Rajaships being divided into two primary groups; one containing twenty-two, the other twenty-four, districts. Here, however, as before, there will be some unimportant uncertainties as to the distribution. The majority will belong decidedly and undoubtedly to one of the two divisions. For the parts, however, where they meet there will be a few doubtful, or equivocal, names.

The twenty-two will be called, as they are in many maps, the Baisi; the twenty-four, the Chaubisi, Rajas.

Of the two divisions, the Baisi is more western. It begins when we leave Kumaon for Nepal. The Chaubisi group extends from the eastern frontier of the Baisi to the parts about Kathmandu, or Nepal proper; Nepal in the limited sense of the term; Nepal, the occupancy of the Newar.

The list is as follows:—the Rajaships being taken in their order from west to east. Those at the beginning of the list are most undoubtedly Baisi, those at the end most undoubtedly Chaubisi. The doubtful ones are those of the middle.

Baisi and Chaubisi Rajaships.

1. Yumila
2. Acham
3. Duti
4. Cham
5. Dipal
6. Chhinachin
7. Jajarkot
8. Bangpai
9. Rughun
10. Muiskot
11. Satatala
12. Malaneta
13. Dang
14. Salyana
15. Palabang
16. Khungri
17. Bingri
18. Piutana
19. Gajal
20. Jahari
21. Bilaspur

22. Roalpa
23. Malebum
24. Kalagong Ghurikot
25. Balihang
26. Gutum
27. Dharma
28. Galkot
29. Isma
30. Durkot
31. Argha
32. Kachi
33. Gulmi
34. Palpa
35. Garahang
36. Poin
37. Satahung
38. Birkot
39. Nayakot
40. Kaski
41. Dhor
42. Gajarkot
43. Rising
44. Ghiring
45. Tanahung
46. Lamjun
47. Tarki
48. Musikot
49. Gorka.

Of these the most important are, Malebum, Yumila, and Gorka. Malebum belongs to the debateable land between the two divisions. The Raja of Yumila was a sort of Kaiser, or emperor, to the rest. They all, or nearly all, acknowledged his supremacy. They took from him the *tika*, or mark of authority. They allowed him to interfere in their private quarrels when the balance of power was endangered. On the other hand, they yielded as much actual obedience as their inclinations, regulated by their power of resistance, prompted. Still, the Raja of Yumila was the Raja paramount. Besides admitting the supremacy of a head, the chiefs formed amongst themselves subordinate confederations. Thus; Lamjun marched with Tanahung and Kaski; Tanahung being followed by Dhor, and Kaski by Satahung. Birkot, in like manner, headed Garahang, Poin, and Nayakot. And so acted others towards others. There was a league called Athabhai, or the eight, another called Satbhai, or the seven, brothers. The brotherhood, in these cases, might be real or imaginary.

In regard to its constituent population, the Rajaship of Yumila is the most Bhot, about one-fourth being Hindu, and three-fourths Tibetan.

Yumila, so far as it is other than Hindu, seems to be, to a great extent, Tibetan.

Malebum, so far as it is other than Hindu, seems to be, to a great extent, Gurung.

In Malebum, however, we find the name Jareya; it being believed that an impure chief of that name had once great power in Malebum. His daughter married a Gautamiya (Buddhist) Brahmin, by whom she had twenty-two sons, *i. e.* the twenty-two Rajas of the Baisi group.

The term Jareya points to Rajasthan; indeed, Rajput blood (either real or pretended) still continues to be the rule.

In the ordinary maps Malebum is the most conspicuous name for these parts. It is, in reality, the name of the State, which, until the rise of the Gorka dynasty, was the head of the forty-six Rajaships.

As Malebum and Yumila rose at the expense of the petty States around them, Gorkha rose at the expense of Malebum and Yumila.

Gorkha, so far as it was other than Hindu, seems to have been chiefly Magar. The details of its history, as a sovereign dynasty, are given by both Hamilton and Kirkpatrick.

Of the Hindus of Nepal, the blood seems to be, for the most part, either Rajput or Brahminic. The descendants of a Brahmin father and a native mother take high rank in Nepal. Lower than their fathers, higher than their mothers, they take the rank of Kshetriya; bear the title of the father and wear the thread.

The Khas fall into divisions, being Thâpa, Bishnyat, Bhandari, Karki, Khânkâ, Adhikari, Bisht, Kunwar, Baníah, and the like. They fall, too, into sub-divisions, *e. g.* the

Bagyal	Gagliya
Takuryal	Suyal
Palami	Maharaji
Laminchanya	Khulal
Powar	Sunyal
Ghimirya	Khapotari
Gudar	Parajuli

Deoja

are members of the Thâpa.

Akin to the Khas, yet differing in the real or supposed details of their origin (inasmuch as their fathers were Kshetriyas rather than Brahmins, and their mothers Hindu rather than Nepalese), the Ekthariah fall into the

Buratlioki	Bohara
Raya	Chiloti
Ravat	Dangi
Katwal	Raimarjhi
Khati	Bhukhandi
Maghati	Bhusal
Chohan	Khutal
Boghati	Dikshit
Khatil	Pandit
Bavan	Parsai
Mahat	Chokhal
Barwal	Chohara

Durrah

sections; differing only in the details of their origin from the Thakuri, whose blood is royal, their ancestors having been the dynasts of some petty principality. The divisions of the Thakuri are—

Sahi	Sena
Malla	Singh

Maun	Hamal
Chohan	Ruchal
Chand	Jiva

Rakshya.

These details will not have been superfluous if we allow them to stand as a sample of the division and subdivision, which both the soil and the social system undergo in countries like Nepal—where the systems of both cast and tribe meet, and where the physical geography gives us hills and valleys.

Populations of doubtful or equivocal position.—The difficulties of determining the exact details of the Indian and Bhot (or Nepalese) frontier have already suggested themselves. Sometimes there is the loss of some notable characteristic, such as creed or language. Sometimes there is an actual intermixture of blood. Physical form, our best guide, is by no means, infallible. A Bhot from the higher Himalayas is, undoubtedly, a different being from a Rajput or Brahmin. But who will say that a Bhot from the jungles or the *turai* is the same, in skin and feature, as his congener from the snow-levels, or that he is so very different from the Kol, or Khond ? Our best authority, on these matters, Mr. Hodgson—zoologist and physiologist, as well as philologue—by no means commits himself to any very trenchant lines of demarcation ; indeed, he has, on one occasion, shown great and laudable candour in admitting that a certain language belonged to the Bhot group, whereas the physical conformation of the men who spoke it had been previously described by him as Tamul.

Beginning at the Sutlej, and moving eastwards, we find the following populations belonging to the class under notice. To each and all of them the following questions apply—Are they in the same category with the lower class

Hindus? Or are they in the same category with the Chepang, Dhimal, and Bodo tribes? Or are they a *tertium quid?*

Chumars.—These have already been noticed. They occupy parts of Kunawer; and (Bhot fashion) practise polyandria.

Domangs.—In the same districts as the Chumars. Word for word, Domang is

Dom.—The Doms of Kumaon have already been noticed. So have the

Rawat of the same country.

The Tharu.—These are the occupants of the *turai,* or belt of forest at the foot of the Himalayas. The Tharu first show themselves in Oud, and extend far eastwards.

In the western half of Nepal, and on the alluvia of the rivers which form the Gunduk, lie

1. The Denwar
2. — Durri
3. The Kumhal
4. — Manjhi
5. The Bramho.

These have been described by Mr. Hodgson as dark-skinned, light-limbed, oval-faced, and high-featured men; more like the Khonds than the Tibetans or Nepalese. They consider themselves Hindus; and belong chiefly to the Magar frontier.

Further to the east, where the Nepalese populations are Murmi, Limbu, and Kirata, and where the Hindus are the Hindus of north Bahar, lie (along with certain Tharus, whom they resemble) the

Gangai, chiefly in Morang; the

Bhawar, an impure tribe, once dominant; the

Batar, and the

Aniwar, once extended far beyond the frontier of Bahar. The

Rajbansi Kooch have already been noticed. They are succeeded by the Dhimal, Bodo, and Gharo; congeners of whom must originally have extended to the Ganges, or even beyond it. It is with Bengalis, on one side, and the Lepchas and Lhopa, on the other, that these most especially come in contact.

That the whole of Asam, even where the language is Bengali, and the creed Brahminic, is Bhot or Burmese in blood, has already been stated.

The heterogeneous character of the tribe and cast names of Nepal requires a special analysis. The lists given above are only a few out of many. What is general, what special; what natural, what artificial, should be distinguished.

CHAPTER XXI.

The Mahrattas.

THE present section is pre-eminently a natural one; differing, in many significant respects, from all the preceding. In the first place, the Mahrattas are the most southern members of the group to which they belong. In the next, they belong to a broken, if not a mountainous, country. Deserts like those of Bikanir, alluvia like those of the Gangetic districts, find no place within the Mahratta area. At the same time, none of its levels are so high as the mountain-basin of Cashmír.

Again, the Mahratta country faces the sea; the sea that connects India with Persia, Arabia, Africa, and Europe. It will, therefore, not surprise us if we find African and Mahratta elements in contact.

The main *differentiæ,* however, lie in the relations of the Mahrattas to the populations whose language is akin to the Tamul. Up to the present time, the northernmost members of this class appear as intruders upon the proper Hindu areas. That they are not this we reasonably infer; the inference being that the intrusion has been on the other side. It was the Bhíls and Kols who were the aborigines, the Rajputs and their congeners who were the strangers. At the same time, as the map now stands, the Kol and Bhíl districts take the appearance of exceptional prolongations from the south. Their occupancies indent the Hindu and Gujerathi frontiers. They only, however, indent them.

Now, instead of merely indenting the Mahratta districts, the aboriginal localities surround them. There are both Bhíls and Kols to the north of the northernmost Mahrattas. There are Kols in Gujerat, and there are Bhíls in Rajputana. There were Bhíls, indeed, on the very edge of the valley of the Indus. That in some cases the Mahratta language comes in direct contact with both the Hindí and the Gujerathi, is true. But it is also true that, as a general rule, its northern frontier is Bhíl and Kol, its eastern, Gond and Telinga, its southern, Tulava and Canarese.

The physical form of a Mahratta is most usually contrasted with that of the Brahmin and the Rajput; by the side of which it shows to disadvantage. As a general rule, writes Elphinstone, the lowest of the Rajputs wear an air of dignity. As a general rule, the highest of the Mahrattas comports himself meanly. The latter, however, are hardy and active, and, if somewhat undersized, well-proportioned. Their skins are dark, and their features irregular. The best commentary, however, upon their physical and moral constitution is their history.

They are Sudras (so-called) rather than either Kshetriyas or Brahmins. The fact of their being so has, perhaps, disparaged their personal appearance. They should be compared, not with the Rajputs and Brahmins, but with the lower casts in general of the rest of India.

Their language is, undoubtedly, in the same category with the Hindí, whatever that may be, *i. e.* its affinities are with the Gujerathi and Bengali, rather than with the Tamul and Telinga. It is, however, a somewhat outlying member of the class; so much so, that, in the hands of those writers who deny the Sanskrit origin of the group in question, the Mahratta has been the chief instrument of criticism. "The others are what the Mahratta is; and the Mahratta is more Tamul than Sanskrit." Such is the train of reasoning.

The alphabet is a derivation from the Devanagari, which it closely resembles. It does this because it has been but recently adopted. The literature it embodies is unimportant.

The historical area of the Mahrattas is far wider than the ethnological. Its extension, however, is recent. It began in the reigns of Shah Jehan and Aurungzeb, being founded by Sivaji, whose blood seems to have been mixed, *i. e.* Rajput as well as Mahratta. He was the son of Shahji, who was the son of Maloji, who was the son of Bapji, who was the husband of a lady of the very respectable Mahratta family of the Bhonslay. Maloji entered the service of a chief who, though, perhaps, in fact a simple Mahratta, had fair pretensions to some Rajput blood. At any rate, he bore himself as a man who is, at once, proud and practical. When Shahji, a child, was presented to him, his own daughter (a child also) was also in his presence. "What a fine couple they would make," was his observation—heard by Maloji, and hoarded-up in the treasure-house of his memory until some years had passed, and a public occasion brought him before his chief, and gave him an opportunity of reminding him of what he called a betrothal of his (the chief's) daughter to his (Shahji's) son. As Shahji had risen in the world, his version of the story was admitted, the marriage was effected, and Sivaji, the most prominent hero of all India, was the offspring. If the details of his career are withheld from the reader, it is not because they are foreign to ethnology. The biography of the representative men of the ruder portions of mankind is pre-eminently an ethnological subject. The life, however, of Sivaji belongs to Indian history in general. In the way, however, of extending the political power of his nation, his father did a little before him. He carried it southwards. In the service of, and (perhaps) second in command to, the Raja of Bejapúr, he received a grant of land and power in the Carnatic. This brought him to the parts about Madras, where the Polygar of Mudkul was at war with the Raja of Tanjore. Shahji joined the former, helping him to conquer his opponent; quarrelled with him about the spoils; defeated him; so that the descendants of Shahji were Rajas of Tanjore when that district became a British dependency. Sivaji himself turned his sword northwards. At first the captain of an organized body of banditti, then the zemindar of Punah, then a self-imposed potentate to the districts of his immediate neighbourhood, he is invited by Aurungzeb to join him in the war against his brothers. He plays his own game, however, and refuses to connect his fortunes with those of the imperial bigot; of whom, however, it was his future fate to hear and see more than enough. He plays his own game; with the Raja of Bejapúr as his first opponent. From him he wins more than one valuable fortress. He, then, takes the important towns of Kalian and Surat, extending his power to the sea. An Indian navy is first heard of in the days of Sivaji. It is, however, employed against him. We shall notice it in the sequel, when the sub-African districts of the western coast of India come under notice; when the Sidis of Abyssinian blood appear as elements of the heterogeneous population of Hindostan. The eventful life, however, of Sivaji draws towards its close, and he dies master of the whole of the Konkan, and of a large block of territory in the interior. This he leaves in a strong position, and in an aggressive attitude; fresh and full of vigour, and (as such) strongly contrasted with the decrepit empire of the Moguls. It was eminently a Hindu rather than a Mahometan organization.

The Mogul empire is breaking up. It has strength enough to reduce the kingdoms of Bejapúr and Hyderabad; but not strength enough to defend them against the Mahrattas. Neither are the southern districts of the Rajput country free from the Mahratta inroads. Berar on the Gond, and Kandeish on the Bhíl country, are plundered. Meanwhile, the districts of Aurungabad, Beder, and parts of Berar, are consolidated by the Nizam-ud-Mulk into a kingdom destined to retain the title of the founder, but not destined to be held by his successors. The dominion of the Nizam will become Mahratta. The founder, however, of the name was a Turk, Kulich Khan, son of Ghazi-ud-Khan. The Turks, who had been introduced into India by the conquest of Baber, were simply Moguls. The Turks who, from time to time, were introduced as mercenaries, were distinguished as Turani (or Turanian) Moguls. Kulich Khan was the chief o the Turani Moguls of the Dekkan. He effects the sepa ration of the Nizam districts from the empire. He fails to keep them free from the Mahrattas, who, about the same time, conquer Gujerat.*

The empire grows weaker and weaker. Delhi is sacked by Kuli-Khan. A.D. 1732.

A few years later the power of the Rohilla Afghans is established in the immediate neighbourhood of the capital, and Rohilcund becomes the seat of disturbance and the source of danger. A.D. 1745-47. Indeed, the Afghan aggressions have a double origin, Rohilcund and Afghanistan itself. The Durani dynasty is rising in power; and the two representatives of the Patan name unite in hostility to the Moguls. The weakest of the successors of Akbar calls in the treacherous aid of the Mahrattas, who now find their way to the parts beyond the Ganges, to Allahabad, to Delhi, to Oud. They make common cause with the Rohillas: quarrel with them; make common cause again. Still they are essentially antagonistic to the Duranis. The latter win the great battle of Paniput; with which ends the history of the Mogul India.

A.D. 1760.

The area of the Mahratta language extends along the coast from the Damaun Gunga river to Goa—there or thereabouts. In the interior, however, it is spoken somewhat further to the north—indenting the Gujerat area, upon which it seems to have encroached. Eastward it extends into Hyderabad and Berar, where it comes in contact with the Gond and Telinga. Southward it is bounded by the Tulava and Canarese.

The Mahratta blood must be, to a great extent, Bhíl.

The Mahratta creed is, to a great extent, Jain.

The foreign settlements ou the Mahratta area are numerous. These are chiefly

Parsi, as in Gujerat.

African, as in Cambay and Jinjira.

The Africans of these parts agreeing with those of Sind, in being called Sidi,* are, in other respects, very different. They are not only free but dominant. In the time of Aurungzeb, the admiral of the fleet was a Sidi.

Jewish.—In Kolaba.

Portugueze, chiefly in Sawuntwara, and the parts about Goa.

In the way of politics, the Mahratta area is very variously distributed. It contains several petty (very petty) independent States. The greater part of Portugueze India is Mahratta.

* Also Hubshesh.

The Guicowar, Sindia, and Holcar territories, are the same.

Specimen of the language.

English.	Marathi.	Gujerathi.	Hindostani.
Man (homo)	manúsh	jana	ādmi
—— *(vir)*	purush	mānus	mard
Woman	baiko	bāyadī	randī
Head	doksheh	māthum	sir
Hair	kes	nimālo	bāl
Eye	doleh	ānkh	ānkh
Ear	kan	kān	kān
Nose	nakh	nāk	nak
Mouth	t'hond	mohodum	munh
Tongue	jib	jubh	jībh
Tooth	dant	dānt	dānt
Hand	hat	hāth	hāth
Foot	paie	pag	pānw
Sun	suria	sūraj	sūraj
Moon	tshundr	chānd	chānd
Star	tshandaní	tāro	tārā
Day	vuas	din	din
Night	ratr	rāt	rāt
Fire	vistú	āg	āg
Water	panni	pānī	pānī
Tree	dzad	jhāda	per
——	bruksh	——	——
Stone	duggud	patthar	patthar.

The numerals, like those of the Bengali, Uriya, &c., are Hindí.

CHAPTER XXII.

The populations whose language is akin to the Tamul.—The Rajmahali mountaineers.—The Kols.—The Khonds.—The Sours.

It has already been stated that the Tamul populations and their congeners have been called the natives of *southern* India. It has also been suggested that this term is inaccurate. That the parts about Cape Comorin are Tamul is true; and true it is that the Dekkan, or southern half of India, is what may be called Tamiliform. But it is by no means true that these districts constitute the whole of the Tamul area. This extends not only far beyond them, but far beyond them *to the north.* At one point it actually touches the Ganges, and that *at the present time*, and in an unequivocal manner. More than this, it all but touches the southern limit of the Bhot and Burmese areas—a fact to which attention has already been directed. The occupants of

The Rajmahal hills, on the southern bank of the Ganges, in the parts about Bogilpur, have long been known as a population whose language and manners differ from that of the ordinary Hindu of the districts around. In the Asia Polyglotta, a specimen of their dialect stands by itself, isolated on all sides, *i. e.* with no Hindu, no Tamul, no Tibetan affinities—the Garo being isolated also. No wonder. When the Asia Polyglotta was written, the Tamul class was limited to the south of India, the Khond, Gond, and Kol forms of speech being wholly, or all but, unknown.

The extent to which it agrees with these may be inferred from the following comparison of the pronouns.

English.	Râjmahal.	Tamul, &c.
I	en	nân, en
Thou	nin	nîn
He, she, it	ath	âta
We	nam	nâm
——	om	ôm
Ye	nina	nim
They	awar	avar
This	îh	î
That	âh	á
Here	ino	inge
There	âno	ange.

For a long time the Rajmahali mountaineers were the terror of the neighbouring districts. They robbed, they levied blackmail. A strong bamboo bow with a poisoned arrow was their weapon. With this they made themselves formidable to the Mahometan powers, troublesome to the Company. With this they defended their dense jungles, or rather the jungles defended them. Every arrow was unseen, certain, fatal. The Company failed in their measures of coercion, as the Mahometans had failed before them.

Kindness was then tried, and it was successful. The epitaph of Cleveland, bearing date 1784, records that "without bloodshed or the terrors of authority, employing only the means of conciliation, confidence, and benevolence, he attempted and accomplished the entire subjection of the lawless and savage inhabitants of the jungleterry of Rájamahal, who had long infested the neighbouring lands by their predatory incursions, inspired them with a taste for the arts of civilized life, and attached them to the British Government by conquest over their minds, the most permanent, as the most rational, mode of dominion." The tomb on which it is inscribed was erected at Bhagulpur by order of the Governor-General and Council of Bengal.

The skin of the Rajmahalis is dark, their face broad, their eyes small, their lips thicker than those of the men of the plains. That features of this kind suggest a variety of illustrations is what we expect *à priori*. "The Rajmahali physiognomy is Mongol," writes one. "The Rajmahali physiognomy is African," writes another.

The creed is, more or less, Hindu; its Hinduism being of an imperfect and degenerate character. *Bedo* is one of its gods; word for word, the *Batho* of the Bodos; word for word, the *Potteang* of the Kukis; word for word, *Buddha*. Their priesthood, like that of the Bodos, consists of Demauns and Dewassis; men whose functions have been already explained.

The nearest congeners to the Rajmahali mountaineers are the speakers of

The Uraon dialects, whose occupancy is the hilly country to the south and south-east. Word for word, *Uraon* seems to be *Uriya*.

English.	Uraon.	Rajmahali.
Man	alla	male
Head	kuk	kupe
Hair	chutti	tali
Ear	khebda	khetway
Eye	khan	khane
Blood	khens	kesu
Bone	khochal	kochal
Foot	dappe	kev
Hand	khekhah	sesu
Sun	dharmi	ber
Moon	chando	bilpe
Star	binka	bindeke
Fire	chek	chiche
Water	um	am.

The Kols.—That Kol is a word which is applied by the

Hindus to certain populations distinguished from themselves, and that it is also a term of general application, has already been stated; the Kols of Gujerat having been brought under notice when the ruder tribes of western India commanded our attention. Word for word, the two names are identical. Between the eastern Kols of Monghir, Ramgurh, Chuta Nagpúr, Gangpur, Sirgujah, and Sumbhulpúr and the Uraon and Rajmahalis the chief difference seems to be that of dialect.

The divisions and subdivisions of the Kol name are numerous.

The Sontals, indigenous to Chuta Nagpúr and the parts about Palamow, have, since the beginning of the present century, intruded themselves into some of the Rajmahali occupancies, which now contain two separate populations, allied to each other, though speaking languages which are said to be mutually unintelligible. It was with these northern and intrusive Kols that the recent disturbances arose. Like Kol, the name Sontal is found in western, as well as eastern, India. There was a Sontalpúr in Gujerat.

According to the Sontal mythology, the first two mortals bore the names of Pilchu-hanam and Pilchu-brudhi, one being a male, the other a female; being also brother and sister to each other, and the children of a duck's egg. A deity named Lita, or Marang Buru, brought them together as man and wife. In Orissa, this Lita, or Marang Buru, is very specially worshipped, and that both privately, as a domestic deity, and in public, by means of feasts and festivals. Of this god there is a stone image at Sikar-ghat, a place of resort and ceremony. It stands on one of the feeders of the Ganges, which receives in its waters, twice a year, a bone of some deceased Sontal, thrown in by one of the surviving relations, who makes a pilgrimage to the spot for the purpose of doing so. Other ceremonies accompany this act—lustral, or purificational, in character.

Maniko is the elder brother of Marang Buru, and is invoked once a year by the Naikis (mark the word) or priests, who sacrifice to him fowls—Bodo and Dhimal fashion. His sister's name is Jaherera.

Connected with every Sontal village is a grove called Jaher, in which the Manjhi-hanam, or the founder of the village, is periodically worshipped.

The domestic gods are called Odah-Bonga. Bonga means deity. Abge Bonga is the name of a god who is worshipped twice a year. The offerings to him consist of rams, he-goats, and red cocks, upon which all the males (but none of the females) regale themselves—burning the leavings.

Rankini, a bloody-minded female, is said to be occasionally propitiated by human sacrifices.

The Sontals swear by the skin or by the head of the tiger. They swear also by their gods and by the lives of their children.

The Ho.—The Ho are the best known of all the Kols; not, however, because they have been visited by the greatest number of Europeans, but because they have been made the subject of a valuable monograph by Lieutenant Tickell in the Journal of the Asiatic Society of Bengal.* The parts about Singbhúm are their locality.

The Ho are locomotive agriculturists; *i. e.* they sow the soil, and work it with the hoe; but are unskilled in the art of manuring. Hence, the lands on which they settle soon become exhausted, and fresh clearings are required. Their villages, too, are small, though the houses of which they consist are well-built. The walls are of

* Vol. ix. part ii.

mud, but strong and solid. The roofs are of thatch, well laid on. The veranda is supported by wooden pillars, rudely carved. The residence of the family consists of three rooms, one for eating, one for sleeping, one for stores. The outhouses are at a little distance; some for pigs, some for poultry, some for servants.

The Ho dress but lightly, some of them wearing next to nothing. The women work. The men hunt—or rather hawk; for falconry is both their business and their pastime. The bow is the chief weapon.

A Ho bridegroom buys his bride; or rather, his father buys her for him, the price being so many head of cattle. Whether, however, the match is to take place at all depends, to an inordinate extent, upon the omens that the parties concerned meet in their way from house to house. Should anything unlucky present itself, a sacrifice of fowls is made, and prayers put up to Singbonga (of whom more will be said hereafter), to the effect that, if the parties still wish to be united, better omens may attend their next negotiation. After looking over Captain Tickell's list of evil auguries, I wonder that Ho marriages ever take place. It contains almost everything that either runs or flies. If a vulture, crow, magpie, oriole, woodpecker, jackall, hare, bee, snake, &c., pass behind the negotiator, there will be a death. If a certain kind of ichneumon drag a certain kind of spider across the road, the bride will be dragged away by a tiger the first time she goes out for wood or water. If a hawk seize a bird, the same. If a certain kind of vulture fly singly, or in front of its flock, death to one of the four parents—death to the bride's parent if the village of the bride, to the bridegroom's if his village, be the nearest—death to a father if the bird be a male, to the mother if a female. If the great wood-hawk hover overhead, death to both mother and son at childbirth. Should a branch fall from a tree, death. The dung-beetle rolling dung portends hard work and little reward. Such are a few of the evil omens. There are some good ones to set against them. Upon the whole, however, the signs of bad luck preponderate. That the marriages are attended by feasts is what we expect *à priori*. There are feasts and ceremonies as well. There are ceremonies, too, at the birth of children, at the naming of them, at burials. There are ceremonies in abundance; but of a definite recognized priesthood very little. The following is a Ho dirge:—

We never scolded, never wronged you;
Come to us back;
We ever loved and cherished you, and have lived long together
Under the same roof;
Desert it not now!
The rainy nights, and the cold blowing days, are coming on;
Do not wander here.
Do not stand by the burnt ashes; come to us again!
You cannot find shelter under the peepul when the rain comes down.
The saul will not shield you from the cold bitter wind.
Come to your home!
It is swept for you, and clean; and we are there who loved you ever;
And there is rice put for you; and water;
Come home, come home, come to us again!

Dead bodies are interred, and gravestones placed over them. This, however, is insufficient to keep down the spirits, which are believed to walk about during the day, and to keep within-doors at night. A certain spot, upon which is placed an offering, is kept clean for them. According to the Ho mythology—

Ote Boram and Sirma Thakoor, *i. e.* Sing Bonga, or God, were self-created. Sing Bonga is the sun. After them the moon was self-created.

Ote Boram and Sirma Thakoor then made the earth; after that they clothed it with grass, trees, rocks, water; they then made cattle, which were first born in Bogo Bochee; after them all wild animals. They then made a little boy and a little girl, at the bottom of an immense ravine, and as they had no houses to live in, the gods told them to inhabit a huge crab's cave (Katkomoá). They grew adult, and Sing Bonga came to see them every day, and called them his grandchildren; but at length seeing no hopes of any progeny, from their extreme simplicity, he taught them the art of making Eely (rice beer), the use of which caused those sensations, which were in due time the means of peopling the world.

After the creation of man, Sing Bonga, or the sun, married Chandoo Omol, or the moon, from whence sprung four sons and numerous daughters. Now the four sons kept with their father, and the daughters lived with their mother, and as the sun rose every day, with his four hot, fiery sons in addition, the whole world began to burn; and all the animals and man perishing with heat, entreated the moon to save them: so the moon resolved within herself to destroy the sun's sons, and went, and accosting the father, said, "Our children do much harm to the world, and will soon destroy your labour. I am determined to eat mine; do you also devour yours." The sun promised he would follow the moon's example; and so when she hid all her daughters, and came and told him she had devoured them, he destroyed and eat all four of his children; after which the moon released her daughters from confinement. This artifice so enraged the sun, that he drew his sword and cut the moon in half, but repenting afterwards of his anger, allowed her to get whole in certain days, though she still remained condemned to be in half at others, and so she remained, and all her daughters, with her, which are the stars.

Now, some time after the first man and woman had lived together and known each other, Sing Bonga came down and asked them what progeny they had; they say unto him, "Grandfather, we have twelve sons and twelve daughters." These twenty-four lifted up their voices and said, "Great grandfather, how can we brothers and sisters all live together?" Sing Bonga said, "Go you and make preparations and make a great feast, rice and buffaloes' flesh, and bullocks' flesh, goats, sheep, pigs, and fowls of the air, and vegetables;" and they did so: and when the feast was prepared, Sing Bonga said, "Take ye two by two, man and woman, that which shall please you most, and that shall ye have for share, to eat all the days of your life, apart from the rest, so that none shall touch his brother's share."

And so when the feast was prepared, the first pair and the second pair took buffaloes' and bullocks' flesh, even as much as they could carry, and these became the Kol and Bhoomij race; then a pair took the rice; and other pairs, male and female, rice and vegetables, and these became Bramins, Rajpoots, Chuttries, and other Hindoos; and others took away the goats' flesh and fish, and became other kinds of Hindoos; the Bhooians took the shell-fish. Lastly, when nothing was left but the pigs' flesh, came two pair and took it away, and these are Sontals and Koormees to this day; and when all the feast was cleared away, there remained one pair who had nothing, and to them the Kols gave of their share, and these are Ghassees to this hour.

And so all these went and lived separately, and peopled the world, and multiplied exceedingly, and Sing Bonga taught those who lived in far countries other languages, and he gave people of different trades their implements.

And after this from the Kols, from their senior house, sprung the English, who also eat of bullocks' flesh. But they are the senior children, and the Kols the junior!

And after the world was peopled, Sirma Thakoor destroyed it once, with the exception of sixteen people, because people became incestuous, and unmindful of God, or their superiors.

Wicked men are born again as dogs, pigs, or lizards. Suttees never are born again, but remain burning for ever in their pits, and come out at night, wandering about, still burning. Good people after death are born again in some better condition in life than formerly. And this order of things will remain for ever and ever.

When men die, their spirits go to the Sing Bonga, who asks them how they have lived, and judges them. The wicked he whips with thorny bushes, and sometimes buries them in great heaps of human ordure, and after a while sends them back to be born in this world as dogs, cats, bullocks, lizards, &c. The good man he sends back to be born a still greater and better man than he lived before, and all that he had given away in charity, Sing Bonga shows him heaped up in heaven, and restores it to him.

Other deities are Nagé Erra, Desa Uli, Marang Bonga, and Pangúra, his wife—village gods;

Chanala Desum Bonga, whose wife is also Pangúra, the god of married women;

Horaten Ko, a god of the roads;

Mahli Bonga and Chandu Omol;

Jaer Buri is the wife of Desa Uli.

Pigs and fowls are the chief offerings. Idols are wholly wanting. There is singing, dancing, and drinking at the festivals, some of which degenerate into orgies. Of domestic worship there is not a little. Every case of sickness involves a sacrifice, and an application to the soothsayer. That the Ho is eminently addicted to superstitions is clear. Whether he be more so than the rest of the rude world is doubtful.

The name for a Ho tribe is *kíli*—word for word, the Afghan *kheil*. A man cannot marry a woman of his own *kíli*, nor eat with a man of a different one.

The Bendkars.—The Bendkars form a single tribe consisting of about 300 individuals, their occupancy being the Bendkar Buru or the Bendkar hills. These lie to the north of Keonjur and the south of Kolehan.

The Bendkars speak either the Ho or the Uriya; are half Hindus; worshippers of Kali; eat neither pork nor beef; drink water from a Ho's hand, but will eat with neither Ho nor Hindu. They burn their dead.

KOL DIALECTS.

English.	Singbum Kol.	Sontal.	Bhumij.	Mundala.
Man	ho	horh	horro	horl
Hair	ub	ub	ub	up
Head	bo	buho	buho	bohu
Ear	lutur	lutur	lutur	lutur
Eye	met	met	met	med
Blood	myun	myun	myun	myun
Bone	jang	jang	jang	jang
Foot	kata	suptijanga	kata	kata
Hand	thi	thi	thi	tihi
Sun	singi	singmanal	singi	singi
Moon	chandu	chandu	chandu	chandu
Star	epil	ipil	ipil	ipil
Fire	sengel	sengel	sengel	singil
Water	dah	dah	dah	dha
One	mi	midh	moy	miha
Two	barria	barria	barria	baria
Three	apia	pia	apia	apia
Four	upunia	ponia	upuria	upnia
Five	moya	monegotang	monaya	moria
Six	turia	turingotang	turrya	turia
Seven	iya	iairgotang	* sath	* sath
Eight	irlia	iralgotang	* ath	* ath
Nine	area	aregotang	* nou	* noko
Ten	gelea	gelgotang	* das	* dasgo.

As far as I can judge from some short vocabularies from

* Hindu.

Gondwana, the affinities of the Kol dialects (of which the Ho is one) run westwards rather than eastwards, whereas *The Khond* dialects extend east and south, in the direction of Orissa and the Telinga frontier. Fuller and more elaborate than Lieut. Tickell's paper on the Ho is that of Captain Macpherson on the Khonds; or rather on their religion, their human sacrifices, and their female infanticide. It is the great repertorium for our knowledge of the superstitions of the so-called aborigines of India. Pagan we can scarcely call them, inasmuch as, in the following notices, it is impossible to overlook the existence of ideas introduced from both ordinary Hinduism and Parsiism. The chief Khond deity, Bura Pennu, created for himself a consort whose name was Tari. He also created the earth. He walked abroad upon the earth—Tari, his wife, with him. But her affections were cold, and when Bura asked her to scratch the back of his neck for him, she refused. There were other causes of quarrel as well, but this refusal was one of them. And now Bura determined upon creating beings that should truly and warmly serve and love him, and, to this end, he made man. Tari opposed him as much as she could, but not effectually.

Man, when made, was pure, good, and healthy. But Tari envied his purity, goodness, and health, and sowed the seeds of sin and evil, "as in a ploughed field." Physical evil Bura met by antidotes, but moral evil he left mankind free to either choose or reject. A few rejected it at once and from the first. To these Bura said, "Become ye gods! living for ever, and seeing my face when ye will, and have power over man, who is no longer my immediate care." The greater part, however, chose evil, and had it as mankind has it now.

Tari, then, is the evil, Bura the good principle; and

whilst the sect of Tari holds that she will eventually win, the sect of Bura believes in the final prevalence of good. Meanwhile, the struggle goes on, the weapons being hail, and rain, and wind, and lightning, and thunder. The comet of '43 was watched by the Kols with intense interest. They took it for a new weapon.

The first class of the minor gods of the Khond Pantheon is the offspring of Bura and Tari, and their offices (which may be collected in detail from the subjoined list) are to meet the primary wants of man—wants originating out of the introduction of evil. There are

Pidzu Pennu = the God of Rain.

Burbi Pennu = the Goddess of New Vegetation and First Fruits.

Petterri Pennu = the God of Increase and Gains.

Klambo Pennu = the God of the Chase.

Loha Pennu = the Iron God, *i. e.* the God of War.

Sundi Pennu = the God of Boundaries. These are invoked in all ceremonials next to Baru and Tari.

The sinless men, who, having at once and from the first rejected evil, were taken up by Bura, form the next class. They are tutelary to the different Khond tribes.

The third class consists of deities sprung from the gods of the other two—*e. g.*

Nadzu Pennu = the Village God.

Soro Pennu = the Hill God.

Jori Pennu = God of Streams.

Idzu Pennu = House-god.

Munda Pennu = Tank God.

Suga Pennu = God of Fountains.

Gossa Pennu = God of Forests.

Kutti Pennu = God of Ravines.

Bhora Pennu = God of New Fruits.

Dinga Pennu, the Judge of the Dead, is the only one of the Dii Minores who does not reside on the surface of the earth, or a little above it; for the ordinary habit of the other deities is to move about in atmospheric space, invisible to human eyes, but not invisible to the eyes of the lower animals. Of the spirits, then, Dinga Pennu is one; but he is not one of the spirits that walk abroad upon the earth. He resides in the region beyond the sea, where the sun rises, upon a rock called Grippa Valli = the Leaping Rock. It is smooth and slippery, "like a floor covered with mustard seed," and a black unfathomable river flows around it. To this the souls of men speed after their death, and take bold leaps in order to get on it. Hence its name. Some of these leaps succeed, but the greater part fail, in which case the limbs may be broken, or the eyes knocked out by the attempt, and when this happens, the deformity thereby contracted is communicated to the body next animated. Upon Grippa Valli sits Dinga Pennu writing the register of the deeds of men, and casting-up the account of their good and evil actions. Should he adjudge immediate beatification, the soul passes at once to the world of happy spirits. Should the evil, however, outweigh the good, it is recommitted to earth, and sent to its own proper earthly tribe to be re-born. Men have four souls. First, there is the one which is capable of happy communion with Bura. Secondly, there is one attached to the tribes on earth, and, in each particular tribe to which it belongs, it is re-born as often as it dies. Upon the birth of a child the priest determines who it is whose soul, having previously departed in death, has thus returned. Thirdly, there is a soul that is punished for sins done in the flesh; and, fourthly, there is one that dies with the body. Under such a thorough system of metempsychosis as this is, it is only natural for the different degrees of earthly prosperity or adversity to be looked upon as so many degrees of reward or punishment. Hence, the inflictions most dreaded are neither more nor less than the penalties of a former course of vice. Of these the most terrible are poverty, bodily deformity, epilepsy, cowardice, and the want or loss of male offspring. The chief sins are—

1. To refuse hospitality.
2. To break an oath or promise.
3. To speak falsely, except to save a guest.
4. To break the pledge of friendship.
5. To break an old law or custom.
6. To commit incest.
7. To contract debts, the payment of which is ruinous to a man's tribe, the tribe being responsible.
8. To skulk in time of war.
9. To divulge a public secret.

The chief virtues are—

1. To kill a foe in public battle.
2. To die in public battle.
3. To be a priest.

To these add, amongst the sacrificing tribes,—

To be a victim to the Tari.

A strong feeling of pedigree, blood, or tribe, is indicated in this code, and it is no wonder that, in all feastings and ceremonies, a long array of ancestors is invoked. Neither is the belief wanting that the kindest and worthiest of the departed spirits may be prevailed upon to intercede with Dinga Pennu for a discretionary and merciful exercise of his formidable jurisdiction.

It has been stated that Dinga Pennu, the judge of the

dead, is the only one of the Khond Dii Minores who does not inhabit either the earth or the atmospheric space immediately above it. He does not do this. Neither do Tari and Bura, but they are no Dii Minores; but on the contrary, the parents of the Pantheon. The remainder, then, are of the earth, but not earthly. They are shaped, too, as human beings, though their tissues are other than human. They have bodies of human form, but of ethereal texture. And they have also human passions, out of which legend upon legend has been evolved.

Such is the general view of the Khond divinities. The general view of their cultus is as remarkable for what we miss in it as it is for what it displays. There are no Khond temples. There are no Khond images. The stream, the grove, the rock, the glen, with the sky only above them, constitute the Khond shrines. The Khond priest is called Janni. Of the Janni there are two classes; one exclusively priestly, the other free to do anything but fight.

Deferring, for awhile, the notice of the cultus of the two primary divinities, Bura and Tari, I lay before the reader a sketch of the more curious amongst the rituals for the worship of the divinities of the second and third orders,—the worship of the beatified and deified beings, who, choosing good rather than evil, were taken up to Bura, at the beginning being unfrequent and (probably) simple.

The first two may be taken together. Pidzu Pennu is the God of Rain, and Burbi Pennu the Goddess of New Vegetation. Their functions being easily confused, their rites are similar. When Pidzu Pennu has to be invoked, the elders traverse their village and cry "Vessels Ho!" which means that vessels of arrack are to be brought out. These are carried to the tree or stone sacred to *Burbi*

Pennu. Pidzu Pennu then comes upon the priests when the offerings are deposited under the tree, and the meeting is seated, and the great Janni, with two minor assistants, performs the following worship apart.

The Janni first calls on Bura and Tari, and then on Pidzu Pennu, and all or most of the other gods, who (it is hoped) will exert their influence with him. Then follows the prayer, after which they kill the sheep, and either give its flesh away or leave it on the field. The liquor they drink. The Janni stays a little longer than the rest, in case any god may have to question him concerning any omission or imperfection of the ceremonial. "If we have unconsciously omitted to do honour on this occasion to any god, we pray of the other deities to intercede for us, and pacify him."

The God of Increase and Gain is Petterri Pennu, worshipped at seed-time. A rude car is made of basket-work and bamboo. This the Janni drags to the head of the tribe that takes precedence, and obtains from him a little of each kind of seed and some feathers. Having made a circuit of the village with a like object, the car is then accompanied to some appointed field by the young men of the village beating each other and the air with sticks. The seed thus carried out is the share of the evil spirits, who are held to be driven out with the car. The next day a hog is killed, and Petterri Pennu invoked. After this the hog is eaten; only, however, by the elders; for the young men went afield with the car. They have, however, their revenge for their exclusion, and waylay the feasters on their return, pelting them with jungle fruit. On the third day the head of the chief tribe sows his seed, after which the rest may do so too.

A stone in the neighbourhood of each village is dedicated to Klambo Pennu, on which the huntsman lays offerings, and also sharpens his axe or arrow, Klambo Pennu being extreme to mark any neglect of himself, or any violation of the rules of the chase.

Loha = Iron, and Loha Pennu, the god of war, is, literally, the Iron God. In the grove sacred to Loha Pennu is buried a piece of iron, or an iron weapon. When war threatens it appears above the surface, emerges further on the eve of battle, and subsides when peace is made. Loha Pennu, however, presides only over the wars between Khonds and enemies other than Khond, or (at any rate) over those between different tribes. Quarrels within the tribe he leaves alone. The offering of a fowl, rice, and arrack, within the precincts of a holy grove and in the presence of the assembled warriors, precedes the invocation to Loha Pennu.

And now, when all have snatched up their arms, the priest commands silence, and recites a hymn, concluding by the words "Arm and march." They march, and the priest accompanies them to the enemy's boundary, over which an arrow is shot, by some one indicated by the divining sickle. Thirdly, a branch of some tree growing on the enemy's soil is cut off, and carried away to the spot where the exsertion of the iron indicates the invisible presence of Loha Pennu. Here it is clothed like one of the enemy, and, with certain invocations, thrown down on the symbol or shrine of the divinity. The enemy has full time given him for the completion of similar rites.

The declaration, then, of a Khond war is a matter of no small form and ceremony. So, also, are the overtures for peace and the ratifications of treaties. When one of the two belligerent parties is weary of war, the intervention of some friendly or neutral tribe is requested. If this be successful, a kind of mixed commission of two old men on each side is appointed in order to ascertain the will of Loha Pennu as indicated by certain divinations. In a basket of rice an arrow is placed upright. If it remain so, war proceeds. If it slant, the ceremonies that bring in peace are continued. The population makes a procession. The priest, with rice and two eggs, calls on Loha Pennu. They now fill a dish with hog's fat, and place a cotton wick in it. They light this, and if the flame be straight, the augury is for war; if not, for peace.

The peace-dance is one of long duration, and frantic excitement.

Sundi Pennu, the God of Boundaries, may be invoked by two hostile parties on the same occasion, inasmuch as, *ex vi termini*, he is common to them both. He may not, however, be so invoked on the same day. Hence, when a quarrel as to boundaries arises, there must be at least two days before the fighting begins, for (as has been seen in the case of Loha Pennu) it is part and parcel of the military code of the Khonds for each belligerent to allow the other time for his ceremonies.

Of the ceremonials for the divinities of the third class the two selected for notice are those for

1. The Village God, Nadzu Pennu.
2. The God of Fountains, Sugu (or Sidruju) Pennu.

A stone under a cotton tree is the place of worship for Nadzu Pennu. The tree is planted when the village is founded, and when the village is founded the priest says to the tree, "I bring you by order of Bura Pennu, who commanded us to build the village, as did also ——and—— and——" (naming some ten or twelve divinities).

The people feast and the tree is planted.

A day or two afterwards the Janni meets the villagers again, when an old man, stupid and clownish for the occasion, gets up, with him, the following dialogue:—

Old man.—What, I pray you, may be the meaning of the planting of this stick?

Janni.—If you don't know, friend, you must assuredly be a great block—a mere jungle-stick, yourself. And how, O friend block, may I ask, did you find legs to bring you hither? You must have acquired them in some wonderful way. But since you are come to us, I will enlighten you, and make a man of you. Know, then, that when Boora Pennu first ordained that villages should exist, he gave us the tree which you now see planted, for a model in all these respects. That our families should spread like the branches of this great tree, strongly and widely. That our women should resemble its lovely and glowing red flowers. That, as the birds are attracted by the love of those sweet flowers, so the youths of neighbouring tribes should come, attracted by our young daughters. That, as of the flowers of this tree not one falls barren, but all unblighted bear fruit, so should it be with our women. That our sons should, in their youth, be rough, sharp, and keen, like the young branches of this tree, which are covered with thorns; but that, as those thorns disappear with age, so should they become smooth and cool when youth is past. And lastly, this tree is given us as an example that we should live as long as it, a most long-lived tree. Boora Pennu thus ordained, and gave us this model tree.

Old man.—And for what purpose, I pray, is this hog (or buffalo, as the case may be)?

Janni.—One places things which are of value on a stand. We place flesh upon leaves, rice in vessels of earth or of metal; a man rests upon a couch; and this animal is an offering upon which the commands of the deity may rest.

The victim is then killed, and some of its dung mixed with straw and put on the tree-top.

When a spring dries up no divinity is the object of more earnest prayer than Sugu (or Sidruju) Pennu, the God of Fountains. Failing in his ordinary invocations, the Janni takes the cocoon of a silkworm, empties it, and, at the dead of night, repairs, at the risk of his life, to some spring, situate in a different village, or belonging to other proprietors, and tries to wile away its waters to his own dried-up water-course. To this intent he mutters prayers or spells, fills the cocoon, and walks back. At the well which has gone dry, the elders of the village await him—the elders, but no women or youths. The scanty contents of the cocoon are now poured into it, and a sheep or a hog is sacrificed to Sugu Pennu. If all goes favourably a stream of water will have passed from the full well to the empty one, underground, and along the line that the priest took in his way back.

Salo = a cattle-pen, and kallo is the name of a certain spirituous liquor. Hence, the Salo-kallo is the liquor prepared in the cattle-pen, or the Feast of the Cattle-pen-liquor. It is a great yearly festival, and Bura Pennu is the divinity in whose honour it is held. Every branch of every tribe, every member of every village celebrates it, and it is at the time of the rice-harvest that such celebration takes place. It lasts five days; during which the celebrators eat freely, and over-freely, of the kennah, which is fermented rice, with intoxicating, stimulant, or narcotic properties. The Salo-kallo is a period of great licence. The most serious part of it consists in the recitation by the Janni of the doctrines or legends of the Khond Cosmogony, the origin of Evil, the Antagonism of Tari and Bura, &c. A hog is the sacrifice.

The next great festival in honour of Bura is the Jakri, or Dragging; the origin whereof is as follows:—

The woman, Umbally Bylee, appeared as a tiger, and killed game every other day, and all ate of it. There was at that time a fight between the people of Kotrika and those of Mundika. But it was private strife, carried on in womanish fashion, before the art of taking life and that of public battle were known. Umbally Bylee said, "I will kill any one of your enemies you please." They said to her, "Kill so and so;" and she went as a Mleepa tiger, and killed him. Then the people placed unbounded faith in her, and said to her, "Teach us this new knowledge, and show us the art of killing." She replied, "I will teach you; but thenceforward you must do one thing." And she accordingly taught the art of Mleepa to a few, so that they practised it; and she then said, "Now you must worship me by the sacrifice of men, or the earth shall sink beneath your feet, and water shall rise in its place, and I will abandon you." The earth heaved terribly—as some think, from the wrath of Boora Pennu; some, in obedience to the power of the Earth Goddess. Fear filled the minds of all, and, as directed, they set up a pole beyond the village, and brought human victims, and all was prepared for the sacrifice. But now the God of Light sent a god bearing a mountain, who straightway buried Umbally Bylee therewith, and dragged forth a buffalo from the jungle and said, "Liberate the man, and sacrifice the buffalo. I will teach you the art of Mleepa in every form." And he taught that art, and the art of pnblic war.

So, the buffalo having been dragged from the jungle, the festival took the name of the Dragging.

But what is *Mleepa?* Mleepa is a kind of tiger. The ordinary animal is believed by the Khonds to be good rather than bad, a friend rather than an enemy. This is because when he hunts down some other wild animal, and eats only a part of it, the Khond, who may find the remainder, has the benefit of its predaceous propensities. It is only when it is other than an ordinary animal that the tiger kills men; when it is either a tigriform man, or, perhaps, even Tari herself metamorphosed. Tigers of this kind are *Mleepa* tigers.

Tari is malevolent and must be propitiated, and in the necessity of appeasing an evil-minded, rather than in the spontaneity of feeling that delights in doing homage to a kind being, lies the chief difference between the worship of Tari and Bura. In other respects, what applies to the one applies to the other also. The sect of Tari, like that of Bura, believes that the latter has provided remedies for the consequences of the introduction of evil; but it holds that these remedies are only partial, incomplete, and insufficient, that although the soul after death may enjoy happiness under Bura, the body during life may be sorely afflicted by the ill-nature of Tari.

Such earthly good as Tari permits is on the express condition of her being worshipped with human sacrifices, upon which she feeds. The sacrifices are made periodically and publicly, also on certain occasions by individuals. The tribe, the subtribe, the village, may offer them. At the periodical sacrifices each head of a family procures a shred of the human flesh. The victims are provided by the tribe, each member contributing according to his means. When special occasions demand a special victim, whoever furnishes it receives its value, and is exempted from contribution for the next time of offering. Should an individual lose (say) a child, carried off by a tiger, the tiger will be held to have been Tari, and the priest will be invoked. After certain formulæ he will declare that Tari must be pacified, and the father will bind himself to find a victim within the year—a victim called *Tokki*, or *Keddi*, by the Khonds themselves, *Meriah* by the Oriyas. The Tokki, to be acceptable, must be the full and unimpeached property of the offerer, acquired by purchase. It is better still if his father has been a victim before him, or if he has been devoted to the gods as a child. The purchase of victims is made from the men of one of two casts, the Panwa (or Dombanga) and the Gahinda, some of such wretches being attached to each village. They procure them by kidnapping from the Hindus. Sometimes they sell their own offspring. A long interval may elapse between the purchase of a victim and its immolation.

The Tokki (or *Keddi*), being brought blindfold to the village for which he is destined to become the offering, is lodged with its head-man, in fetters if an adult, at liberty if a child; and here he is honoured as a being consecrated and hallowed, and, on the whole, scarcely unhappy. Everyone welcomes him, and should he grow, and have intercourse with any of the village females, the father or husband is only too thankful for the distinction. Sometimes a female, herself a victim, is specifically awarded to him, along with a portion of land and stock. The condition of the parents is now inherited by the offspring, and the children of such unions are liable to be sacrificed, when called, which is not always. Escape is rare, nothing being more sedulously inculcated on the victim than the conviction that his death will bring him to immediate happiness, his flight to certain and well-deserved misfortune. And now the time of oblation comes on. The victim, hitherto unshorn, has his hair cut off, and the village performs the ceremony called bringa. By this they make the vow that a sacrifice shall be effected. All wash their clothes and go out of the village, headed by the priest, who invokes Tari.

The first day and night of the festival thus horribly solemnized is devoted to drunkenness, frantic dances, and all kinds of impure excitement, excitement which it is deemed to be impious to resist. Upon the second morning the victim is led forth to some grove solemn and shaded, and never violated by the axe, and to some stream sacred because it flows through it. Such are the spots that so many superstitions love and choose; choose for the most unholy rites. A post is now sunk in the ground, and the victim fastened to it, anointed with oil and ghee, daubed with turmeric, adorned with flowers. So he remains till the third morning, when a little milk and sago is given him. At noon the barbarities by which he is deprived of life begin. His limbs are broken, for, as he must die unbound, he must also be prevented from escaping. The ritual varies—the following, the fullest, in the possession of Captain Macpherson, is given *in extenso*, notwithstanding its length.

The Priest's Invocation.

O Tari Pennu! when we omitted to gratify you with your desired food, you forgot kindness to us. We possess but little and uncertain wealth. Increase it, and we shall be able often to repeat this rite. We do not excuse our fault. Do you forgive it, and prevent it in future by giving us increased wealth. We here present to you your food. Let our houses be so filled with the noise of children that our voices cannot be heard by those without. Let our cattle be so numerous that neither fish, frog, nor worm may live in the drinking ponds beneath their trampling feet. Let our cattle so crowd our pastures that no vacant spot shall be visible to those who look at them from afar. Let our folds be so filled with the soil of our sheep that we may dig in them as deep as a man's height without meeting a stone. Let our swine so abound that our home fields shall need no ploughs but their rooting snouts. Let our poultry be so numerous as to hide the thatch of our houses. Let the stones at our fountains be worn hollow by the multitude of our brass vessels. Let our children have it but for a tradition that in the days of their forefathers there were tigers and snakes. Let us have but one care, the yearly enlargement of our houses to store our increasing wealth. Then we shall multiply your rites. We know that this is your desire. Give us increase of wealth, and we will give you increase of worship.

After this each individual present asks for what he wishes; and the priest continues :—

Umbally Bylee went to cut vegetables with a hook. She cut her finger. The earth was then soft mud; but when the blood-drops fell it became firm. She said, "Behold the good change! cut up my body to complete it!" The people answered, "If we spill our own blood we shall have no descendants. We will obtain victims elsewhere. Will not the Dombo and the Gahi sell their children when in distress? and shall we not give our wealth for them?" and they prayed thus :—

"May the gods send the exhausted Dombo, his feet pierced with thorns, to our door! May the gods give us wealth."

Their prayer was answered. They procured and sacrificed a victim. The whole earth became firm, and they obtained increase of wealth. The next year many victims came for sale, and the people thanked the gods, saying, "You have sent us victims, and have given us wealth." Thenceforward the world has been happy and rich, both in the portion which belongs to the Khonds, and the portion which belongs to Rajahs.

And society, with its relations of father and mother, and wife and child, and the bonds between ruler and subject arose. And there came into use cows, bullocks, and buffaloes, sheep, and poultry. Then also came into use the trees and the hills, and the pastures and grass, and irrigated and dry fields, and the seeds suitable to the hills and to the valleys, and iron and ploughshares, and arrows and axes, and the juice of the palm-tree, and love between the sons and daughters of the people, making new households. In this manner did the necessity for the rite of sacrifice arise.

Then, also, did hunting begin. A man brought in a rat, a snake, and a lizard, and inquired if they were fit to eat. Then the Earth Goddess came and rested on the Janni, and said to him, "Give names to all the wild animals, distinguishing those that are fit and those that are unfit for use, and let men go to the jungles and the hills, and kill the sambur and spotted deer, and other game, with arrows and with poison." And men went to hunt.

While hunting, they one day found the people of Darungabadi and Laddabarri (tribes of the Souradah Zemindary, adjacent to Goomsur, which do not offer human sacrifices) offering sacrifice. Their many curved axes opened the bowels of the victims, which flowed out. They who went to the hunt said, "This ceremony is ill-performed. The goddess will not remain with you." And the goddess left these awkward sacrificers, and came with our ancestors. These people now cut trees only. The deity preferred the sacrifice at the hands of our forefathers, and thenceforth the whole burden of the worship of the world has lain upon us, and we now discharge it.

Tari Pennu in this way came with our ancestors. But they at first knew only the form of worship necessary for themselves, not that necessary for the whole world. And there was still much fear; and there were but few children, and there were deadly snakes and tigers, and thorns piercing the feet. They then called upon the Janni, to inquire the will of the goddess, by the suspended sickle. He said, "We practise the rite as it was first instituted, worshipping the first gods. What fault, what sin is ours?" The goddess replied, "In a certain month, wash your garments with ashes, or with stones; make kenna; purchase a child; feed him in every house; pour oil on him and on his garments, and ask for his spittle; take him into the plain, when the Earth Goddess demands him; let the Janni set him up; call all the world; let friendship reign; call upon the names of the first people; cut the victim in pieces; let each man place a shred of the flesh in his fields, in his grain store, and in his yard, and then kill a buffalo for food, and give a feast, with drinking and dancing to all. Then see how many children will be born to you, how much game will be yours, what crops, how few shall die. All things will become right."

We obeyed the goddess, and assembled the people. Then the victim child wept, and reviled, and uttered curses. All the people rejoiced, except those with whom the child had dwelt, and the Janni. They were overwhelmed with grief; their sorrows prevailed entirely over their expectations of benefit, and they did not give either their minds or their faith to the gods. "The world," said they, "rejoices, we are filled with despair;" and they demanded of the deity, "Why have you instituted this miserable heart-rending rite?" Then the Earth Goddess came again and rested upon the Janni, and said, "Away with this grief. Your answer is this: when the victim shall weep, say to him, Blame not us, blame your parents who sold you. What fault is ours? The Earth Goddess demands a sacrifice. It is necessary to the world. The tiger begins to rage, the snake to poison, fevers and every pain afflict the people; shall you alone be exempt from evil? When you shall have given repose to the world, you will become a god, by the will of the gods."

The victim answers:—

Have you no enemies, no vile and useless child, no debtor to another tribe who compels you for his debts to sell your lands; no coward who in time of battle skulks with another tribe? Have you none of these to seek out and sacrifice?

The Janni.—We have acted upon quite different views. We did not kidnap you on the road, nor while gathering sticks in the jungle, nor when at play. The souls of those whom you would have us sacrifice can never become gods. They are only fit to perish by epilepsy, falling in the fire, or by ulcers, or other dread diseases. Such sacrifices would be of no avail. To obtain you, we cleared the hill and the jungle, fearless of the tiger and the snake. We stinted ourselves to fill your parents, and gave them our brass vessels; and they gave you to us as freely as one gives light from a fire. Blame them! Blame them!

The Victim.—And did I share the price which my parents received? Did I agree to the sale? You now tell me this. No one remembers his mother's womb, nor the taste of his mother's milk; and I considered you my parents. Where there was delicate food in the village, I was fed. When the child of any one suffered, he grieved; but if I suffered, the whole village grieved. When did you conceive this fraud, this wickedness to destroy me? You, O my father, and you,—and you,—and you,—O my fathers! do not destroy me.

The Mullicko, or chief of the village in which the victim was kept, or his representive, now says:—

This usage is delivered down to us from the first people of the first time. They practised it. The people of the middle time omitted it. The earth became soft. An order re-established the rite. Oh, child, we must destroy you. Forgive us. You will become a god.

The Victim.—Of this your intention I knew nothing; I thought I was to pass my life with you. I assisted to build houses and to clear fields for my children. See! there are the palm-trees I planted. There is the mowa tree I planted. There is the public building on which I laboured—its palings still white in your sight. I planted the tobacco which you are now eating. Look behind you! The cows and the sheep which I have tended look lovingly at me. All this time you gave me no hint of my intended fate. I toiled with you at every work with my whole mind. Had I known of this doom, I had still toiled, but with different feelings. Let the whole burden of my soul's grief, as I remember the past, lie upon you.

The Chief.—You are about to become a god. We shall profit by your fate. We cannot argue with you. Do you not recollect that, when your father came to claim your uncompleted price, you snatched up a shining brass vessel; that we said, "That is your father's," and you threw it at him, and ran away amongst the sheep? Do you not recollect the day on which we cut your hair, devoting you to sacrifice? And do you not recollect that when many were sick, and the Janni brought the divining sickle, he declared "The earth demands a victim?"

Then several persons around say, "I should have told you, and I, and I;" and several give answers such as "I thought of our hard labour to acquire you, which had been wasted, had you escaped from us;" and,—"You might have known all well."

The Victim.—It is true I did observe something of this; but your aged mothers, and your wives, and your beautiful children, my brothers and sisters, assured me that you were humane, and would never kill one so useful and so beautiful as I. "They will rather," said your mothers and children, "remembering your acts and your ways, sell these fields, and these trees, and that tobacco, to procure a substitute." This I believed, and I was happy and laboured with you.

The Chief.—We cannot satisfy you. Ask your father, who is present. I satisfied him with my favourite cattle, my valuable brass vessels, and my sheep, and with silken and woollen cloths, and axes. A bow and arrows, not four days old, I gave to his fancy. Your parents, forgetting your beauty, forgetting the pleasure of cherishing you, turned their hearts to my cattle and my brass vessels, and gave you away. Upbraid them. Heap imprecations upon them. We will curse them with you, imprecating upon them—that all their children may be similarly sacrificed. That they may lose, within the year, the price for which they sold you. That they may have a miserable and forlorn old age, lingering childless and unfed. That when they die in their empty house, there may be no one to inform the village for two days, so that, when they are carried out to be burned, all shall hold their nostrils. That their own souls may afterwards animate victims given to hard-hearted men, who will not even answer their death-plaints consolingly. Curse them thus, and we will curse them with you.

The victim will now turn to the Janni, saying:—

And why did you conceal my fate? When I dwelt with the Mullicko, like a flower, were you blind, or dumb, or how were you possessed, that you never said, "Why do you cherish, so lovingly, this child—this child who must die for the world?" Then had I known my doom and leapt from a precipice and died. Your reason for concealment—living as you do apart from men, is—that you thought of yourself. "I am great. The whole world attends on my ministrations." But, world, look upon him! What miscreant eyes! What a villainous head, with hair like a sumbully tree! And see how enraged he is! What a jabber he makes! What a body he has got, starved upon worship which depends upon men's griefs!

—A body anointed with spittle for oil! Look, O world! Look, and tell! See, how he comes at me, leaping like a toad!

The Janni replies :—

Child! why speak thus? I am the friend of the gods; the first in their sight. Listen to me. I did not persuade your father or your mother to sell you. I did not desire the Mullickos to sell their fields to acquire your price. Your parents sold you. These Mullickos bought you. They consulted me, inquiring, "How may this child become blessed?" The hour is not yet over. When it is past how grateful will you be to me! You, as a god, will gratefully approve and honour me.

The Victim.—My father begot me; the Mullickos bought me, my life is devoted, and all will profit by my death. But you, O Janni! who make nothing of my sufferings, take to yourself all the virtue of my sacrifice. You shall, however, in no respect profit by it.

The Janni.—The Deity created the world, and everything that lives; and I am his minister and representative. God made you, the Mullicko bought you, and I sacrifice you. The virtue of your death is not yours, but mine; but it will be attributed to you through me.

The Victim.—My curse be upon the man who, while he did not share in my price, is first at my death. Let the world ever be upon one side while he is on the other. Let him, destitute and without stored food, hope to live only through the distresses of others. Let him be the poorest wretch alive. Let his wife and children think him foul. I am dying. I call upon all—upon those who bought me, on those whose food I have eaten, on those who are strangers here, on all who will now share my flesh—let all curse the Janni to the gods!

The Janni.—Dying creature, do you contend with me? I shall not allow you a place among the gods.

The Victim.—In dying I shall become a god, then will you know whom you serve. Now do your will on me.

The cruelties of the absolute immolation are now drawing nearer and nearer still, and, in a few minutes, the victim will be torn to pieces, quivering with life, by the fanatic and maddened crowd around him. The exact spot for the sacrifice has been determined beforehand, *i. e.* the night previous, and by a strange kind of divination. A number of persons are sent in the dark with sticks in their hands, and with orders to probe and poke some portion of the ground about the village in order to find a crack or opening, for such is the spot indicated by the Earth Goddess as the exact locality for the sacrifice. This being found, a short post is fixed in it, in the morning. Round this they place four larger ones, and in the middle the victim. The arm of a growing tree is now riven half-way down, and the victim, forced into the cleft, like Milo, is left for it to close on him; the natural elasticity of the timber being assisted by ropes round its open extremity. These the priest, with his assistants, draws tighter and tighter. He then wounds the victim slightly with an axe, and leaves him to the crowd. They throw themselves on him, and strip the flesh from the extremities and trunk, leaving the head and intestines untouched.

Such are the usual rites; subject, however, to variations in the way of detail. In one district the victim is slowly burnt to death, with horrible cruelties besides. A low stage with a roof-like ridge is raised, and the victim fastened to it. Fire is then applied in such a manner as to make him writhe and struggle up and down the two slopes alternately. The more tears he sheds the more abundantly will Tari allow a supply of rain. The next day he is cut to pieces.

None but the worshipper can approach the victim. Stroug parties guard his remains against wild beasts the night after the sacrifice, and, the next day, the chief and priest consume them along with the whole carcase of a sheep, on a funeral pile. The ashes are scattered over the fields, or made into a paste, and plastered over the barns and granaries.

Two formalities are indispensable :—

1. To the father or seller of the victim, as the case may be, a *dhulj* is given. This is a bullock, equivalent to a payment in full satisfaction of all demands.

2. A bullock is sacrificed and made a feast of, with the following prayer to Tari :—

O Tari Pennu! You have afflicted us greatly; have brought death to our children and our bullocks, and failure to our corn;—have afflicted us in every way. But we do not complain of this. It is your desire only to compel us to perform your due rites, and then to raise up and enrich us. We were anciently enriched by this rite; all around us are great from it; therefore, by our cattle, our flocks, our pigs, and our grain, we procured a victim and offered a sacrifice. Do you now enrich us. Let our herds be so numerous that they cannot be housed; let children so abound that the care of them shall overcome their parents—as shall be seen by their burned hands; let our heads ever strike against brass pots innumerable hanging from our roofs; let the rats form their nests of shreds of scarlet cloth and silk; let all the kites in the country be seen in the trees of our village, from beasts being killed there every day. We are ignorant of what it is good to ask for. You know what is good for us. Give it to us.

When the victim has been cut to pieces, the deputies, who have been sent from the several villages to receive a shred of its flesh, return home. At home, the few who have remained behind, keep fast till their arrival. The bearer of the flesh rolls it up in the leaf of the guglut tree, and, when he gets near the village, lays it on a cushion of grass, and deposits it in the place of the public meetings. He then divides and subdivides it amongst the heads of families, saying:—

O Tari Pennu! our village offered such a person as a sacrifice, and divided the flesh among all the people in honour of the gods. Now, such a village has offered such a one, and has sent us flesh for you. Be not displeased with the quantity, we could only give them as much. If you will give us wealth we will repeat the rite.

Other formulæ and feastings defer the full completion of the ceremony until the fourth day from the return of the Janni and his distribution of the flesh. A buffalo is then slaughtered and feasted on, its inedible parts being left for the spirit of the victim (Tokki, Keddi, or Meriah). Nor is this all. A year afterwards a hog is sacrificed to Tari Pennu with this invocation: "O Tari Pennu! up to this time we have been engaged in your worship, which we commenced a year ago. Now the rites are completed. Let us receive the benefit."

The practice of female infanticide amongst the Khond tribes is at least as common as that of human sacrifices; indeed, there is no part of the population where it is utterly unknown and unpractised. At the same time some sections of the population are more infanticidal than others. Of these the most conspicuous are certain of the sect of Bura—not of Tari, as we might at first expect. To such an extent is the practice carried among the more extreme adopters of it, that, except when a mother's first child is a girl, no female infant is allowed to live. So deadly is the effect of this pernicious custom that villages of more than a hundred houses may occasionally be seen without a single female child.

The religious view of the practice is as follows:—Bura found so little comfort in his own wife, Tari, that he came to the conclusion that women were only to be tolerated as necessary evils, and gave his instruction, advice, or injunctions to mankind accordingly. He gave them, in short, an express admonition to bring up as many females as were necessary for the good of society, and no more.

Other reasons lie in the belief that the amount of soul assigned by Bura to a given generation is limited, and that the less there is for women the more there is for men.

Is it because the social position of the woman is unnaturally low that this practice of female infanticide thus predominates? By no means. So far from the condition of Khond females being bad, or even indifferent, the very reverse is the case. They have many and high privileges, privileges which are believed to be the highest and most numerous amongst the tribes that most especially practise infanticide.

One of these privileges is a very near approach of polyandria. Whilst infidelity on the part of a married man is punished by fines and other penalties, little or no constancy is required on the part of the wife. A wife, too, may quit her husband, and take another, at any time, except when she is *enceinte*, within a year of her marriage, or within a year of the birth of a child. Nor is this all; her property goes with her, being reclaimed by her father. But the tribe at large is answerable for the debts of its individual members. Hence, when wives are capricious the community suffers. "To any man but a rich and powerful chief, who is able to make large and sudden restitutions, and to his tribe, a married daughter is a curse. By the death of our female infants before they see the light, the lives of men without number are saved, and we live in comparative peace."

The Sours.—Long as have been the notices of the Kols and Khonds, they are but extracts from still more elaborate descriptions. Of the Sours I can give no such accounts, having no *data* of equal or even approximate magnitude to refer to. As a general rule, they are said to form the third or (counting the Uraon and Rajmahalis) the fourth section of one great class, the so-called aborigines of the eastern Ghauts, as opposed to the Bhíls and Kols of the west, and the Gonds of the centre. With these they, in all probability, agree in most of the points wherein they differ from the ordinary Hindu. Their area begins where that of the Khonds ends, and is extended as far south as the Pennaur—there or thereabouts. It is succeeded by that of

The Chenchwars—an allied population, lying along the mountains that run southward, between the Kistna and the Pennaur.

In one important respect both the Sours and the Chenchwars differ from the Khonds, Kol, and Uraon. They lie within the true Tamul area, and, so doing, present no notable contrast, in the way of language, to the populations around them. Their languages are represented by the following lists, in which the Chentsu (word for word Chenchwar) presents the most Hindu forms—indeed, as far as the following list is evidence, it is actually Hindí.

English.	Khond.	Savara.	Gadaba.	Yerukala.	Chentsu.
Man	lokka	mandra	lokka	mumisam	manus
Head	tlavu	ahobumu	bo	talayi	mund
Eye	kannuka	amu	ollo	supan	ayenkhi
Ear	kirru	luv	nintiri	soyi	kan
Mouth	sudda	amuka	tummô	vayi	mu
Tooth	ahamu	ajagna	ginna	pallam	dat
Blood	rakko	miyamo	yignam	regam	lahu
Bone	pasu	ajagna	vondramgoyi	yamaka	had
Hand	kaju	asi	titti	ky	hat
Foot	vestamu	aji	adugesananu	keru	khoju
Day	vujjagu	tamba	simmya	pammaru	din
Sky	mudengi	agasa	konda	menu	sarg
Sun	bela	vuyu	singi	beruli	bela
Moon	layidi	vonga	arke	tarra	masu
Star	sukala	tute	tsukka	tsukka	bhudaka
Fire	nade	togo	sungol	nerupu	agin
River	jodi	nayi	roggilu	aru	ladi
Stone	viddi	aregna	birel	kellu	paththar
Tree	mranu	anebagna	sunabbo	chede	gats
——	——	——	——	marom	——
One	rondi	aboy	vokati	vondu	* yck
Two	jodeka	bagu	rendu	rendu	* duyi
Three	tinigota	yagi	mudu	mume	* tin
Four	sari	vonji	nalugu	nalu	* char
Five	panchu	mollayi	ayidu	anju	* panch
Six	——	kudru	aru	aru	* chhe
Seven	* sata	gulji	yedu	yegu	* sat
Eight	* ata	tamuji	yenimide	yettu	* ath
Nine	* nogatta	tinji	tommidi	ombadu	* lo
Ten	* doso	galliji	pade	pottu	* das.

As for the Kol forms of speech, they seem to extend considerably towards the west, inasmuch as more than one of the dialects from Gondwana, and (as such), *eo nomine*, Gond is decidedly Kol. Such are the Cúr and Chunuh

* Hindí.

specimens. The details, however, of the line of demarcation are obscure.

The Gonds.—Mutatis mutandis, what applies to the Sours and Chenchwars applies to the Gonds—they are Kol, Khond, or Uraon in the points wherein they most especially differ from the Hindus. Of the details of their creed we know but little. Of the poetry or legend the following is a sample :—

Sandsumjee's Song.

Sandsumjee's song hear, O Father.
Six wives he took, Sing-Baba not born,
Seventh wife took, by her Sing-Baba was conceived.
Of her pregnancy Father was not informed.
Departed Father, his kinsfolk being assembled together.
For this reason to some one it happened to offer a sacrifice to a God.
Hereupon Sing-Baba began to be born.
Small wife was sleeping, the other six were there.
Said they, grain basket's mouth into her head let us introduce.
In our house child is born,
So said, so done, into mouth her head introduced,
And Sing-Baba was born.
Sing-Baba having taken up, into buffaloe's stable threw,
And a puppy instead placed,
And said, a puppy is born.
A puppy having brought forth,
Crows to frighten they set her,
Sing-Baba, buffaloes said, that him let none hurt,
Nor blow strike, and into his mouth milk having poured him suckled.
The six wives said, let us go and see him, is he living or dead?
Sing-Baba was playing.
Thence indeed having taken him into cows' stable threw.
The cows said Sing-Baba let no one hurt
Or blow strike, into his mouth milk pouring him suckled,
Therefore information they sent to seek, is he living or dead ?
Sing-Baba was playing.
Thence having taken well into threw.
On the third day having gone to see, is he living or dead?
Sing-Baba there indeed was playing.
Thence indeed having taken, tiger's path upon.
They threw him, tiger's female and male were coming;
Sing-Baba's cries they heard.
Tigress compassion felt, "my child it is."

Having said so, took him away. Their den came to and their pups from apart set,
Meat bringing their pups to feed
Their pups weaning, with milk Sing-Baba suckled,
So continuing to do, Sing-Baba grew up.
One day his mother her whelps
Together brought, and to whelps began to say
Yourselves among together stay, fight not.
The third day Sing-Baba said, my body is naked
To me a dhoty, dohur, and pugrey give.
She going Bazar road seated remained.
A muslin-maker and cloth-maker that way came
Having got up ran, they their bundles having thrown away fled,
She having taken up brought Sing-Baha took and put on
And his mother's feet kissed,
Staying staid then one day indeed began to say
That to me a bow give. She again went
Seated remained a sepoy armed with a bow that way came.
She ran having cried out. Bow thrown away, he fled.
She having it came and to Sing-Baba gave;
Sing-Baba big brother little brother together played.
Birds shot big brother little brother to them gave to eat
So continuing to do, Sandsumjí home returned with his friends
And Sandsumjí began to say has any one become inspired, let him arise;
God into any one not entered? Then Sing-Baba inspiration received.
Sing-Baba was coming, big brother little brother together were
Coming came, in the midst was a bráhman
Him Sing-Baba required to get up, he refused;
Big brother became angry, the bráhman eat up
Sing-Baba the image took up.
All began to say, that you who are you?
He said that you the buffaloes and cows ask
And to his little brother said, mother go and call.
He ran and called.
These three species before the punchait assembled came.
Then Sing-Baba said that them question,
From them they asked, this one who is he?
First the buffaloes said this Sandsumjee's son is.
They said, you how understand? These said
In our house two days staid. How did he remain?
These said thy six wives having taken into our house to kill threw
And there not injured, then cow's house into threw
From these asked, How into your house Baba came?
The cows said, At our house two days stayed.
These six wives thence having taken into well threw,

There indeed not injured, thence taking I know not where took.
Sing-Baba they questioned that thence you went where ?
He said of my mother ask.
They mother-tigress asked
You where found ? She said
On my road these six wives threw away ?
I having taken brought, my whelps weaning,
Milk him suckled and here there with prey
My young fed. All-understood, tigress'
Feet embraced, and her a God established.
And these six wives to this Tigress gave.
That day Sing-Baha illustrious became
And Tigress indeed as a God established became.
Of Sandsumjee Baba this song is,
Of Bhirry bamboo jungle Bhirri the song is.

In the original the first ten lines run thus :—

Sandsumjee-na sáka kuyât, ro Bábân,
Sark ask kítur, Sing-Baban hillé pûttúr,
Yirrún ask kítúr, awíté Sing-Bábán autarietúr.
Aulár yétana Baban púnwakê.
Taksítún Baban, tunwa pari sumpté kiálé
Bariké bouke aie penk putta sika.
Hikké Sing-Baban putti-lé-ai latur.
Loro askna sowatí, sarún mutta.
Awítun, koti aunâté tulla dúrissí, "assun inga chawa putti,"
Ud it, ahé kint annâté tullatún durritún.

The Kol or *Kúlis of Gujerat.*—These differ from the Ghonds, &c., in speaking a language, that (in the present state of opinion) is held to agree with the Hindí rather than the Tamul ; in other words, they are tribes who, from being in closer contact with the Gujerati, and Mahratta Hindus, have either unlearned their own tongue, or adopted so many Hindí words as to disguise it. Miscellaneous notices concerning them have already been given.

The Mairs.—These seem to be the Kols, Bhíls, Khonds, or whatever else we choose to call them, of Marwar, as

The Minas are those of Mewar ;

The Moghis being those of Amber or Jeypur.

That their occupancy is the hill country rather than the plains, and that it reaches the Ganges has already been stated. They are the hill men of the Aravulli.

The Bhíls.—These also have already been mentioned. They extend far towards the north. In the desert to the north and north-west of Marwar, they approach the frontier of Sind.

In Marwar itself they are numerous. Between Sirohi and Udipur they constitute the chief population, being the occupants of a hilly district, in small communities under leaders with the title *Rawut*. The Rawut of Oguna, when Tod was in his country, could muster as many as 5000 bows. He was in all but name independent, paid no tribute, obeyed no one. One of the Colonel's men, who penetrated into these parts, found that the Lord of the Mountain was dead, his men abroad, his widow alone in the hut. He told his story, and asked for a passport. This was an arrow from the quiver of the late chief. It carried the bearer safe through the whole country. The symbolic power of the arrow has already been noticed. Mahmúd of Ghuzni was told what it meant in Turkistan, when he held his dialogue with the Tshagatai chief.

In Malwa the Bhilalahs are Bhíls, with a certain amount of real or reputed Rajput blood. They "combine the pride and pretensions of the Rajput, with the cunning and roguery of the Bhíls, and appear to be, without exception, a debauched and ignorant race, often courageous from constant exposure to danger, but invariably marked by an equal want of honour and shame. Many remarkable instances of their being of this character came within my knowledge. The Bhillalah and Sundi chiefs were the only robbers in Malwa, whom under no circumstances travellers could trust. There are oaths of a sacred but obscene kind amongst those that are Rajputs, or who boast their blood, which are almost a disgrace to take, but which they assert the basest was never known to break before Mundrúp Singh, a Bhilalah, and some of his associates, plunderers on the Nerbudda, showed the example."*

The great centre, however, of the Bhíls is Kandeish, itself the alluvium of a river, but encompassed with mountains. To the north lies the Satpúra range, the watershed to the Nerbudda and the Tapti. To the south the Satmalla and Ajunta ranges give an easterly spur to the Ghauts. This is what the Bhíl country is in the way of physical geography. Politically speaking, the space between them is bounded by portions of the Guicowar, by portions of the Holkar, and by portions of the Nizam territory. Three agencies, however, are British.

1. The north-west }
2. — north-east } Bhíl agency.
3. — southern }

The Bhíl districts take in a portion of the area between the Ghauts and the sea,—the Daung or Dang country, a land of forest and jungle. Hence, we must be prepared to hear of the Dang Bhíls. So we must of the Satpura (or northern), and Ajunta (or southern) Bhíls. The Mahabarata mentions the Bhíls. The Mahometan histories of Gujerat and Malwa mention them. The Kandeish records say little about them. The inference is, that the latter are late in date; in other words, that all Kandeish before it was Mahratta, was Bhíl, rude and unlettered. Another fact in favour of this view is the circumstance of many Bhíl tribes being Mahometan. This means that Mahometanism was the first powerful influence that acted on them. In Baglan, to the north and north-west,

* Malcolm's Central India, vol. ii. p. 156.

they are cultivators. There are Bhíls in Bugswara, on the other side of the Ghaut. The general title of a Bhíl chief is Naik. Few Naiks belong to an old dynasty.

It was under Aurungzeb that the majority of the Mahometans became proselytes, of whom many relapsed. This should teach us to look for traces of an abortive Mahometanism amongst them.

They are agricultural rather than industrial or commercial. They are graziers rather than farmers. Yet they are scarcely to be called graziers or herdsmen. They are rather the analogues of the sub-Himalayan tribes like the Kooch and Bodo, who are locomotive agriculturists. They sow and reap, but before they reap or sow they clear the land by burning the trees upon it. They clear and manure. They then crop and exhaust. They exhaust and leave. A great deal is said about the extent to which, when disease or accidental death is superstitiously accounted for, they are ready and willing to migrate. I think that the exhaustion of the soil may have something to do with their readiness. They are hunters and fowlers, their architecture being of the rudest. Their huts are compared to bee-hives. This means that they are low and rounded, made of wattles. The village system is fully developed among them. The Jagla is the head of the village, the Naik of the tribe. The village watchman is, by theory, appointed by the Naik; by practice, by the head man of the village.

The chief Mahometan Bhíls in Kandeish are—

The Turví, on the north-east; well-made, fair-complexioned.

The Nirdhi, to the south, on the Ajunta range.

Then, in the scale of civilization, come

The Mutwari,

The Burda,

The Dorepi, and

The Khotíl, of the north-west, basket-makers, cultivators, and gum-collectors. It is to the wax and gum collectors in general that the term Khotíl is applied. Then come, ruder still, allied in wildness, but separate in occupancy,

The Nahal, on the Turvi frontier.

The Bhíls drink. They marry as many wives as suits. They rob. They reverence their chiefs. They swear on a strangely-foul mixture of salt, cow-dung, and jowaré. They have the credit of keeping oaths thus sworn. They play on an instrument which Scotchmen compare to the bagpipe.

The Kalapurruj, Durio, Naiko, and Chowdri are Bhíls, who, from the western side of that jungly part of the Ghauts which is known as the Dang Forest, have spread themselves over some of the lower levels, especially over parts of Bugswara. They are small-made, bright-eyed, dark-skinned; shy and locomotive; skilled in the use of the bow; professors of sorcery. Their chief respect they show to trees and stones remarkable for either size or shape. The death of a child, a cow, or even a few fowls, will make a whole family migrate from the village in which it took place to some less ill-omened spot.

The Wáráli.—The Wáráli have Marathi names and speak the Marathi language. When asked What are the names of your wives? the answer was, "We never mention the names of our wives." When further pressed, each man gave the name of his neighbour's, no one that of his own wife. Girls marry at twelve or thirteen, boys at sixteen or seventeen. The dialogue, conducted by Dr. Wilson and the Rev. J. Mitchell on one side, and some Wáráli of the parts about Umargaum in Havoli pergunna (a Portuguese dependency) on the other, from which the preceding statements have been taken, thus proceeds :—

Do you give any instructions to your children? Yes, we say to them, Don't be idle, Work in the fields, Cut sticks, Collect cow-dung, Sweep the house, Bring water, Tie up the cows.

Do you give them no more instructions than these? What more do they need?

Don't you teach them to read or write? No Wáralís can either read or write.

Do you give them any instructions about God? Why should we speak about God to them?

What God do you worship? We worship Wághiá (the lord of tigers).

Has he any form? He is a shapeless stone, smeared with red lead and ghí (clarified butter).

How do you worship him? We give him chickens and goats, break cocoa-nuts on his head, and pour oil on him.

What does your God give to you? He preserves us from tigers, gives us good crops, and keeps disease from us.

But how can a stone do all this for you? There is something besides the stone at the place where it is fixed.

What is that thing? We don't know; we do as our forefathers showed us.

Who inflicts pain upon you? Wághiá, when we don't worship him.

Does he ever enter your bodies? Yes, he seizes us by the throat like a cat, he sticks to our bodies.

Do you find pleasure in his visits? Truly, we do.

Do you ever scold Wághiá? To be sure we do. We say, You fellow, we have given you a chicken, a goat, and yet you strike us! What more do you want?

Do you never beat Wághiá? Never.

Whether do you bury or burn your dead? We burn them.

What interval occurs between the death and the burning? We allow no interval when the death occurs during the day. When it occurs during the night, we keep the body outside till the break of day.

Why are you so hasty in the disposal of your dead? Why should we keep a corpse beside us?

Where does the soul go after death? How can we answer that question?

When a man dies in sin, whither does he go? How can we answer that question?

Does he go to a good place, or a bad place? We cannot tell.

Does he go to heaven or to hell? He goes to hell.

What kind of a place is hell? It is a bad place; there is suffering in it.

Who are in hell? We don't know what kind of a town it is.

Where do good people go after death? They go to Bhagaván.
Don't they go to Wághiá? No, he lives in the jungles.
Where is Bhagaván? We don't know where he is, and where he is not.

The Wárâli believe that the country which they now occupy has always been theirs. A line drawn from Damaun to Jowar cuts their country. So does a line drawn from Jowar to the Dhano creek. In many places they come within a few miles of the sea. This means that the hills which give its southern feeders to the Damaun and its northern to the Surya rivers are Wárâli. Some belong to British, some to Portuguese, India; some to the independent State of Jowar. The tribual system prevails amongst them, the tribes being numerous. There are, amongst others, the

Ravatia	Meria
Bantria	Wangad
Bhangara	Thakaria
Bhavar	Jhadava
Sankar	Kharbat
Pileyane	Bhendar

Kondaria, &c.

No man marries a wife of his own division.

The Kathkuri or *Katodi.*—These take their name from the *kath* or *cat-echu,* of which they have almost the exclusive preparation. They are small and dark, with low foreheads and curly hair. They have a belief that they are descended from the monkeys and bears which Adí Narayun, in his tenth incarnation of Rama, took with him for the destruction of Rawun, king of Lanka. Him he conquered. Meanwhile, the promise was made to his ursine and simious allies that in the fourth age they should become human beings. They object to mentioning the name Rama, except on their death-beds;

when they mutter it as long as they can. The Dhor Kathkuri eat the flesh of the cow. The Mahratta Kathkuri, though they abstain, have no natural repugnance to it. They abstain because if they did not they would be forbidden to enter a Hindu village. We have the names of five of their tribes—

1. Helam
2. Powar
3. Gosavi
4. Jadavi
5. Sindhi.

These are Hindu.

They acknowledge the existence of a supreme being named Tsher. They have their domestic gods and goddesses. They practise incantation, and encourage the awe with which the Hindu regards their imprecations; for a Hindu believes that a Katodi can transform himself into a tiger.

The women are on an equality with the men. Their marriages are conducted without the intervention of any Brahmin. The bride chooses her husband. A few twigs are stuck on the heads of the couple. A few words of ceremony are muttered. A feast follows, at which anything or everything may be eaten, and at which much is drunk, for the Kathkuris are amongst the least temperate of the Mahratta populations, and most of what they earn by their catechu goes to the shop of the Parsí liquor-merchant. They name their children on the fifth day, generally giving an ordinary Mahratta name. The dead are burned. If wood be wanting, they are buried along with a pot of rice. Some time after the interment the bones are taken up and burned. Persons dying of cholera are always buried first, their bones being burnt afterwards.

Like the gutta-percha hunters of the Malayan peninsula, the Katodi have a sort of slang of their own.

English.	Katodi of Kolaba.	English.	Katodi of Kolaba.
Call	akh	*Hawk*	moregai
Boiled rice	anuj	*Take*	lí
Hedgehog	ahída	*Give*	wope
Kite	alav	*Turban*	salú
Crab	kírlú	*Dog*	súna
Fowl	kúkdai	*Boy*	sora
Iguana	gohur	*Girl*	sori
Arrow	chúmbotí	*Crow*	hadia
Munjus	nagúlia	*Man*	hodus
Crane	bugad	*Woman*	hodis.

The miserable huts of the Katodi stand outside the villages. The brown-faced monkey is one of the few animals whose flesh they hesitate to eat. They say that it has a human soul.

The Mhars, like the Katodi, live on the outskirts of villages, and are abhorred by the Hindus. They cut wood and grass. They measure land. They remove carcases from the towns, eating those of buffaloes and bullocks.

CHAPTER XXIII.

The Telinga, Canarese, Tulava, Malayalam, and Tamul districts.

When the Mahratta area, on one side, and the Uriya, on the other, have been left behind us, the continuous and homogeneous character of the remaining population can no longer be overlooked. There is no longer a question as to whether the proportion of Sanskrit vocables in the languages be sufficient to either disguise their character or effect a transformation. Whatever may be meant by Hindu affinities, the affinity itself is now out of sight. Neither are there any populations like the Kols and Bhíls, the Mairs and Minas; where the language and blood are believed to differ, the former belonging to the north, the latter to the south. All south of the Mahratta and Uriya districts is, in speech at least, either Tamul or Tamuliform.

There are derivatives from the Sanskrit in abundance; but these derivatives are not only foreign to the original language in the way that the French of the Norman conquest is foreign to the speech of England, but are admitted, on all hands, to be so. The creed, however, is Hindu.

The creed in the Tamul districts is Hindu, even as it is Hindu in Rajputana or Bengal.

But it is not wholly and exclusively Hindu in either Bengal or Rajputana. Neither is it in the Dekkan. There are mountains and forests in both areas, and the mountain and the forest have ever been the fastnesses in which the older creeds, the older habits, the older physiognomies, and the older dialects of a country, resistant to the encroachments that change the ethnology of the level plains, longest linger. The analogues of the Kol and Khond, the Wárâli and Katodi, are numerous in southern India. In southern India, however, their language belongs to the same class as that of their more-civilized neighbours, and (so doing) fails to create contrasts. To some extent, however, contrasts exist; and, to some extent, they will be noticed.

Again—in even the most Hindu parts of the districts under notice there are customs and beliefs which, if found at all in the other parts of India, are, by no means, very prominent and characteristic. In other words, there is Hinduism in the south in abundance, but there is also much that appears to be other than Hindu—other, and apparently older.

As a general rule, the Tulava and Malayalam countries exhibit extreme forms of the Telinga, Canarese, and Tamul peculiarities.

As a general rule, such peculiarities as appear in an extreme form in the Tulava and Malayalam districts, and in a moderate one in Canara and Malabar, are to be found, in some shape or other (either fragmentary or rudimentary), in northern India. This means that the differences are differences of kind rather than degree.

At the same time, the Dekkan is Indian in the way that Brittany is Parisian, or Wales English. The political relations and the creed agree. The blood disagrees to a great extent, the language to a greater extent still.

Of predial slavery there is more in Tamuliform India than in Hindostan proper.

So there is of the Jain, or semi-Buddhist, creed.

So there is of the Sudra cast, as opposed to the Kshetriya and Brahminic.

So there is of what may be called, for want of a better name, the *no-cast* system. Few Asiatic terms are commoner in Europe than the word *Pariah*. It is generally translated *outcast*. But, as the past participle of the English for the Latin word *jacio*, and the Portuguese word *cast* have no etymological connection, and as the link between the two words is *nil*, and as their relationship is neither closer nor more distant than that between the English word *sparrow-grass* and the Latin *asparagus*, the correspondence is no correspondence at all, and the translation is exceptionable. Hence it is best to speak only of Sudras and the classes below them. Now the Sudras are the chief cast of the Dekkan, the Sudras being, according to theory, the lowest of all casts. In a Brahminic district this inferiority is possible. In a Kshetriya district it is possible. In a Vaisya district (if such a thing existed) it would be possible also. But what in a district where the Sudras themselves are dominant? It is improbable, to say the least. The lowest man in his own country always discovers an inferior in a strange one. As parasites are fed upon by parasites; as the lowest depth leads to a deeper still; as—but why go on with metaphors? The Sudras are powerful in southern India; and their inferiors are, perforce, other than Sudra. In their own eyes they are the lowest of four casts. If so, their serfs and slaves must be of no cast at all. Such is the Sudra view. The Pariahs are below them—*ergo*, the Pariahs are without cast.

But what say the Pariahs? Do they ignore the principle of cast? By no means. In the first place, there is the great right and left hand struggle, as bitter as was that of the green and blue factions of the Constantinopolitan Circus, as to whether they or the Pallas move on such or such a side at such and such processions. Then there are some half-dozen lower groups with members of which no Pariah will intermarry or eat. But each of these groups is equally exclusive. What is the true interpretation of this? This has already been suggested. The four great divisions are *genera;* the minor classes, whose name is legion, are *species.* If the Pariahs are anything, they are instances of a fifth *genus. Outcasts* or *abjects* they may be. They are not men *without cast.*

Whatever they are, they are the most numerous, *eo nomine,* at least in southern India—in southern India, where the standard of the highest is but low; in southern India, where the magnates are Sudra.

The characteristic, however (if it be one), which has commanded the most attention is that of polyandria. In the present work it has already been noticed. It is Tibetan and Tamul, but it is North American as well. It is more or less African. It is more or less a practice of many countries. I am unwilling to give it a general character. I prefer to exhibit a few concrete instances. Amongst the Moylar of the Tulava country, a widow, tired from celibacy, but restrained from re-marriage, may go to a temple and eat some rice. She may then choose between living in the temple or out of it. If she decide upon being an indweller, she takes a piece of cloth and a daily allowance of rice. She then is bound to sweep the temple, fan the idol with a yak's tail, and submit herself to the embraces of men of her own cast only. The sons of Brahmin women are called Moylar. They wear the Brahminical thread, and employ themselves about the temple. The girls are given in marriage to them.

The out-door prostitutes (for this is what they really

are) may cohabit with any one of pure descent. They pay, however, a sum not exceeding half a pagoda to the temple.

Compare this with the accounts given by Herodotus of the practice in the Assyrian temples.

In the Malayalam country the Nairs are Sudras—Sudras, but often soldiers. They fall into eleven classes, of which three are superior to all the rest, and, more or less, on an equality with each other. Thus, a Kirit may marry the daughter of either a Sudra or a Charnadu, whose profession is akin to his own. The fourth class, however, are palanquin-bearers, and the tenth and eleventh are potters or weavers. The men take their wives before they arrive at puberty. After consummation, husband and wife live apart, the latter in the house of her mother so long as she lives, and in that of her brother afterwards. Doing this, she is free to cohabit with any one she chooses; with any one or with any number of ones. It is only necessary that her lovers be her equals or superiors in cast. The consequence is, that no Nair son knows his own father, and *vice versâ*, no Nair father knows his son. What becomes of the property of the husband? It descends to the children of his sisters. The eldest male manages the landed property. The personal is divided. A man's mother manages his house; when she dies, his eldest sister. Brothers, as a matter of course, live under the same roof. Should one separate from the rest, he takes a sister with him. This is the *descensus per umbilicum*,—part and parcel of polyandria; polyandria being Nair, but not Nair exclusively.

The purity of cast is continually impaired; where is it not? But there are ways and means by which a partial reparation is effected. In many cases the original difference is of no notable amount; and when this is the case, the offspring follows the condition of the lower of its parents. If the mother be higher than the father, the father's cast is the child's also. If the father be the higher, the child goes to the side of the mother.

But what if the difference be great? In this case it is of no importance, provided that the father be the higher of the two progenitors. But if it be the mother, suicide or abortion is the result,—we may almost say the remedy. When the abandonment of cast is on the side of the female, so that a woman of either high or middle rank has conceived by a man of the lower (and that such cases actually happen, is the express statement of Mr. Caldwell), the child never sees the light. The miserable mother either destroys herself, or procures abortion.

English.	Tamul.	Malayalam.	Canarese.	Telugu.
Man	al	al	alu	al
Head	talei	tala	tale	tala
Hair	mayir	talamudi	kudala	ventruka
Ear	kadu	kada	kivi	chevi
Eye	kan	kanna	kannu	kannu
Mouth	vayi	vaya	bayi	noru
Tooth	pal	palla	kallu	pallu
Bone	elumbu	ella	eluvu	emika
Blood	udiram	chora	netturu	netturu
Egg	muttei	mutta	tatti	gaddu
——	——	——	motti	——
Day	pagal	pagal	hagalu	pagalu
Night	ira	rav	iralu	reyi
Sky	vanam	manam	banu	minnu
Sun	pakalon	surya	hottu	poddu
Moon	tingal	tingal	tingalu	——
Star	vanmin	minjawna	chukki	chukka
Fire	neruppu	tiyya	benki	uippu
Water	tanni	vellam	niru	nillu
River	aru	puzha	hole	eru
Stone	kal	kalla	kallu	rayi
Tree	sedi	chedi	gida	chettu
——	maram	maram	mara	——
Village	ur	tara	halli	uru
——	——	desam	uru	——

English.	Tamul.	Malayalam.	Canarese.	Telugu.
Snake	pambu	pamba	havu	pamu
I	nan	gnan	nanu	nenu
Thou	ni	ni	ninu	nivu
He	avan	avan	avanu	vadu
She	aval	aval	avalu	ame
It	adu	ada	adu	adi
We	nam	gnangal	navu	memu
Ye	nir	ningal	nivu	miru
They	avar	avara	avaru	varu
Mine	enadu	enre	nannadu	nadi
Thine	unadu	ninre	ninnadu	nidi
His	avanadu	avanre	avana	vadidi
Our	namadu	nangade	nammadu	madi
Your	umadu	ningade	nimmadu	midi
Their	avarudu	avarude	avarudu	varidi
One	onru	onna	ondu	vokati
Two	irandu	renda	eradu	rendu
Three	munru	munnu	muru	mudu
Four	nalu	nala	nalku	nalugu
Five	anju	anja	ayidu	ayidu
Six	aru	ara	aru	aru
Seven	ezhu	ezha	elu	edu
Eight	ettu	etta	entu	enimidi
Nine	ombadu	ombada	ombhattu	tommidi
Ten	patta	patta	hattu	padi.

When the details of the superstitions of the independent tribes and the lower casts shall have been investigated, an inkling towards the original mythology of southern India will become possible. A belief in *pysachi*, or spirits ; a veneration of a black stone, and a Shammanist diabololatry are the chief phenomena towards which our present imperfect evidence points. There is also a deity named Buta to whom fowls are offered, every man being his own priest, just as is the case with the Bodo and Dhimal.

It is one thing to be a Pariah, or a man of such low cast as to be contemned by the Sudra. It is another thing to be the analogue of the Bhíl or Kol. Of these last the chief occupancy is the Nilgherry Hills and the range between them and the Mahratta frontier. The Nilgherry Hills, however, are the parts which have been best investigated. They give us

The Tudas.—Infanticide polyandrists, who are few in number, and less Hindu than their neighbours:

The Kohatars.—Occupants of the lower ranges, and eaters of beef:

The Curumbars, Curumars, or Curbs;

The Irular—(compare the name *Warali*), and

The Budugurs—all fragmentary, pagan, and semi-pagan populations. In the Tuda creed the black stone has a prominent place. The fuller form of the word is Tudava, apparently, word for word, Tulava.

The Malearasar.—These are the analogues to the Tudas, &c., in the hills of the Malayalam country.

Specimen of Language.

English.	Tuda.	Kohatar.	Budugur.	Curumbar.	Irular.
Man	al	ale, manija	manija	manisha	manisha
Woman	kuch	pemmage	hennu	hennu	ponnu
Head	madd	mande	mande	mande	tele
Eye	kann	kannu	kannu	kannu	kannu
Ear	kevvi	kive	kive	kive	kadu
Tooth	parsh	palle	hallu	hallu	pallu
Mouth	bor	vai	bai	bai	vai
Blood	bach	netra	netru	netaru	latta
Bone	elf	yelave	yellu	yellu	yellambu
Foot	kal	kalu	kalu	kalu	kalu
Hand	koi	kei	kei	kei	kei
Day	nal	nale	dina	dina	nalu
Sun	birsh	potte	hottu	hottu	podu
Moon	teggal	tiggule	tiggalu	tingla	nalavu
River	pa	pevi	holla	niru	palla
Water	nir	nire	niru	niru	dani
Fire	nebb	——	kichchu	kichchu	tu
——	dilth	dije	——	——	tee
One	vadd	vodde	vondu	vondu	vondu
Two	ed	yede	yeradu	yeradu	erndu
Three	mudu	munde	muru	muru	muru
Four	nank	nake	nalku	nalku	naku

English.	Tuda.	Kohatar.	Budugur.	Curumbar.	Irular.
Five	utsh	anje	eidu	eidu	eindu
Six	ar	are	aru	aru	aru
Seven	el	yeye	yellu	yellu	yettu
Eight	ett	yette	yettu	yettu	yettu
Nine	anpath	vorupade	vombattu	vombattu	vombadu
Ten	path	patte	hattu	hattu	pattu.

Of these, the Budugur and Curumbar are somewhat more Hindí than the rest; the Tuda being the most peculiar.

CHAPTER XXIV.

Ceylon.—The Maldives and Laccadives.—Migratory and other populations of Continental India.

In one important point Ceylon differs from Continental India. It is, to a great extent, Buddhist. In Continental India there was only an approach to Buddhism. In Ceylon it actually exists, *eo nomine*, and with its own proper literature; a literature of which the Pali, rather than the Sanskrit, is the vehicle.

That there were traces of what was called Diabololatry, or Devil-worship, in southern India has already been stated. When Siva entered the country (so runs the doctrine), he found himself unable to extinguish the ancient worship of the aborigines, without, to a certain extent, allying himself with it. So he made himself his own son, named Vira Bhadra, whose wife Bhadra Cali is the patroness and mother of the present Shanars, whose business it is to cultivate the palmyra tree, and whose cast is one of the very lowest. They belong to the Continent. Their *cultus*, however, illustrates that of the Singhalese.

When an offering to a devil has to be made, a devil-dancer is sought out from either the head men of the villages, or from some amateur devotees who are often females. There is no regular priesthood. The officiating individual dresses himself as some particular devil, with cap and bells, horns and drum, and, above all, a bow. On the frame of this bow a series of bells is fastened, the bow resting on a pot, and being struck by a plectrum. One musician strikes the string, another produces the bass note out of the brass pot, a third beats cymbals. Meanwhile the devil-dancer gradually works himself into a frenzy; when he is supposed by the lookers-on to have the powers of the devil he represents. As a present deity they worship him, tell him their grievances, reveal their wants, implore his oracles. This is the Shamanism of southern India, as exhibited by the Shanars of Tinevelly.

In Ceylon there is a diabolical literature or liturgy.

I.

Come, thou sanguinary Devil, at the sixth hour. Come, thou fierce Devil, upon this stage, and accept the offerings made to thee!

The ferocious Devil seems to be coming, measuring the ground by the length of his feet, and giving warnings of his approach by throwing stones and sand round about. He looks upon the meat-offering which is kneaded with blood and boiled rice.

He stands there and plays in the shade of the tree called Demby. He removes the sickness of the person which he caused. He will accept the offerings prepared with blood, odour, and reddish-boiled rice. Prepare these offerings in the shade of the Demby tree.

Make a female figure of the planets with a monkey's face, and its body the colour of gold. Offer four offerings in the four corners. In the left corner, place some blood, and for victims a fowl and a goat. In the evening, place the scene representing the planets on the high ground.

The face resembles a monkey's face, and the head is the colour of gold. The head is reddish, and the bunch of hair is black and tied. He holds blood in the left-hand, and rides on a bullock. After this manner make the sanguinary figure of the planets.

II.

O thou great devil Maha-Sohon, preserve these sick persons without delay!

On the way, as he was going, by supernatural power he made a great noise. He fought with the form of Wessamoony, and wounded his head. The planet Saturn saw a wolf in the midst of the forest, and broke his neck. The Wessamoony gave permission to the great devil called Maha-Sohon.

O thou great devil Maha-Sohon, take away these sicknesses by accepting the offerings made frequently to thee.—The qualities of this devil are these: he stretches his long chin, and opens wide his mouth like a cavern: he bears a spear in his right hand, and grasps a great and strong elephant with his left hand. He is watching and expecting to drink the blood of the elephant in the place where the two and three roads meet together.

Influenced by supernatural power, he entered the body of the princess called Godimbera. He caused her to be sick with severe trembling sickness. Come thou poor and powerless devil Maha-Sohon to fight with me, and leave the princess, if thou hast sufficient strength.

On hearing these sayings, he left her, and made himself like a blue cloud, and violently covered his whole body with flames of fire. Furiously staring with his eyes, he said, "Art thou come, blockhead, to fight with me who was born in the world of men? I will take you by the legs, and dash you upon the great rock Maha-meru, and quickly bring you to nothing."

Thou wast born on Sunday, the first day of the month, and didst receive permissiou from the King of Death, and didst brandish a sword like a plantain-leaf. Thou comest down at half-past seven, to accept the offerings made to thee.

If the devil Maha-Sodon cause the chin-cough, leanness of the body, thirst, madness, and mad babblings, he will come down at half-past seven, and accept the offerings made to him.

These are the marks of the devil Maha-Sohon: three marks on the head, one mark on the eye-brow and on the temple; three marks on the belly, a shining moon on the thigh, a lighted torch on the head, an offering and a flower on the breast. The chief god of the burying-place will say, May you live long!

Make the figure of the planets called the emblem of the great burying-place, as follows: a spear grasped by the right hand, an elephant's figure in the left hand, and in the act of drinking the blood of the elephant by bruising its proboscis.

Tip the point of the spear in the hand with blood, pointed towards the elephant's face in the left hand. These effigies and offerings take and offer in the burying-place,—discerning well the sickness by means of the devil-dancer.

Make a figure of the wolf with a large breast, full of hairs on the body, and with long teeth separated from each other. The effigy of the Maha-Sohon was made formerly so.

These are the sicknesses which the great devil causes by living among the tombs: chin-cough, itching of the body, disorders in the bowels; windy-complaints, dropsy, leanness of the body, weakness and consumptions.

He walks on high upon the lofty stones. He walks on the ground where three ways meet. Therefore go not in the roads by night: if you do so, you must not expect to escape with your life.

Make two figures of a goose, one on each side. Make a lion and a dog to stand at the left leg, bearing four drinking-cnps on four paws—aud make a moon's image, and put it in the burying-place.

Comb the hair, and tie np a large bunch with a black string. Put round the neck a cobra-capella, and dress him in the garments by making nine folds round the waist. He stands on a rock eating men's flesh. The persons that were possessed with devils are put in the burying-place.

Put a corpse at the feet, taking out the intestines through the mouth. The principal thing for this country, and for the Singalese, is the worship of the planets.*

That the more impracticable districts of so large an island as Ceylon should contain the analogues of the Bhíls Kols, Khonds, and their congeners, is what we expect *à priori*. We also expect that the analogues of the Pariahs and the so-called outcasts will be forthcoming. There is Buddhism in Ceylon it is true, and it is also true that the Buddhist creed is opposed to many distinctions upon which Brahminism insists. At the same time there is enough of the latter to develope the ordinary phenomena of Hinduism, and these exist to a considerable extent. The population which, on the strength of its pagan or semi-pagan wildness, has commanded the most attention, bears the name Vaddah, a name which is, more or less general, and which is apparently of Hindu origin. It certainly applies to a very rude class of Singhalese. Whether, however, they represent the aborigines of the island, or whether they are the equivalents to the Pariahs, is uncertain. I know of no monograph that gives us the details of their creed. I learn, however, from Dr. Rost, who has kindly favoured me with more than one valuable fact relating to the population under notice, that their language varies but little from the common Singhalese. Now, the common Singhalese is far more Sanskrit than either the Tamul or the Malayalam; far more Sanskrit

* From Callaway's "Translation of the *Kolán Nattannawa*."

than any member of the class to which those languages belong.

English.	Singhalese.	Sanskrit.	Pali.
Man (homo)	manushyayâ	jana	jana
—— ——	minihâ	manush	——
—— *(vir)*	purshayâ	purusha	puriso
—— ——	pirimiyâ	——	——
Woman	strî	strî	itthi
——	gäni	——	——
Head	oluwa	siras	siro
——	isa	——	——
Hair	isakê	kesa	keso
Eye	äsa	——	——
——	aksiya	akshi	akkhi
——	net	chakshuh	——
Ear	kana	——	——
Nose	nâhe	nāsā	nāsā
Mouth	kata	mukham	mukham
Tooth	data	danta	danto
Tongue	dîwa	jihva	jivhā
Hand	ata	——	hattho
——	hastaya	hasta	——
Foot	patula	——	——
——	pâdaya	pada	pādo
Bone	ashtiya	——	——
——	ätiya	——	——
Blood	le	lohitam	lohitam
——	rudhiraya	raktam	——
Day	dawasa	dinam	dinam
Night	ratriya	rātri	rātti
Sun	ira	sūrya	sūriyo
Moon	handa	chandra	chando
Star	taruwa	tārā	tārā
——	târukawa	——	sitārā
Fire	ginna	agni	aggi
——	gindara	——	——
Water	diya	udakam	udakam
——	diyara	——	——
——	watura	jalam	jalam
Tree	gaha	vriksha	rukkho
Stone	gala	prastara	pāshāna
One	ek	eka	eko
Two	de	dwi	dwi

English.	Singhalese.	Sanskrit.	Pali.
Three	tun	tri	ti
Four	hatara	chatur	chatu
Five	pas	panchan	pancha
Six	ha	shash	chha
Seven	hat	saptan	satta
Eight	ata	ashtan	attha
Nine	nama	navan	nava
Ten	daha	dasan	dasa.

The Rodiyas.—A better claim to stand as the representatives of a primitive population can be put in for the Rodiyas,* who exhibit a striking dissimilarity "in their physical characteristics, being much more robust and vigorous." They are found only in the interior, and that as a sporadic population, sometimes in one district, sometimes in another, their numbers being inconsiderable—a thousand (perhaps) in all.

English.	Rodiya.	English.	Rodiya.
Man (vir)	gäwâ	*Hand*	dagula
Woman	gäwî	*Blood*	latu
Head	keradiya	*Sun*	îlayat teriyangê
Hair	kaluwäli	*Moon*	hapa teriyangê
Eye	lâwatê	*Stars*	hâpangawal
Ear	irawuwê	*Fire*	dulumû
Nose	irawuwa	*Water*	nilatu
Mouth	galla	*Tree*	uhälla
Tongue	galagewunu	*Stone*	boraluwa.

That this gives us a wide departure from both the Singhalese and the dialects more especially connected with the Hindí is as manifest. At present, however, it is the only representative of its class.

The Maldive and *Laccadive islanders.*—In language they approach the Singhalese proper, or the Singhalese with its Hindu elements. Their alphabet, however, is Arabic.

* See Paper by Simon Casie Chitty, Esq., in Journal of the Ceylon Branch of the Royal Asiatic Society, vol. xi.

English.	Maldivean.	English.	Maldivean.
Man (*homo*)	mihung	*Mouth*	aga
—— (*vir*)	firihenung	*Eye*	lo
Woman	anghenung	*Day*	duas
Head	bo	*Night*	re
Hair	istari	*Sun*	iru
Hand	aitila	*Moon*	hadu
Foot	fiyolu	*Star*	tari
Tongue	du	*Fire*	alifang
Tooth	dai	*Water*	feng
Nose	nefai	*Tree*	gas.

The chief aliment is from the cocoa-nut-tree; the cocoa-nut-tree and fish.

In all parts of India there are numerous populations of settlers, or colonists, rather than true natives. There are, for instance, Tamul labourers in Ceylon, Telinga families in the Tamul and Canarese countries, Canarese in the Mahratta districts, and *vice versâ*. What occurs, more or less, in most parts of the world occurs to an inordinate extent in Hindostan. The details, however, of these settlements lie beyond the pale of our present inquiry.

Then there are the locomotive, or migratory classes—analogues of the travelling tinkers and pedlars of Europe, analogues to the gipsies of Europe. In Britain the gipsies are wanderers without fixed habitations; whilst, at the same time, they are more abundant in some parts of the island than others. They have no very definite occupation; yet they are oftener tinkers and tinmen than aught else equally legal. They intermarry with the English but little. All this is cast, although we may not exactly call it so. Then, again, they have a peculiar language, although it is so imperfectly known to the majority of the British gipsies as to have become well-nigh extinct.

Of the chief of the tribes in question a good account

is given by Mr. Balfour. This list, however, which is as follows, may be enlarged.

1. *The Bunjaras, or Bunjarris.*—Lumbari is another name for the population. So is Gohur. According to Balfour the latter is the name by which they designate themselves. This is probable; since it means, in their language, *man*. They are bullock-owners; and as the bullock is the chief beast of burden, they are grain-merchants. Their communities are called Tanda, their chiefs Naik. They affecta Rajput descent, and fall into the four following divisions.

a. Rahtor, on the head-waters of the Wurda on the Gondwana frontier; the field of their operations extending to Mysore south, and the Concan west.

b. The Burtiah, to the east of the preceding, from Chicacole to Nellore.

c. The Chouhan, in Mysore.

d. The Powur, in Orissa, and on the east of Gondwana.

Akin to the Bunjaras are—

2. *The Multanis* of the parts about Aurungabad, who emigrated from Multan in 1739. They are Mahometans.

3. *The Beopari* are also carriers and traders of the Deccan.

4. *The Hirn-shikari*, or *Hirn-pardi*, who call themselves Bhouri, are hunters. They fall into the following tribes, two of which bear Rajput names:—

1. Rhator, or Mewar	3. Sawundia
2. Chouhan	4. Korbiar

5. Kodiara.

The chiefs of their communities are called Howlia; their festivals Holi. They steal as well as hunt.

5. *The Tarremuki.*—This is what a class of wandering tinkers call themselves; being also called, by others, Ghissari, Lohar, and Bail-kumbar.

6. *The Korawa.*—In Bejapur, Hyderabad, and Canara, the Bajantri or Gaonka Korawa are musicians, basket-makers, and, real or supposed, thieves, who tattoo themselves.

7. *The Bhatúi* train themselves for the performance of feats of strength, which they wander from village to village to exhibit.

8. *The Muddikpur* earn a "living by catching fish with nets, and their women earn a little by knitting, and by tattooing the dark blue marks on the foreheads of the brahmins and lingaets; but their chief occupation is the exhibition of the transparencies used in representing the battles of the Panch Pandya, five brothers, whose exploits are, we believe, detailed in the Ramayana. The figures are painted on deer-skin with very brilliant colours, and the story being one the Hindu never tires in listening to, in every village after night-fall you may see the representation of the battles, and hear the Keeli Katr describing the heroes' deeds.

"Their females are very virtuous; and one woman has been known to give birth to twelve children. Reading and writing is unknown amongst them. Their dress and food are the same as the Hindus among whom they dwell.

"They live in square huts formed of grass sewed together, the whole being, perhaps, a rupee in value. These they themselves make, and carry with them at their periodical migrations, which custom renders obligatory every three months—a longer stay would, they say, subject them to some dire calamity; and as the third moon passes by, the spot that yesterday was a merry encamping ground, is to-day a desolate and unoccupied waste.

"The Muddikpur seem to have no idea of a Supreme being. They pay their devotions to the transparent figures with which the battles of the Panch Pandya are represented; the box of bamboo containing them is each morning placed on a part of the floor fresh covered with cow-dung; and on the lid being opened to expose the drawings, they burn frankincense, and bow down to the ground in worship:—'Oh Panch Pandya, by you we live, continue to give us our daily bread!'

"They are not restricted to one wife, and they bury all their dead, except lepers, whom they burn." *

9. *The Ramusis.*—Men of predatory habits in the Mahratta country, but Canarese or Telinga in speech and origin; like

10. *The Mangs*—also in the Mahratta country

11, 12. *The Thugs* and *Dacoits*, widely distributed, gang-robbers and thieves.

Last of all (premising that the preceding list is, by no means, exhaustive) I draw attention to—

13. *The Gipsies.*—That these, wherever found, and under whatever names they are described, are in physical form and language, Indians, is now well known.

(1.)

English.	Gohuri.	Bowri.	Taremuki.
Man	gohur	mankhoe	lokro
Woman	gohurni	manussi	chali
Head	mathoe	goddo	mathoe
Eye	ankhi	dolo	dolo
Nose	nak	nak	nak
Ear	kan	kan	kan
Hand	hath	hatha	hath
Foot	pae	——	pug
Water	pani	pani	pani
Stone	bhatta	bhattu	duggru
Earth	jami	bhoe	mattri
Tree	jharr	jhar	jhar.

* E. Balfour on the Migratory Tribes of Central India. Journal As. Soc. Beng. vol. xiii.

(2.)

English.	Korawi.	Bhatúi.
Man	amlún	múns
Woman	punjeri	jo
Head	——	múndhi
Eye	——	akhoe
Nose	——	luk
Ear	——	kunnu
Hand	——	hut
Foot	——	pae
Fire	nerpu	ugg
Water	——	pani
Stone	kellay	pathar
Earth	tirri	bhui
Tree	muru	jhar.

The wandering life of these, and other similar tribes, is not, by itself, sufficient to justify us in separating them from the other Hindus. But it does not stand alone. The fragments of an earlier paganism, and the fragments of an earlier language, are phænomena which must be taken in conjunction with it. These suggest the likelihood of the Gohuri, the Bhatti, and their like, being in the same category with the Khonds and Bhíls, &c., *i. e.* of their being the representatives of the earlier and more exclusively Tamul populations. If the gipsy language of England had, instead of its Indian elements, an equal number of words from the original British, it would present the same phænomena, and lead to the same inference as that which is drawn from the Bhàtti, Bowri, Tarremuki, and Gohuri vocabularies, viz. the doctrine that fragments of the original population are to be sought for amongst the wanderers over the face of the country as well as among the occupants of its mountain strongholds.

(3.)

English.	Ramusi.	Mang.
Eye	kunnul	kewrja
Teeth	pundul	chawur
Sun	goanda	goanda

English.	Ramusi.	Mang.
Moon	phakut	goanda
Fire	dhupa	dhupa
Water	nidul	nir
Stone	ratul	upalla.

The following is a list of words which, apparently, are slang terms :—

English.	Bagwan.	Thug.
One	ungud	udanka
Two	duke	sheluki
Three	ruk	udanu
Four	phoke	pokú
Five	bút	molú
Six	dag	shely
Seven	pnyater	pavitrú
Eight	mung	mungi
Nine	kone	tivsu
Ten	sula	avutaru
Eleven	ekla	ekpuru
Twelve	jewla	habru.

Foreign settlers.—The classes just enumerated were Indian. The following, though occupant of the soil of India, are foreign to it. Some of them have already been mentioned. A long list, however, of alien elements will be given, in order that the very heterogeneous character of the ethnology of India may stand forth in its full due prominence.

1. *Persian.*—Parsis in Gujerat, Mekrani soldiers, &c.

2. *Biluch.*—In Sind and Bahawulpur.

3. *Patan* (*i. e. Afghan*).—In Rohilcund and parts of the Mahratta country.

4. *Arab.*—The Moplahs of the Mahratta and Tulava districts, savage, bigoted, and dangerous Mahometans.

5. *Jewish.*—The Beni Israel of Kolapur. The Jews of Cochin.

6. *Syrian* and *Persian.*—There is, probably, both Syrian and Persian blood amongst the so-called St. Thomas Christians of Cochin.

7. *Armenian.*—In Calcutta, Dacca, &c.

8, 9. *Turk* and *Mongol.*—This is the blood of many of the royal families; also of many settlements originally military.

10. *African.*—The Sidi, &c.

11. *European.*—Portuguese, Dutch, Danish, French, English.

Of these, the Persians, Biluches, Patans, Turks, Mongols, Africans, and Portuguese, have most mixed themselves, by marriage, with the natives; the Jews and Armenians the least.

Such is the sketch of the chief details of the ethnology of one of the most difficult portions of the earth's surface; details which, even when taken by themselves, are numerous, complicated, and, in many cases, obscure. At the same time they are amenable to investigation, and have been well investigated. Of no country is the ethnological literature more valuable, full, and reliable than that of British India. It is not, then, the multiplicity of details that create difficulty. Difficulty and doubt first arise when the broader questions as to the relation between the populations speaking a language akin to the Hindí and the populations speaking a language akin to the Tamul—as to the extent to which the blood and speech coincide—as to the actual character of many of the dialects themselves—and, above all, as to the origin of the Sanskrit language, present themselves. Upon all these points, as well as upon many others, difficulties and doubts have arisen; and I have little hesitation in saying, that, whatever may be the case with the former, the latter are more likely to increase than diminish. More than one opinion upon the higher questions of Indian ethnology demands revision.

That the languages akin to the Hindí contain a great

number of words which, after having been found in the Sanskrit, are again discoverable in the chief languages of Europe, and that the Sanskrit itself, Asiatic as it is in respect to the literature by which it is represented, is, in respect to its grammatical structure, essentially European, are facts which all philologues have admitted and which the most general readers have been informed of. Here, however, the field of actual fact ends. The explanation lies beyond its boundaries. It has, however, been attempted; the current doctrine being that the Greek, the Latin, the Lithuanic, the Slavonic, the German, and the Keltic forms of speech are, one and all, of Asiatic origin: the Sanskrit being the language of (there or thereabouts) the original locality of the primitive mother-tongue. As this is the belief of men learned in the languages of India, it, in all probability, rests upon better reasons than any hitherto published.

Meanwhile, it may be remarked that it is no farther from the Don or Dnieper to the Ganges or the Indus than it is from the Ganges or the Indus to the Dnieper or the Don; and it is quite as easy to derive the Sanskrit from a European, as the Lithuanian from an Asiatic, locality. The fact of the alternative here suggested having been, for all the practical purposes of ethnology, utterly ignored, testifies to the existence of an inordinate and illegitimate amount of assumption. The geographical district which best suits the affinities of the Sanskrit language lies in Europe, *i. e.* on the south-eastern frontier of the Sarmatian (Slavonic and Lithuanic) area. That Persian invasions of India and European invasions of Persia are anything but historical impossibilities, is known to the youngest reader of history. That languages may not only be intruded into distant countries, but that they may permanently establish themselves therein is shown by the Magyar of Hungary. That the deduction of a single language like the Sanskrit from the area of a whole class of languages (for such is Europe to the Greek, Latin, Lithuanic, Slavonic, German, and Keltic tongues) is more reasonable than the deduction of a whole class from the area of a single species, is the dictate of common sense.

For all this, however, the Eastern origin of the languages of Europe is an admitted doctrine, whilst the western origin of the Sanskrit is a paradox. The reason of this I believe to lie in the great number of loose generalities afloat about the East; the East, as the birthplace of mankind—the East, as the source of civilization — the East, as the prolific mother of the chief religions. The East may be all this, and more; yet it is not sufficiently either this or anything else to justify the inordinate amount of assumptions it is permitted to cover. That the elimination of these mischievous elements would lead to recognition of the alternative under notice is certain; and it is equally certain that the recognition of such an alternative would materially modify the existing state of Indian ethnology. At present it is generally admitted that, as far as the greater part of India, in the strict sense of the term, is concerned, the Sanskrit is a foreign language. It came, if not from the north-east of Persia, at least from the north-west of Hindostan. And here I leave it.